IMAGES
of America

NEW RIVER

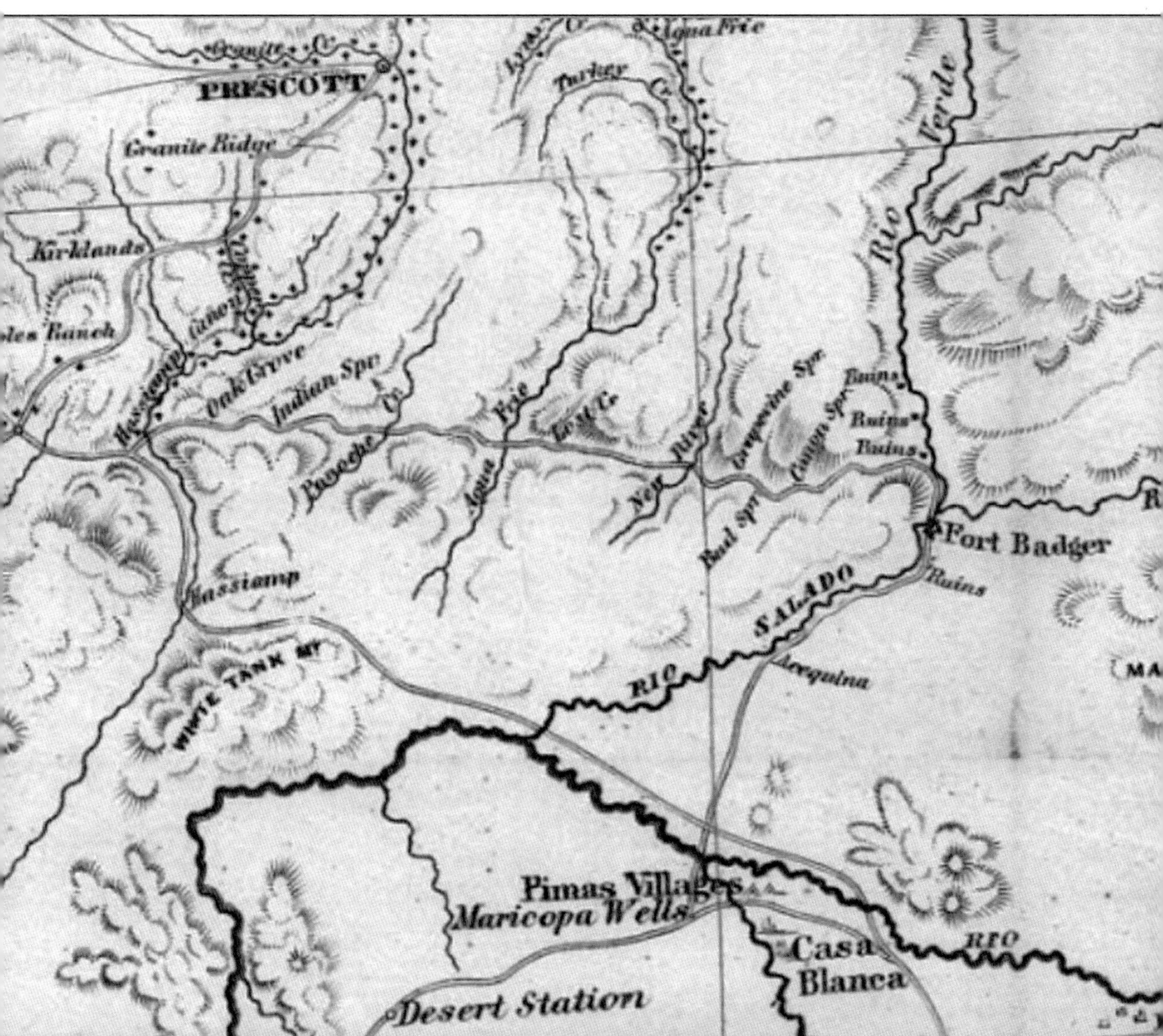

Hartley's 1865 *Map of Arizona* shows the river that gave its name to the community of New River. The road crossing the rivers conveyed troops traveling between forts and other strategic points. Some of the many Hohokam ruins throughout the region dot the map. Note that Prescott is prominently featured while Phoenix—now a sprawling metropolitan area—does not yet appear on the map. (Courtesy of Library of Congress.)

On the Cover: The homesteaders who built New River endured daunting challenges, from extreme summer heat to abundant rattlesnakes, scorpions, and spiny desert plants. Despite the never-ending hard work, Jerry Jacka Sr. and Rose Jacka celebrate Christmas 1931 properly with a decorated tree at the first living quarters at Sun-Up Ranch. Rose's sister Josephine Kubes is at center. This image is from the book *Sun-Up Ranch: An Arizona Desert Homestead*, by Jerry D. Jacka. (Courtesy of Jerry D. Jacka.)

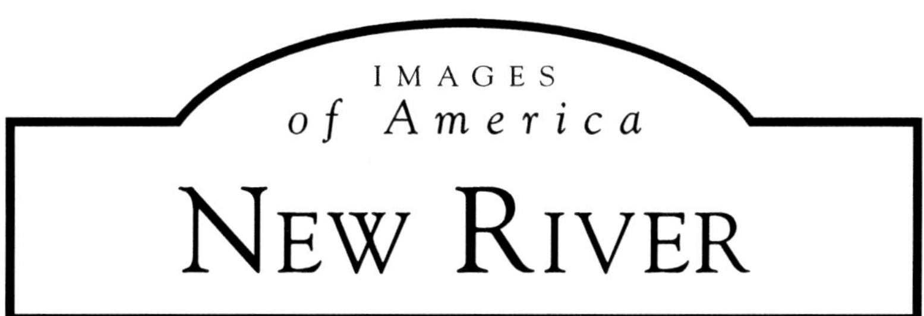

Marcy J. Miller

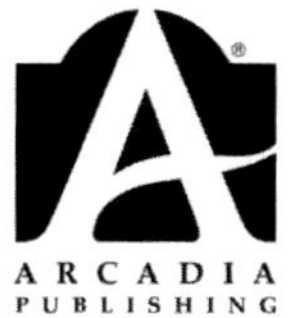

ISBN 978-1-4671-1593-3

Published by Arcadia Publishing
Charleston, South Carolina

Printed in the United States of America

Library of Congress Control Number: 2015950595

For all general information, please contact Arcadia Publishing:
Telephone 843-853-2070
Fax 843-853-0044
E-mail sales@arcadiapublishing.com
For customer service and orders:
Toll-Free 1-888-313-2665

Visit us on the Internet at www.arcadiapublishing.com

To the memory and descendants of the homesteaders and settlers who forged a lasting community from this rugged, beautiful land

Contents

ACKNOWLEDGMENTS

The telling of a history, like the making of it, requires many hands. The making of this book would have been impossible without the help of thoroughly amazing people. Whether sharing trails, photographs, memories, or coffee with me, you have been truly wonderful. My heartfelt thanks go to each of you for your time, kindness, and friendship: John Deegan, June Evans Bond, Rene Faires, Leon and Frances Lann Gee, Lance and Judy Halle, Ann Hutchinson, Bob Nilles, Jerry D. Jacka Jr. and Lois Essary Jacka, and Michael Sandford.

Additional thanks go to Wide World of Maps, the Cave Creek Museum, and to my husband, Russ Lane, who accompanied me not only on several adventures in visiting historical sites, but in the adventure that has been the writing of this book. Special thanks go to Jerry D. Jacka Jr., whose beautiful book *Sun-Up Ranch: An Arizona Desert Homestead* is invaluable to any Arizona history enthusiast, and to his accomplished wife, Lois Essary Jacka, for their gracious contributions.

INTRODUCTION

New River, a rocky, cactus-dotted expanse of rugged terrain on the northern edge of Arizona's Maricopa County, has always defied easy definition. A distinct community with a rural western character, New River is not a town and has thus far stubbornly resisted either annexation or incorporation. Even the name *New River* likely originated as an early cartographer's note indicating a formerly unmapped river. The river itself is a dry riverbed much of the year, with large sections running underground. That, too, likely confused early explorers and mapmakers. The river itself appears as "New River" on the 1865 *Hartley's Map of Arizona*, but is labeled as merely "Dry Creek" on an 1887 territorial map.

It was once home to the ancient Hohokams, and the Tonto Apaches and Yavapais also called the New River area home. Attacks on settlers in the territory were frequent until the US cavalry swept the native people from the Tonto Basin in a 20-year campaign ending in 1886. One conflict occurred at the base of Gavilan Peak following a raid on Charles Morton Mullen's Triangle-Bar Ranch. As part of their efforts, the cavalry built military roads through New River connecting Prescott's Fort Whipple to Fort McDowell. Fragments of these old roads still remain.

By the 1870s, stagecoaches ran regularly through New River on what is now called the Old Black Canyon Stagecoach Road. To service them, stagecoach stations began to spring up along the river. Some were nothing more than change stations for the horses, mules, and oxen, while others offered limited amenities for freighters and passengers. In 1879, Mullen's Station, a stopover on Charles Morton Mullen's Ranch, appeared on county tax rolls. With the daunting desert climate and steep, rough land, the route was already notoriously treacherous. Frequent stagecoach robberies made it even more perilous. Early rancher Frank Alkire described it as "the toughest freight road in all of central Arizona."

As if those challenges were not enough, the forces of nature were often formidable. The river was prone to flooding during the annual monsoon season and spring rains. In 1891, massive flooding struck much of the Salt River Valley. When there was not too much water, there was far too little: from 1892 to 1898, the valley suffered a harsh drought. Frank Alkire (then owner of the Triangle-Bar Ranch) estimated 70 percent of all cattle in Arizona died during the drought. Fire, ever a threat in the desert, often swallowed rangelands as well as structures.

Still, drawn by the availability of public lands thanks to the 1864 Homestead Act, settlers continued to arrive. Cattlemen and sheepmen drove huge herds of livestock through New River, providing a need for resources such as watering sites and shearing facilities. By 1898, officials commissioned a post office. However, would-be postmaster Ephraim "Ray" Tomkinson declined the commission. This may well have been the single act that prevented New River from designation as an actual township, as rural post offices traditionally served as the meeting place and town center of new communities.

The area remained rough. In June 1900, four Mexican bandits murdered station keepers Anton Olsen and T.W. Stewart at New River Wells. The *Arizona Republican*'s next-day report graphically describes the crime, noting that the bodies were "horribly swollen and disfigured, for the chickens had gathered about them and vultures and unclean beasts of the desert." Interestingly, Ephraim Tomkinson discovered the bodies and served on the initial inquest.

The 1920s and 1930s brought New River's biggest influx of homesteaders. Many of them were military veterans taking advantage of government programs to obtain inexpensive tracts of land for the price of hard work and residency. These service-oriented homesteaders founded the chapel, school, guest ranches, cafés and stores that formed the community that thrives today. Many then, as in the 1880s, came west for the reputation the desert had as a "healing" environment for lung disorders from tuberculosis to asthma.

By 1939, the old Black Canyon road remained unpaved. Described by Work Progress Administration (WPA) writers as a "maintained gravel road with many curves and steep grades." By 1947, New River boasted the northernmost paved section of the road. As the nation's culture shifted to one of motoring, more driver-friendly businesses emerged along the highway. From the welcoming Sun-Up Cafe to Elmer King's lively 69er Bar and the tourist-oriented Jackass Acres, New River offered several places to cool off and refresh. New River Station, once a sheep-shearing site, enjoyed its rebirth as a gas station, restaurant, and general store. By 1975, the Roadrunner Saloon—also initially a general store of sorts—gave road-weary visitors a place to relax and enjoy western fare and live music.

The advent of air-conditioning in the hot desert, the paving of the Black Canyon road, and the bridging of the often impassable river crossings permitted further growth. As the rest of the country became intrigued by the Wild West in the 1940s and 1950s, Wranglers Roost operated as a dude ranch, while Jacka's Sun-Up Ranch often hosted both paid and unpaid guests. Eking out a living in the often inhospitable climate and sparsely vegetated land required creativity and constant hard work by every member of the household. Not all of the visitors to the area's guest ranches chose to wear western shirts and boots. The hospitality industry brought another destination that drew out-of-state visitors to New River during the 1950s: the Shangri-La Ranch, a nudist resort.

Today's New River remains a largely rural, horse-friendly community retaining many traces of its early history. From Hohokam ruins to well-preserved homestead houses such as Jacka's Sun-Up Ranch and the still-operational T-Ranch, the area's oldest history is still a visible, tangible presence. This history is representative of the larger history of Arizona itself: a rugged place settled by visionary, tough people who built lasting communities in the wide-open American West. This is a story best told by their photographs and memories.

One

The Vanished Ones

The Native People

From fortresses on its highest peaks to grindstones (metates) found in its lowest washes, New River still bears ample evidence of the prehistoric people who once flourished here. Over 1,000 years ago, the Hohokams occupied the area, living in pit houses built over shallow pits scooped into the rocky earth. The agrarian Hohokams built the first canal system in the Salt River Valley. Appearing about AD 900, the culture peaked at about AD 1300. By 1450, they had vanished entirely. Some theorize they moved on because of water salinization; others blame drought and social conflict. They were likely the ancestors of today's Papago and Pima; the name Hohokam is a Pima word roughly meaning "the vanished ones."

Often making use of ancient Hohokam sites, Yavapai and Tonto Apache people left their own marks on the area. The Yavapais, although a separate tribe entirely, ranged south from the Prescott area and were often misidentified as Apaches. The Tonto Apaches occupied the Tonto Basin to the east of New River and certainly made forays into the area; however, the cavalry dispatched to seize control of the region often failed to distinguish between the two tribes. The Indians raided ranches such as Charles Morton Mullen's Triangle-Bar Ranch and stations along the Old Black Canyon Stagecoach Road.

From 1866 to 1886, the US Army launched a campaign to drive all Native Americans from the Tonto Basin and onto reservations. In October 1870, Col. George Stoneman and a small escort followed an old native foot-path from Fort McDowell to Fort Whipple in Prescott. He hoped the new route would prove viable as a shortcut instead of the commonly used road through Wickenburg to the west. Stoneman's troops later developed the wagon road that became Military Road through Cave Creek. Abandoned by the 1880s, the military road passed through the Triangle-Bar Ranch and continued 40 miles east to Fort McDowell. By 1886, the Apaches and Yavapais were gone—captured, killed, or relocated by the cavalry—and New River was considered safe for Anglo settlement.

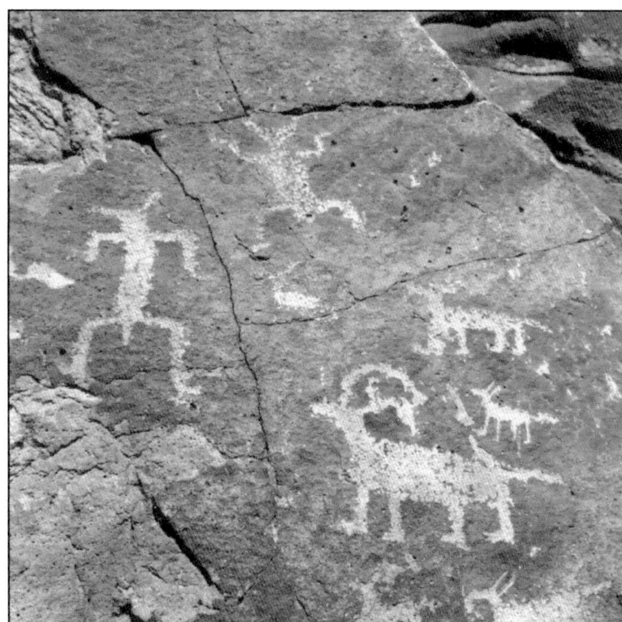

The native people carved rock art and symbols into the rock faces of hills and peaks throughout New River. Like the Hohokams, the bighorn sheep depicted in this petroglyph have since vanished from the region. Many of the petroglyphs have also been destroyed. (Courtesy of Jerry D. Jacka and Lois Essary Jacka.)

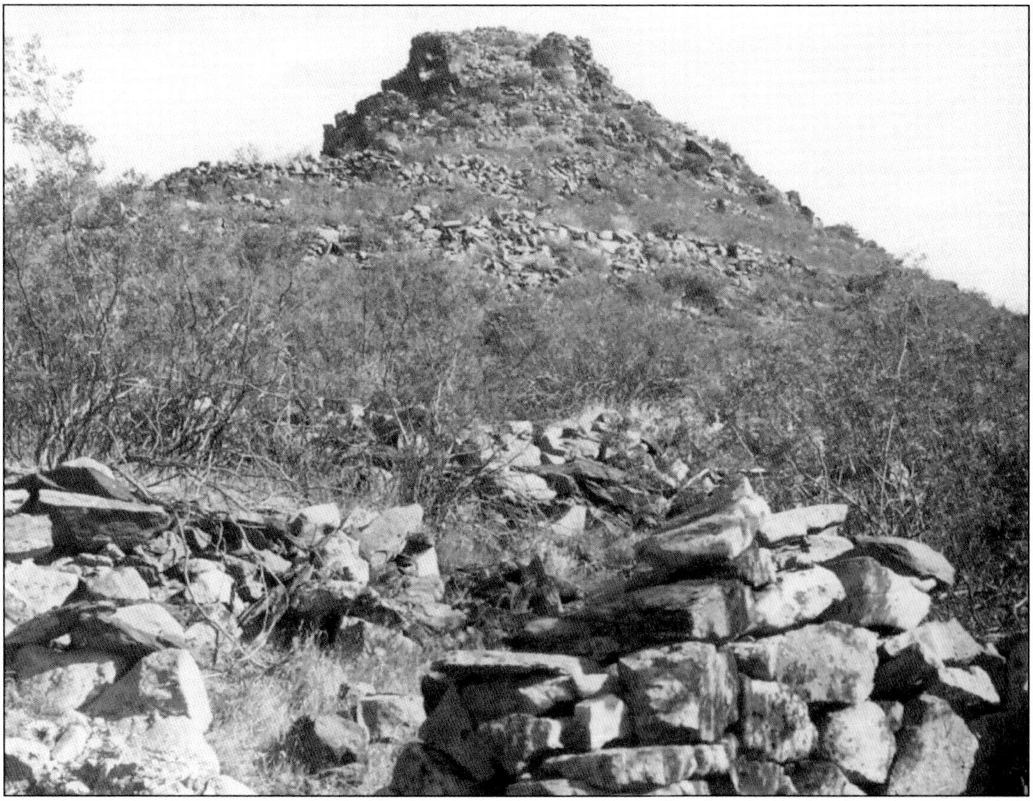

Despite the present of ancient hillside dwellings, rock art, and a peak-top fortress, this small but distinctive peak remains officially nameless and is unidentified on topographical maps. Designated as T:4:8 by archaeologists, it is sometimes erroneously called "Pyramid Peak" by locals. (Courtesy of Jerry D. Jacka and Lois Essary Jacka.)

T:4:8, like many of the New River peaks, was used as a temporary dwelling by the Hohokams. They often hunted in the area before returning to the valley below, where the city of Phoenix is now located. The tactically advantageous pinnacle boasted an excellent lookout over the area. (Courtesy of Jerry D. Jacka and Lois Essary Jacka.)

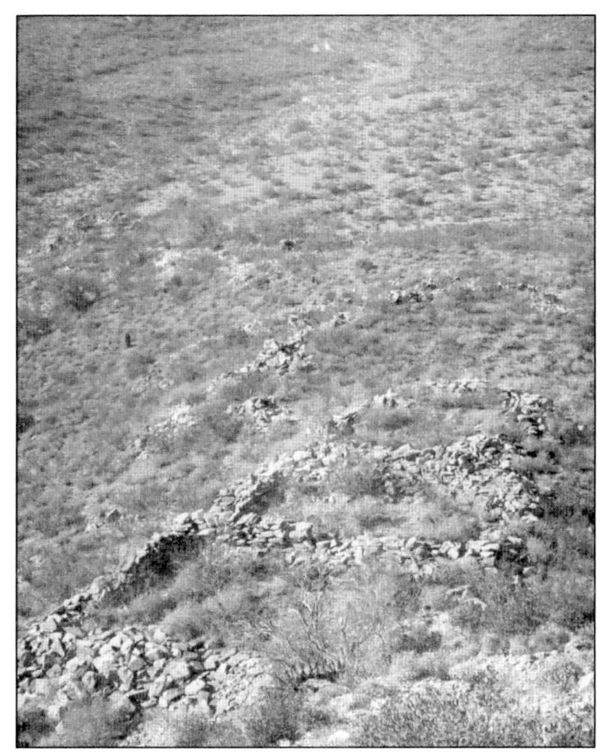

The families who homesteaded New River lived among stunning reminders of the vanished ones. Potsherds and primitive tools were readily found. Here, Bill Essary stands beside the ruins of an impressive prehistoric wall on a hilltop near Black Canyon City, north of New River. (Courtesy of Jerry D. Jacka and Lois Essary Jacka.)

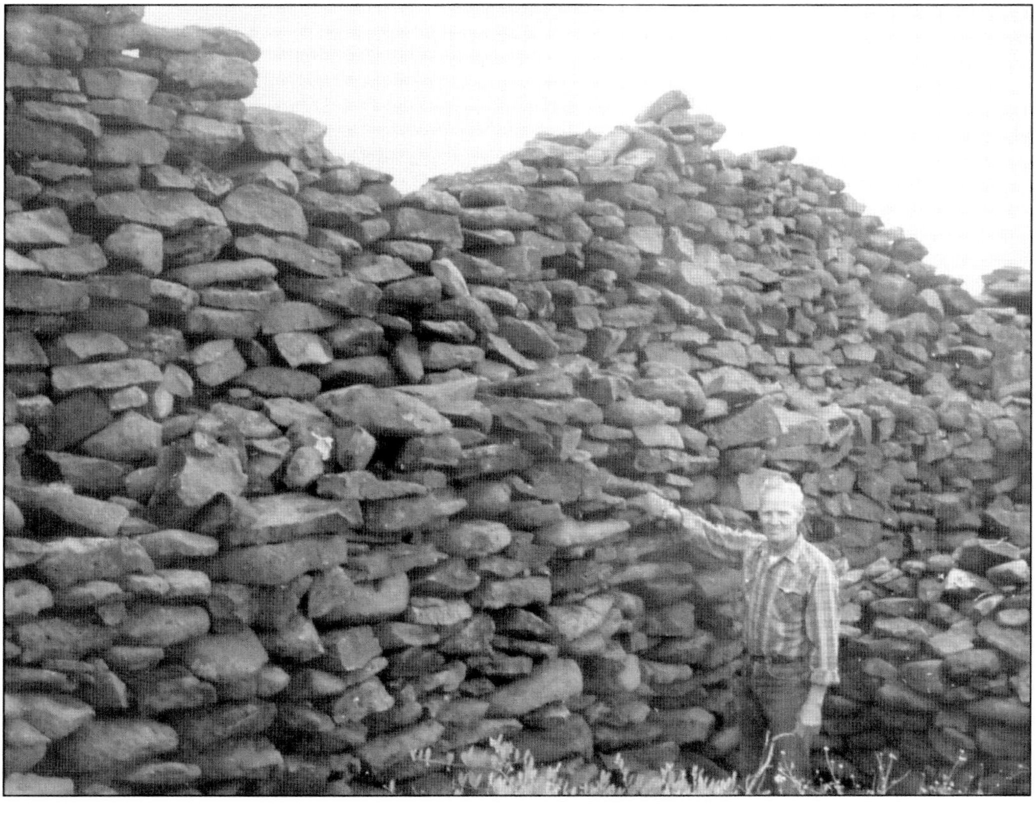

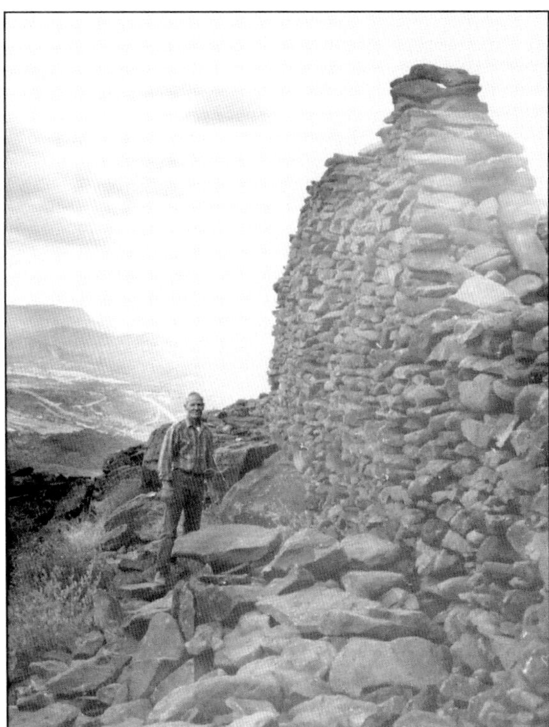

In the background behind Bill Essary, the roads and modern residences of Black Canyon City offer a sharp contrast to the silence of the ancient dwelling place. The loophole visible at the top of the rock wall offered the Hohokams an unobstructed view. (Courtesy of Jerry D. Jacka and Lois Essary Jacka.)

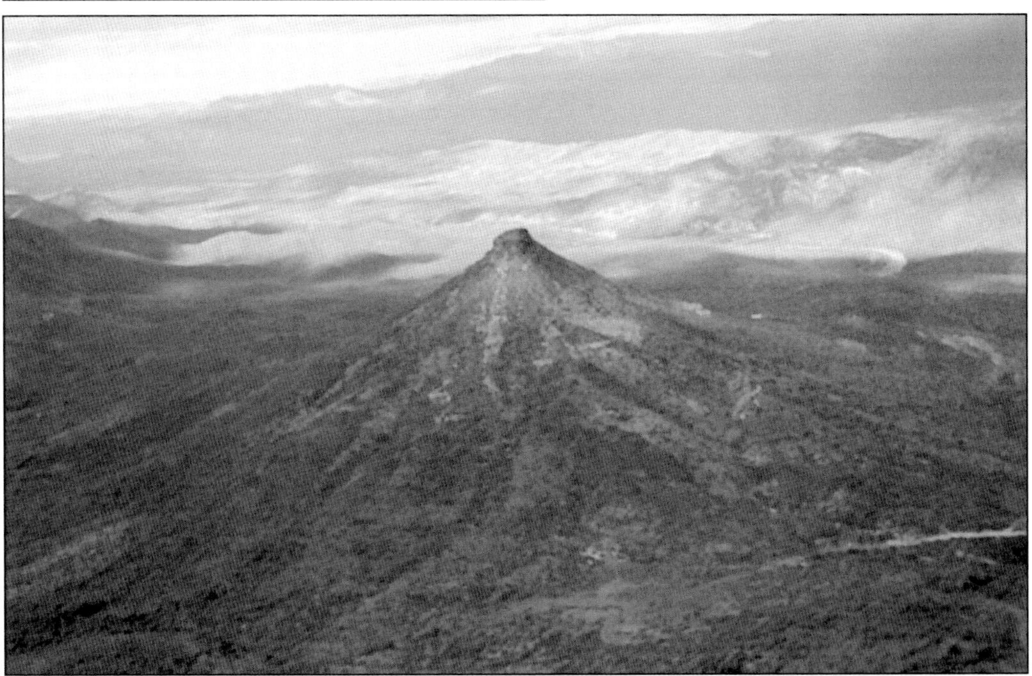

Pepsi Cap Mountain within the Tonto National Forest was once called "Table Top Mountain" by New River locals—not to be confused with Table Mesa, a larger landform not far away. Rowena Essary, one of the original homesteaders, named it Pepsi Cap for its cap-like peak. Archaeologists simply call it T:4:5. Pepsi Cap also boasts an array of Hohokam ruins. (Courtesy of Jerry D. Jacka and Loise Essary Jacka.)

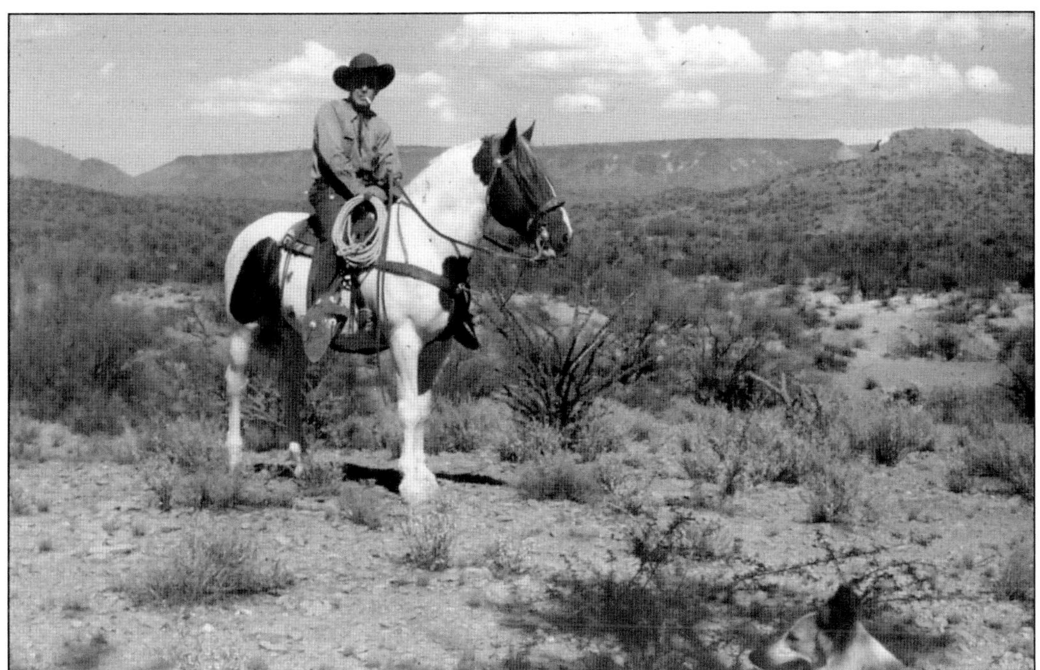

Port Halle, owner of Wrangler's Roost guest ranch, rode among many ruin-topped peaks. To the right is the small mesa locally known as "Indian Mountain" in honor of Hohokam ruins on its flat summit. Potsherds and partial rock walls still remain on and around the peak. New River Mesa, seen in the background, figured in the cavalry's sweep of Apaches and Yavapais from the region in the late 1800s. (Courtesy of Lance Halle.)

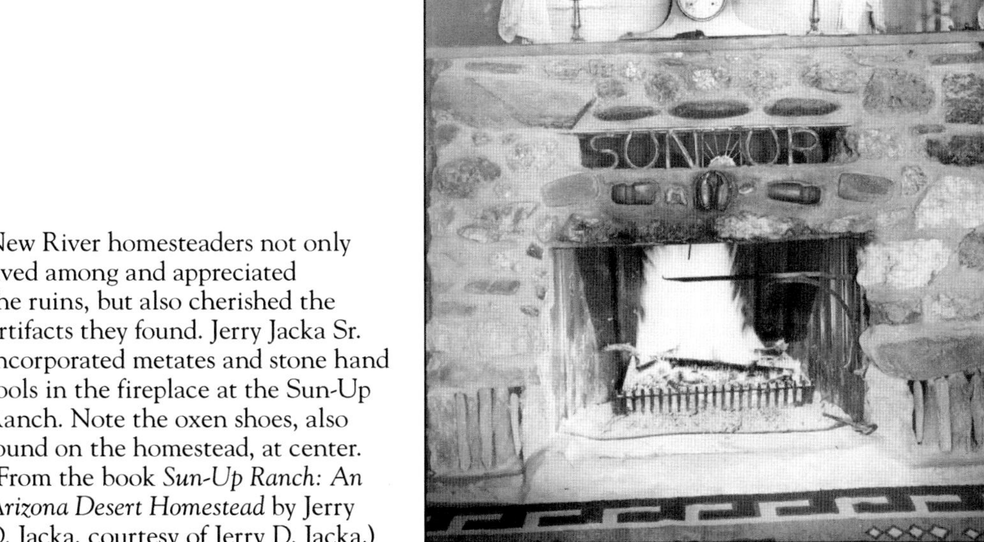

New River homesteaders not only lived among and appreciated the ruins, but also cherished the artifacts they found. Jerry Jacka Sr. incorporated metates and stone hand tools in the fireplace at the Sun-Up Ranch. Note the oxen shoes, also found on the homestead, at center. (From the book *Sun-Up Ranch: An Arizona Desert Homestead* by Jerry D. Jacka, courtesy of Jerry D. Jacka.)

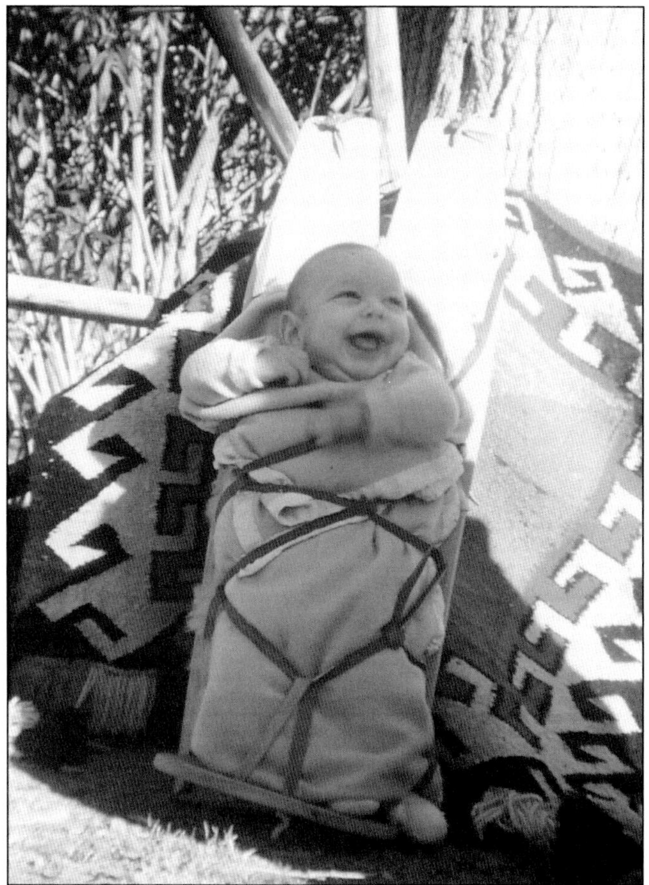

Though the indigenous people had long since vanished or been routed from the area, their cultural influence on later residents remained. Lois Halle of Wrangler's Roost found the traditional Indian cradleboard to be the perfect way to keep young Lance Halle safe as she managed the constant work required to run a guest ranch. (Courtesy of Lance Halle.)

Legends and lore about the Apaches—some valid, some fanciful—are part of the tapestry of New River history. Leon and Frances Gee built this ranch in the shadow of Gavilan Peak. From the other side, the peak resembles an Apache's profile. *Gavilan* means "chicken hawk" in Apache. One legend attributes the name to that of an Apache chief who lived near the peak. (Courtesy of Leon and Frances Gee.)

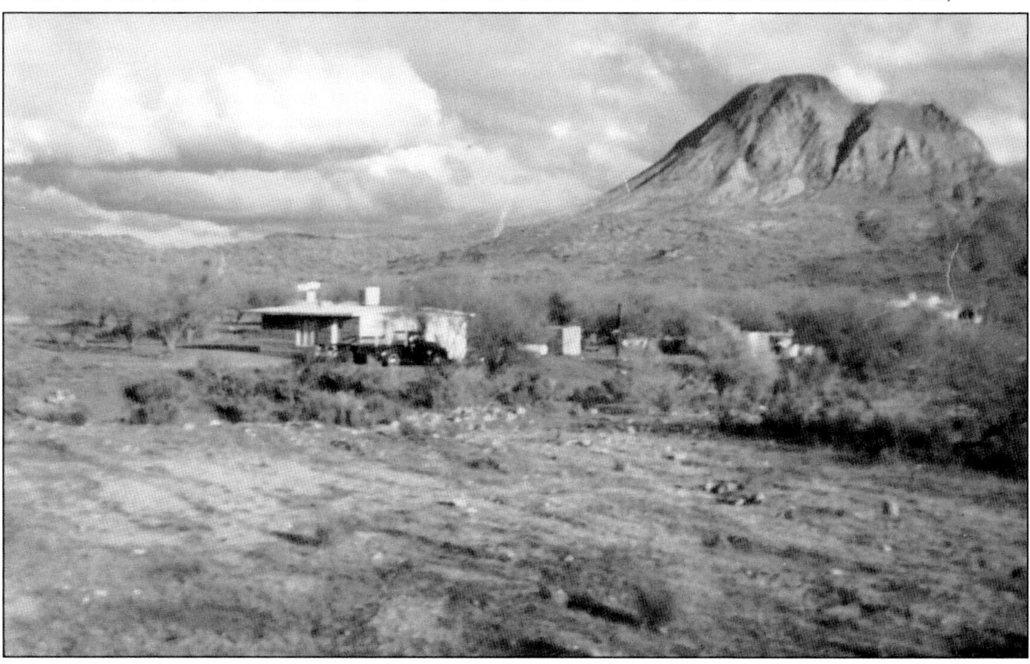

Two

New River Station
A Stop on the Old Stagecoach Road

The "New River Station" mentioned in local histories was not just one but three different sites. One was "Lord" Darrell Duppa's notoriously uncivilized stagecoach stop on the Agua Fria, a considerable distance from the community of New River. That stop, and activities associated with it, were often understandably confused with the stagecoach stop built along New River itself and run by George Hall. The latter was also officially referred to as New River Station.

In 1883, the *Arizona Gazette* wrote that Hall's station was to be "one of the best places on the Black Canyon road," praising the frame stable, hay barn, and chicken house "with a good shake roof . . . to protect his fowls from the coyotes, wildcats, polecats, and owls, which are very thick around there." Hall's stagecoach stop, which included six horses, burned to the ground in 1883. It stood where the small strip mall called Riverside Plaza stands today. Older residents recall the ruins of stone corrals for the livestock across the old stagecoach road (now the freeway frontage road) on the riverbanks to the west.

About a half mile south of Hall's stage stop on the west side of the road is an old building today's residents call "the station." Once a sheep-shearing station, it was built in the 1920s on a 120-acre homestead owned by Charles "Bones" Cable. Upon Bones's death, Frank McCallum inherited the property, selling it in 1946 to Frank and June Evans Bond and June's brother Elwood "Woody" Evans.

In 1957, James and Edith "Edie" Smithart bought the station, which was a Union 76 station and general store by then. Edie ultimately bought out James's share of the business and the remaining land attached to it—about two acres. When Edie married John Henry Cline, they ran the gas station, store, and small café and bar for many years together. Edie Cline sold the station in 1987. It has since endured further remodeling, changing hands, and a variety of identities but is in excellent condition. The original stone walls remain easily recognizable from the busy Interstate 17 freeway, just west. It is still often referred to as by its local name, New River Station.

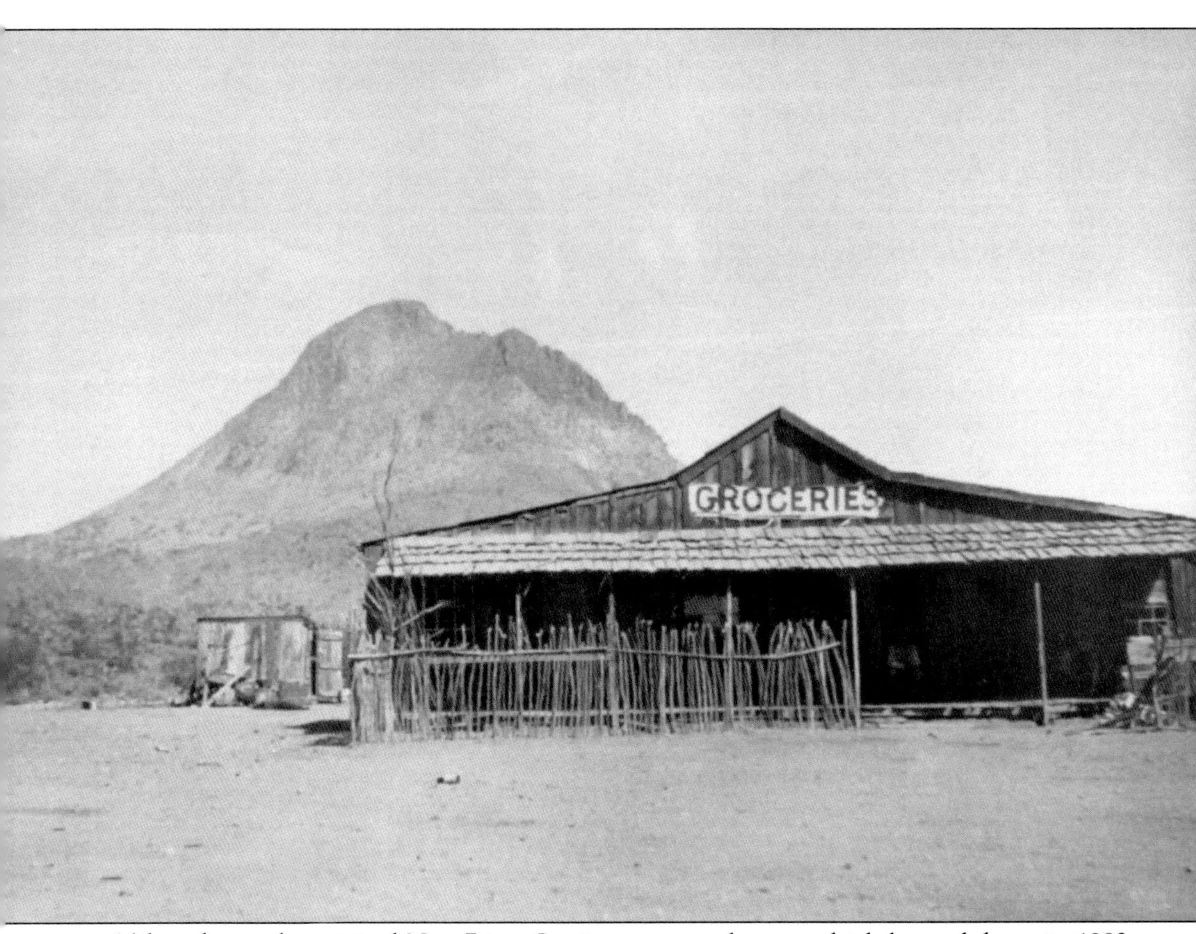

Although not the original New River Station stagecoach stop, which burned down in 1883, the stage stop in this 1902 photograph was built at the same location on the Old Black Canyon Stagecoach Road, just west of Gavilan Peak. The first station, run by George Hall, also had a shake shingle roof. Riverside Plaza, a commercial strip, now occupies the site.

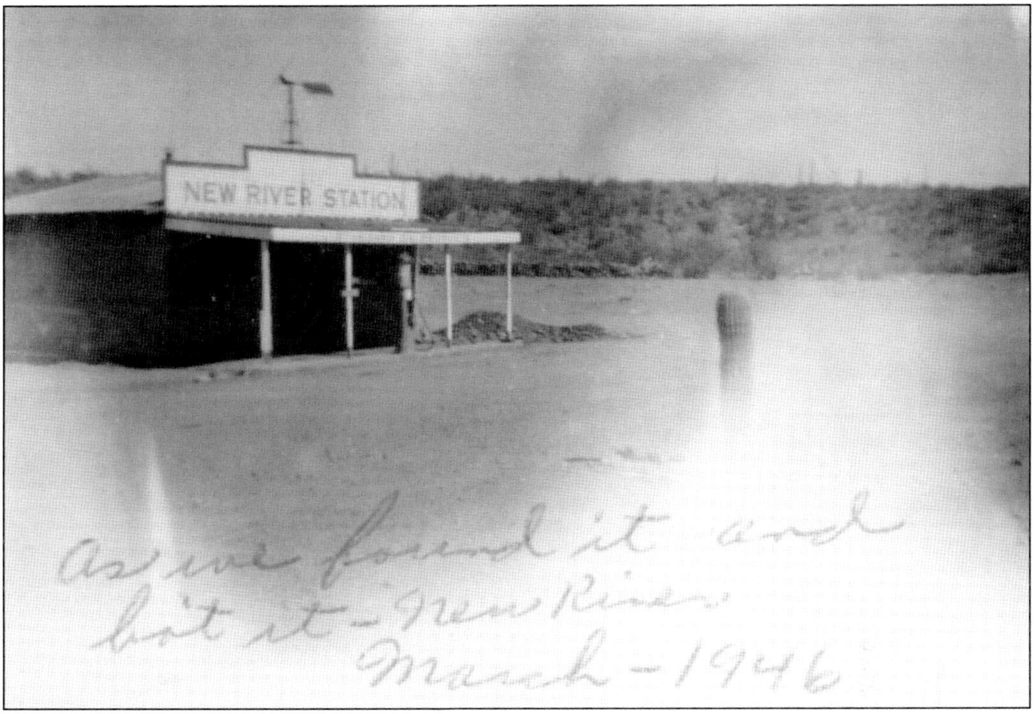

Situated along the sheep drive between seasonal pastures, the building known today as "the station" was once a shearing shed. In the 1920s, homesteader Charles Edward "Bones" Cable turned it into a single-pump gas station. June Evans Bond recalls it being a rough and dirty place when June, her husband, Frank, and her brother Elwood "Woody" Evans bought it in March 1946. Filled with well-used brass spittoons and other evidence of the rough crowd of men who met there to gamble and drink, the station needed a thorough cleaning, disinfection, and renovation. Because of the nature of the place, June's family never traded there when Bones owned it, but saw great potential in the property when it became available after Bones's death. (Both, courtesy of June Evans Bond.)

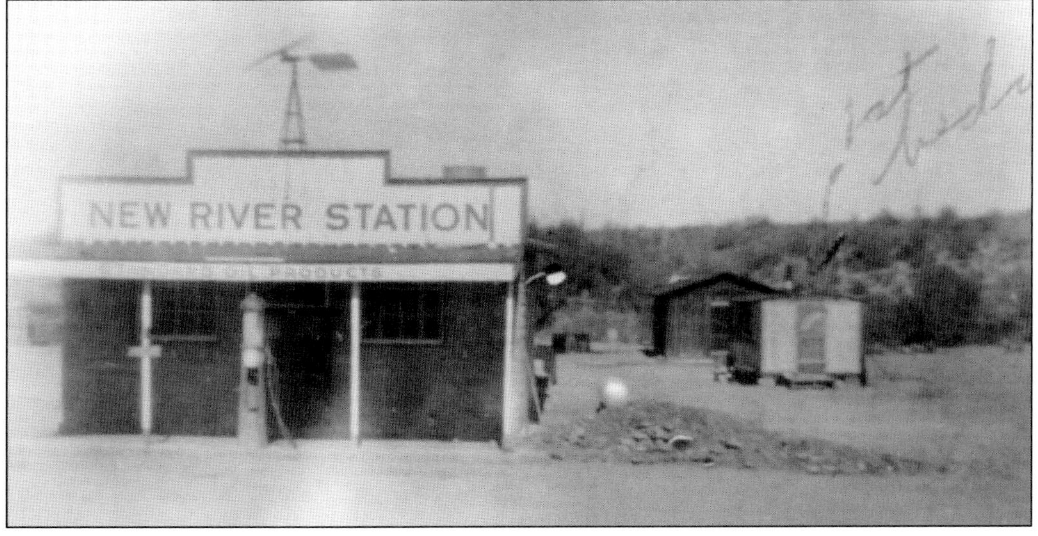

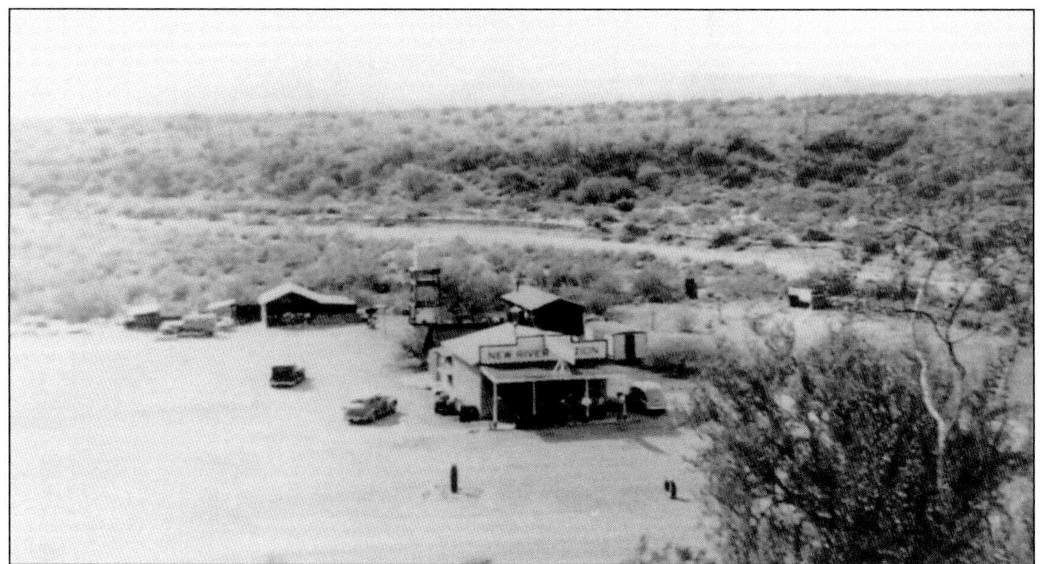

Frank and June Evans Bond lived on the property for several years, keeping livestock in the barn and corrals. June and her sister-in-law Francis Evans were once puzzled by a succession of laughing customers. The women went outside to investigate, only to find that one of their sows had escaped and brought her litter of piglets to the front door where visitors had to step over them to enter. (Courtesy of June Evans Bond.)

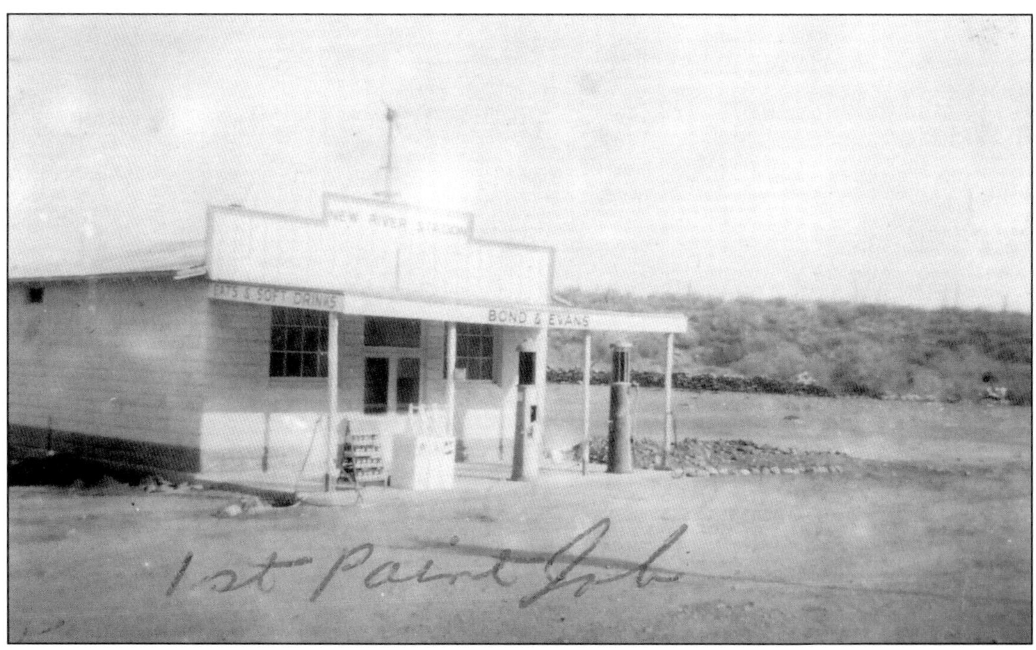

The Bond-Evans partners took great pride in their station, continually expanding and improving the property and the services they offered. This 1947 photograph shows the newly painted station now displaying "Eats & Soft Drinks" and "Bond & Evans" on the eaves and boasting a second gas pump. Note the rock wall to the rear of the building. (Courtesy of June Evans Bond.)

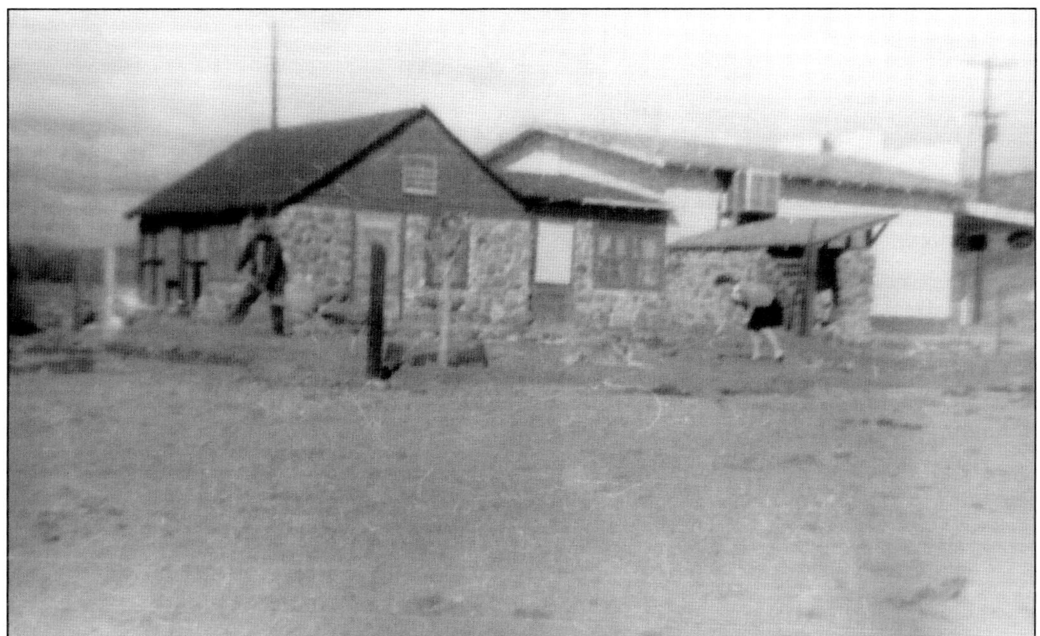

Local stonemason John Gabriel built the stone house attached to the rear of the station. Gabriel also did stonework at Jacka's Sun-Up Ranch along Black Canyon road to the south and built Rock Springs Cafe several miles north. The Bonds are at work on the yard of their new home in this 1946 photograph. (Courtesy of June Evans Bond.)

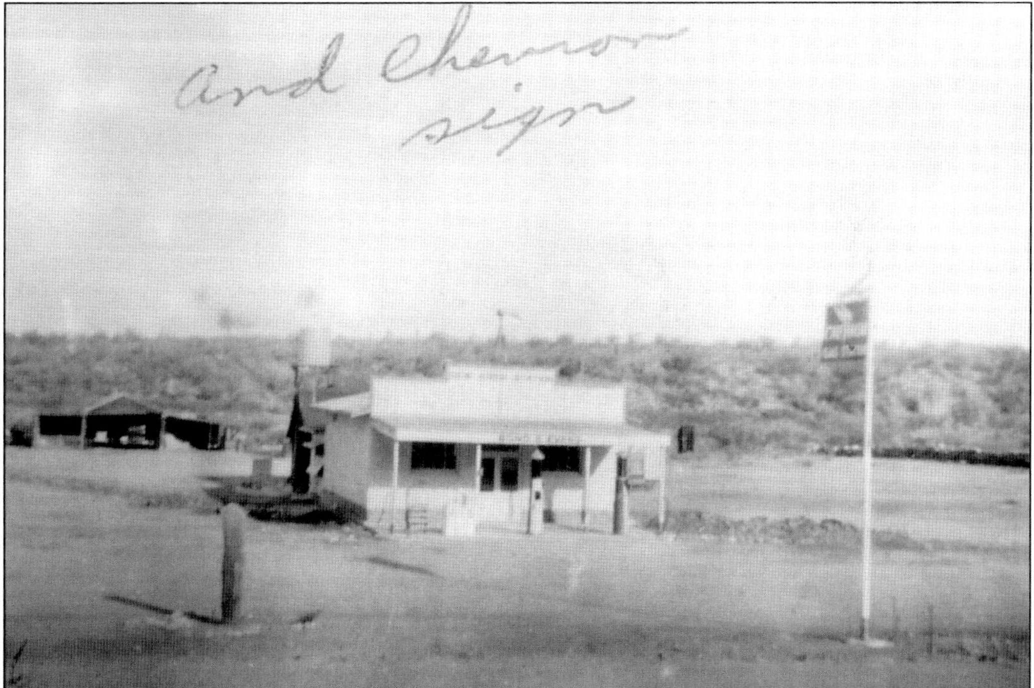

The station changed affiliations with petroleum companies occasionally, boasting new signs to reflect the current vendor. Here, Bond & Evans's station flies the Chevron banner. To the right, the old wooden outhouse still stands. (Courtesy of June Evans Bond.)

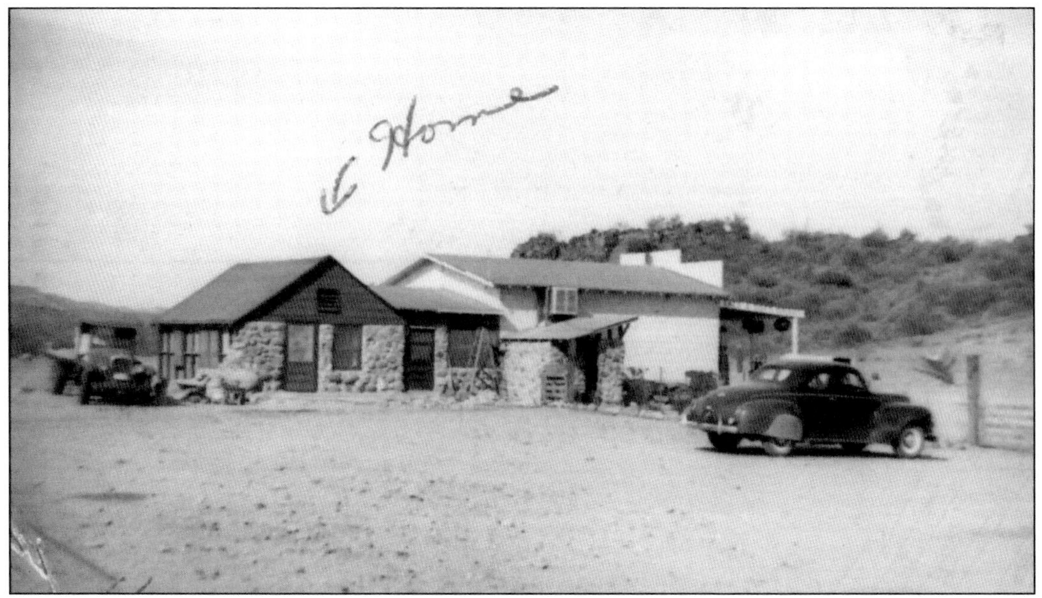

The station's attached stone house faced south. To the right of the ladder is a small doorless bathroom for the customers' use, the entrance angled for privacy. June Evans Bond recalls one female traveler running from the bathroom, screaming, after nearly sitting on a tarantula. The hill across the road, once adorned with rock art, has since been mostly quarried. (Courtesy of June Evans Bond.)

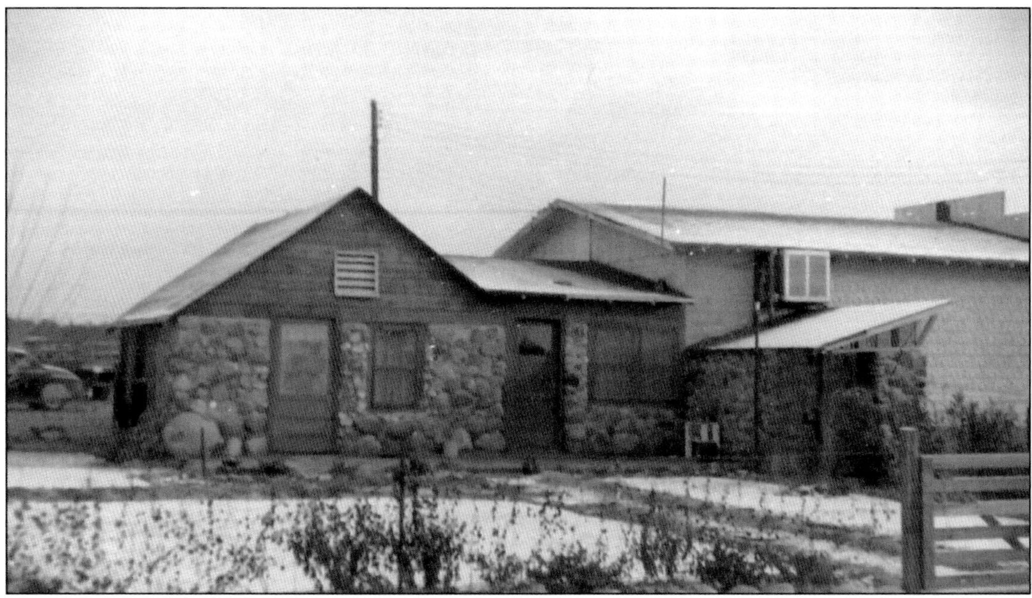

The magic of a rare desert snowfall always led to photographs and fond memories. During five years while living in this house, Frank and June Evans Bond built a larger home nearby. When the Interstate 17 freeway came through, the new home, situated right in its path, was razed. The freeway passed closely behind the station, about where the truck is parked in this photograph. (Courtesy of June Evans Bond.)

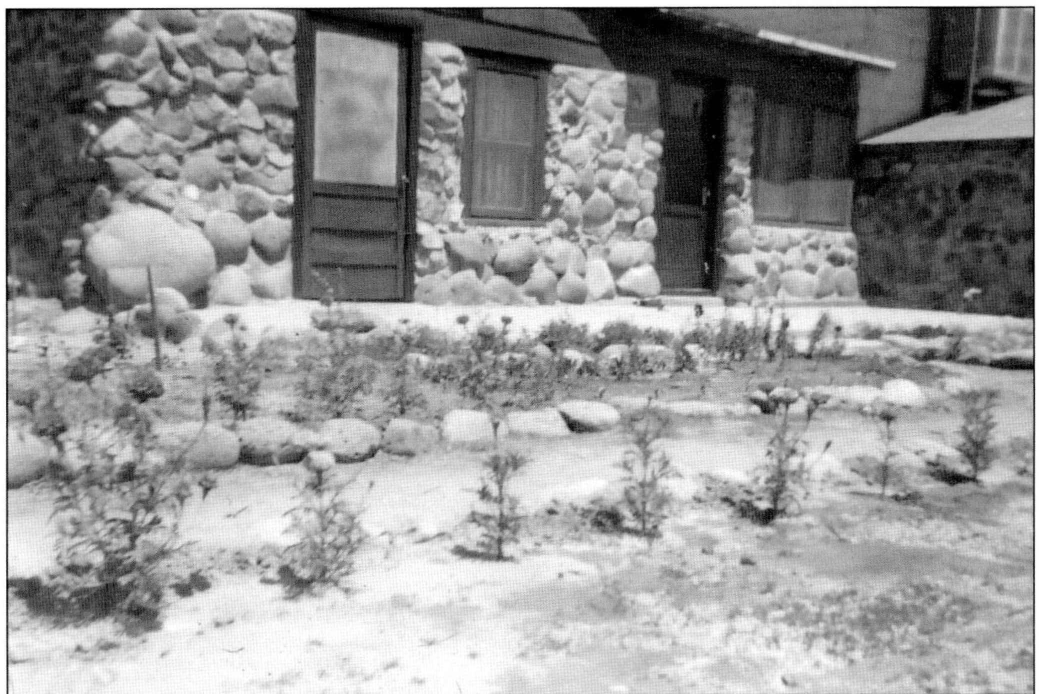

Later in life, June Evans Bond worked for a local plant nursery. Her love of plants and gardening is reflected in this photograph of her newly planted flower beds in front of the house attached to the station. After moving out of this house, June's brother Elwood "Woody" Evans and his wife occupied it. (Courtesy of June Evans Bond.)

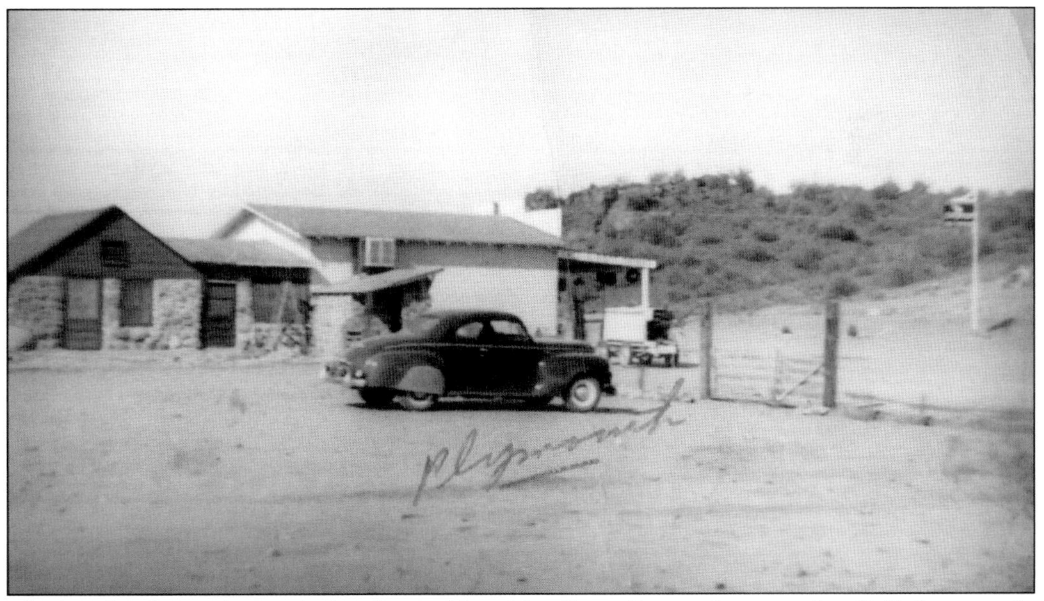

The Bonds' Plymouth is parked in front of their New River Station house in this 1947 photograph. The stone walls shown on the south side of this historic building have since been concealed by wood siding, but the west-facing stone walls are still visible. (Courtesy of June Evans Bond.)

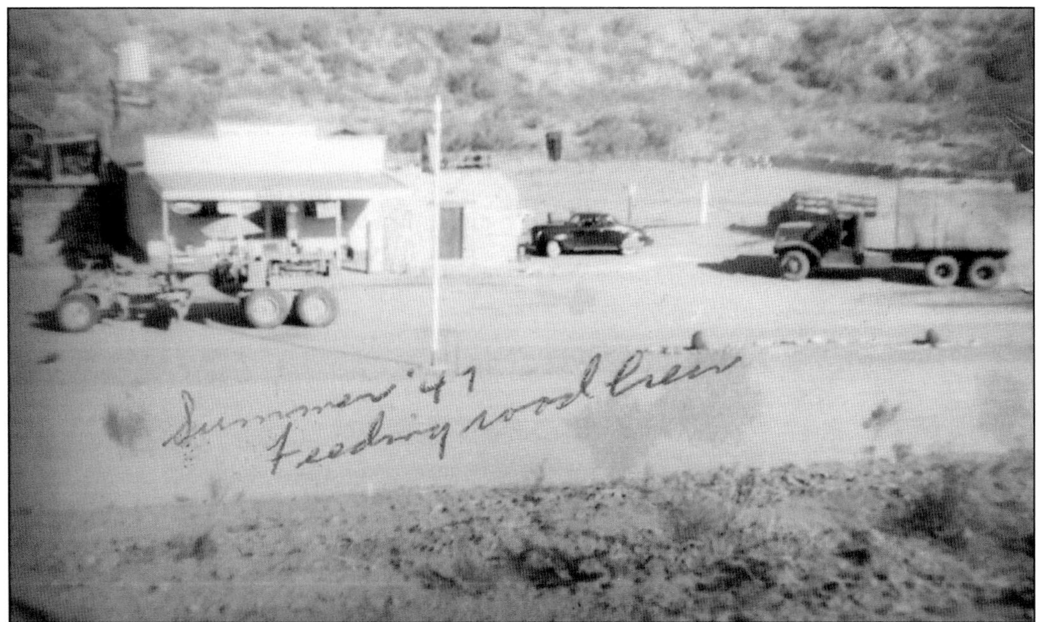

Road crews building the Black Canyon Highway relied on New River Station for many a meal. Their equipment is parked in front of the station in this 1947 photograph. The arduous task of paving the rough, winding, hilly road north from Phoenix took place in stages. (Courtesy of June Evans Bond.)

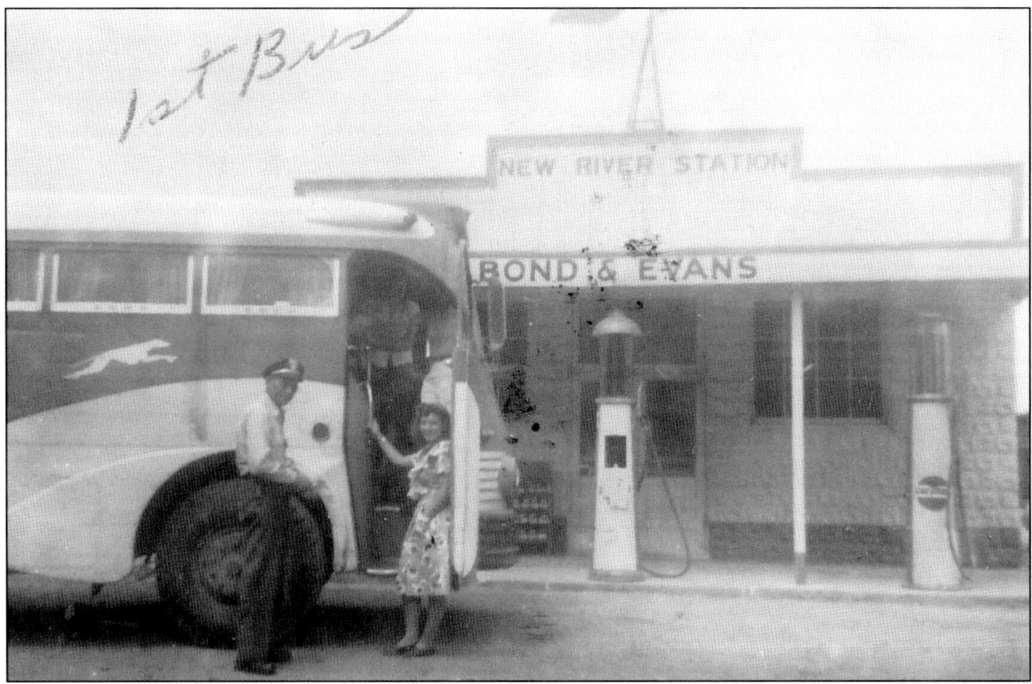

June Evans Bond stands next to Casey, the driver of the first Greyhound bus that, in 1949, traveled from New River Station to Prescott on the Black Canyon road. June said the road was so treacherous, Casey often had to stop and put the bus in reverse to negotiate sharp curves in the narrow dirt road. (Courtesy of June Evans Bond.)

Brothers-in-law, friends, and co-owners of New River Station Frank Bond (left) and Edward "Woody" Evans sit at the station's counter. The mountain lions whose skins adorn the wall were killed in the New River area by Evans's uncle Louis Pyle, a well-known lion hunter. (Courtesy of June Evans Bond.)

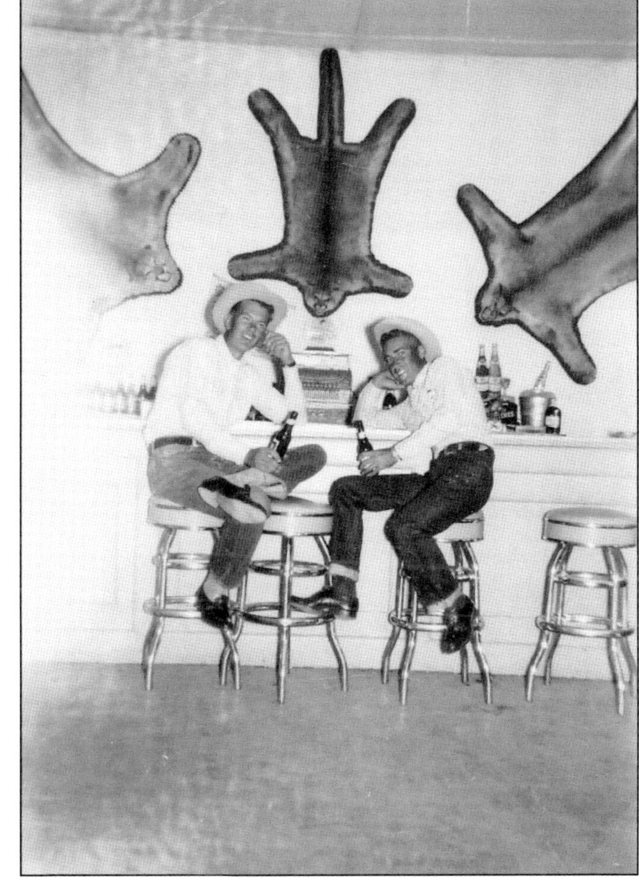

In 1948, crews "broke the hill" in front of the New River Station. The landscape in the immediate area changed dramatically in the 1940s and 1950s as the highway came through and the hill to the east was quarried for rock. Although part of the hill still remains, quarrying continues. (Courtesy of June Evans Bond.)

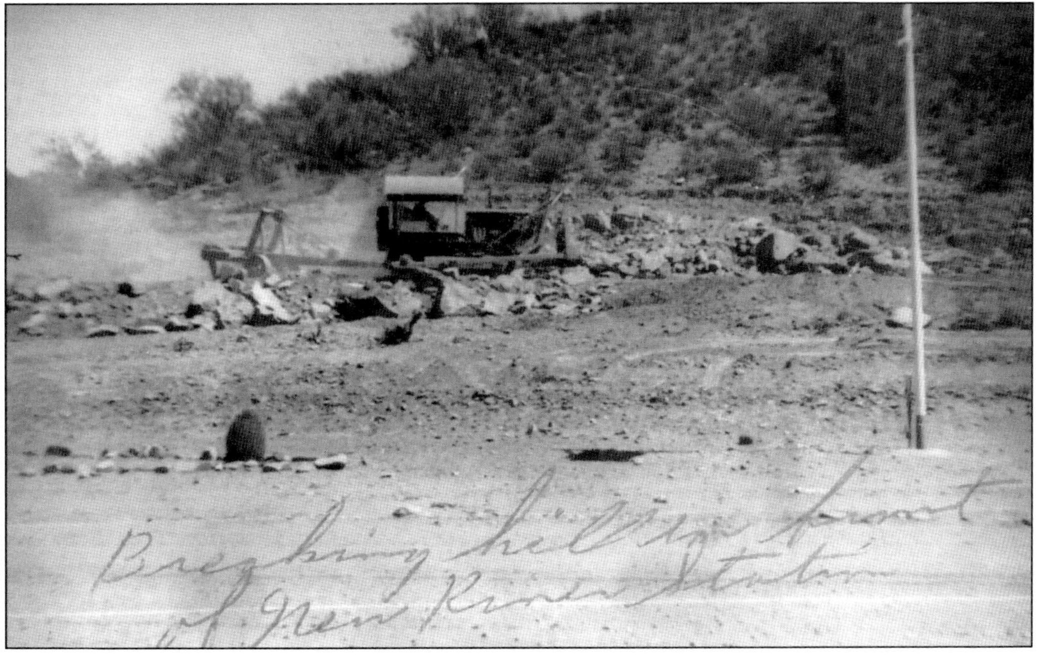

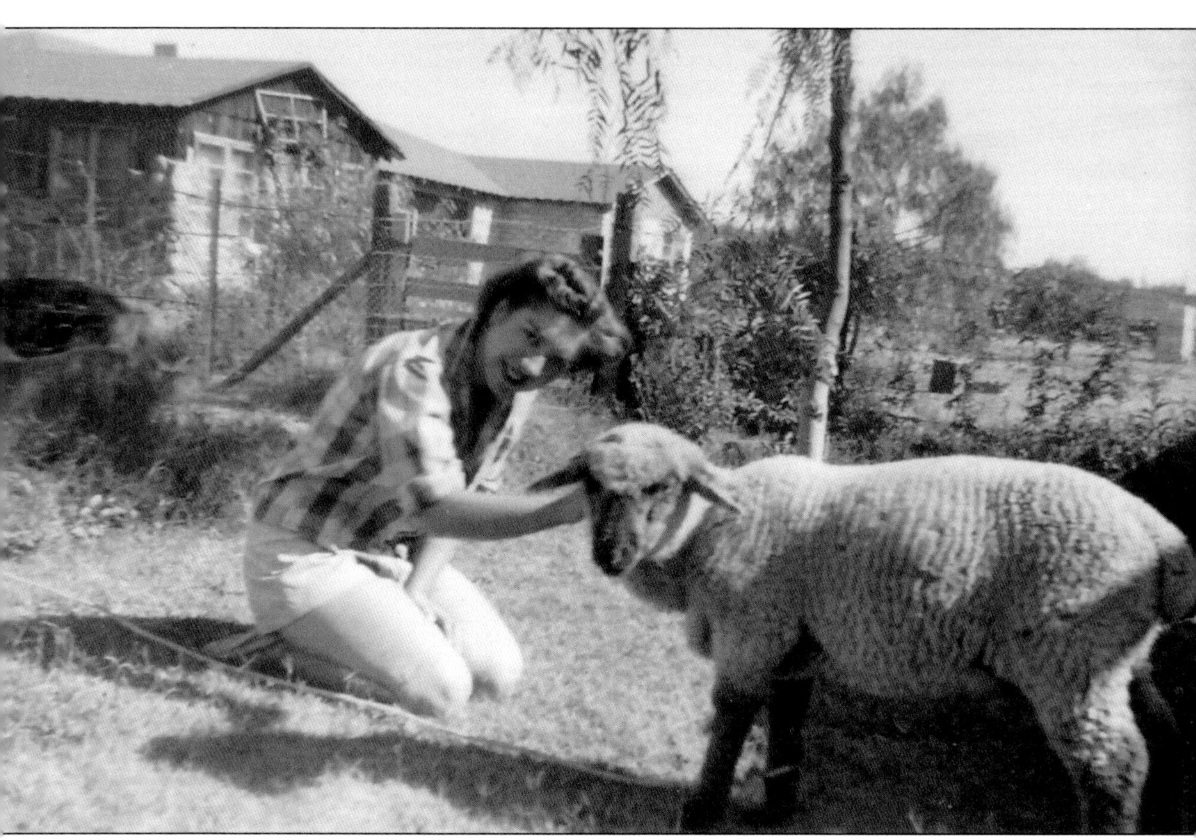

A lifelong animal lover, June Evans Bond once planned to use her scholarship to attend veterinary college in Colorado along with her husband, Frank. Their plans changed when Charles "Bones" Cable died and the heir to New River Station mentioned he did not want the business. June is shown here giving some attention to a sheep. (Courtesy of June Evans Bond.)

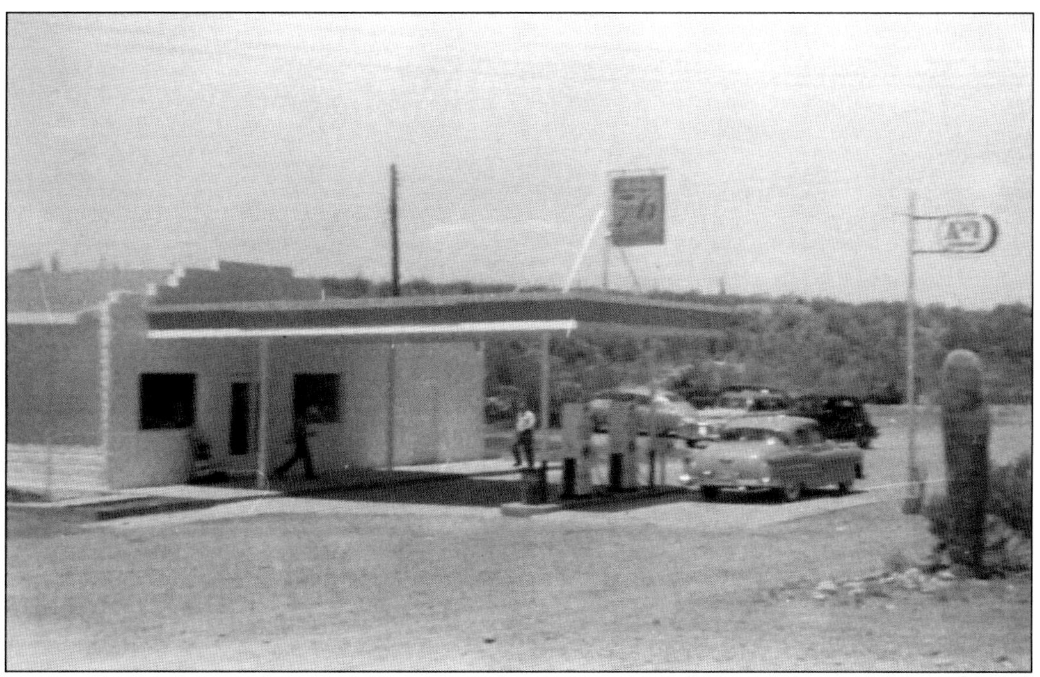

By May 1951, New River Station was a thriving business and a full-fledged Union 76 station with a newly expanded overhang, modernized pumps, and an A-1 beer sign. A-1 was the signature beer of the Arizona Brewing Company and, at the time, the most popular beer in Arizona. Arizona Brewing Company's four-part series of promotional prints, the most famous of which was *A-1 Cowboy's Dream*, were an inevitable part of the decor of the Arizona saloon of the 1940s and 1950s. They are now collector's items. (Above, courtesy of June Evans Bond; below, courtesy of Rene Faires.)

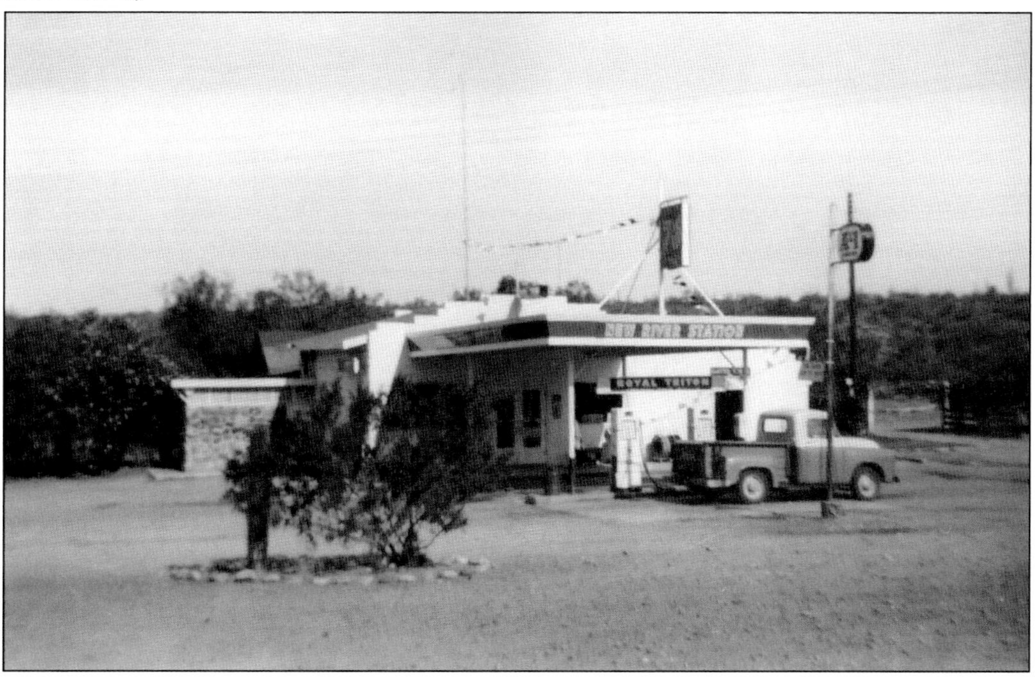

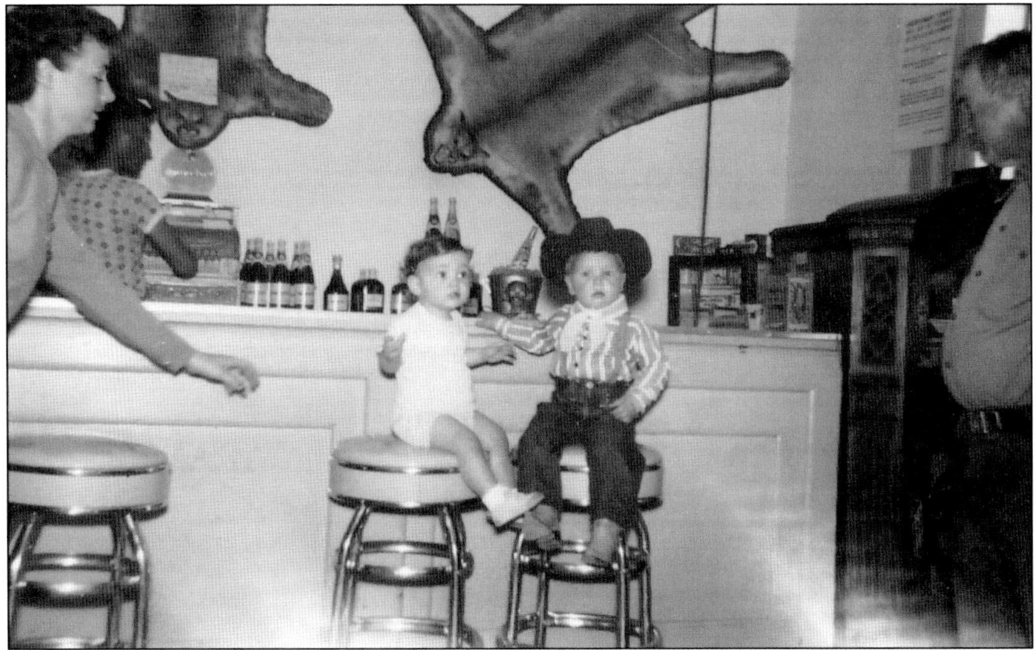

Francis Evans reaches out to her daughter Belinda at the station's counter. The little cowboy to the right is identified only as "Little Basset." Local businesses, few as they were, offered popular gathering places for locals. The station was an important part of the community as well as for travelers along the old Black Canyon road. (Courtesy of June Evans Bond.)

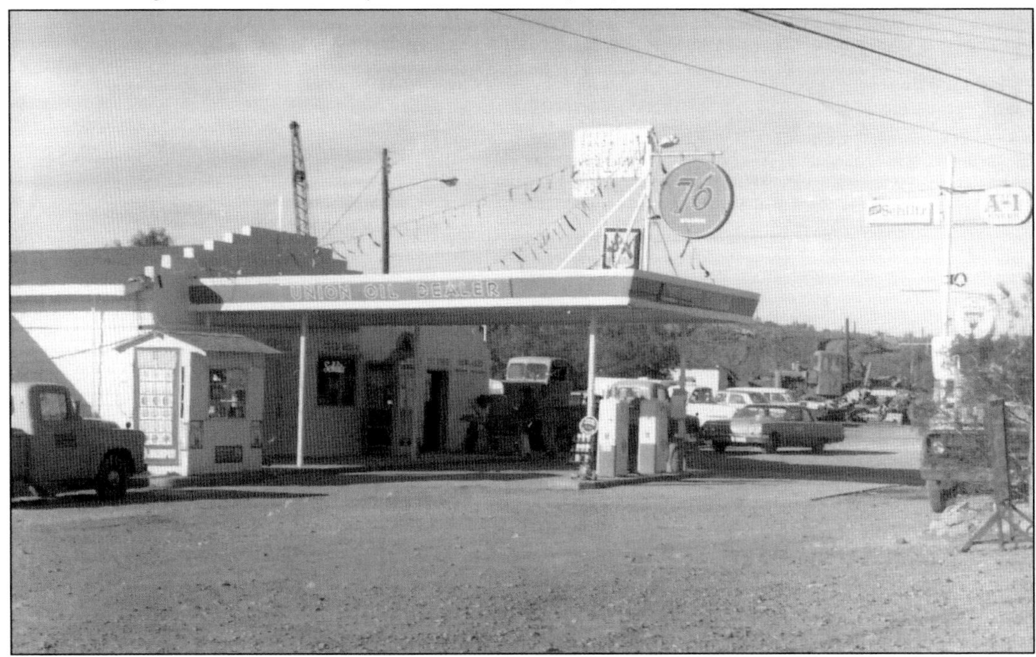

By 1955, telephones had come to New River. Note the Mountain Bell phone booth in front of the station. The large sign reads, in part, "Breakfast Sandwiches Good Coffee." In addition to such fare, the station—now a general store of sorts as well as a service station and café—issued S&H Green Stamps, the popular trading stamps of the time. (Courtesy of Rene Faires.)

In 1957, both Frank Bond and Elwood "Woody" Evans joined the highway patrol. Their wives, June and Francis, ran the station. Highway patrol cars were a regular sight at the station. In an unincorporated rural community with no police department of its own, the presence of law enforcement was a welcome addition. (Courtesy of Rene Faires.)

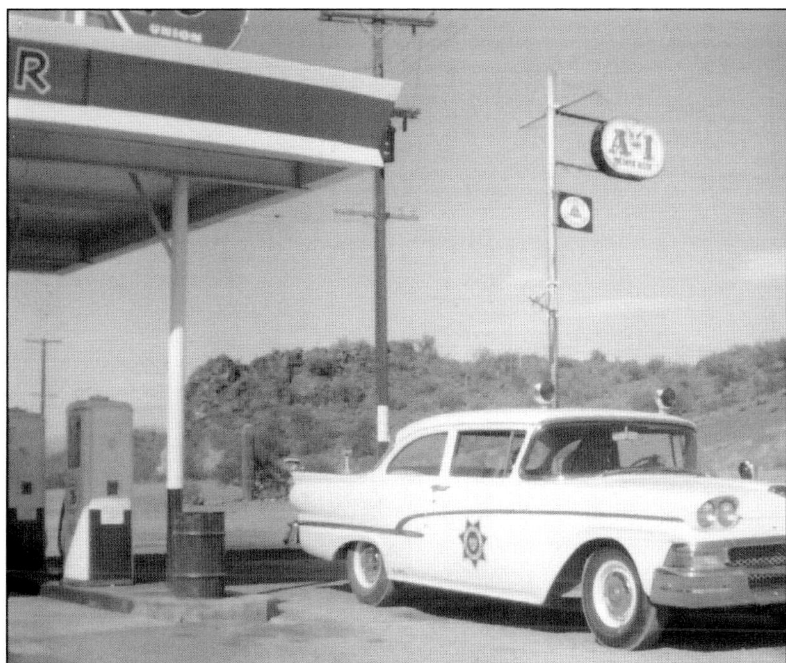

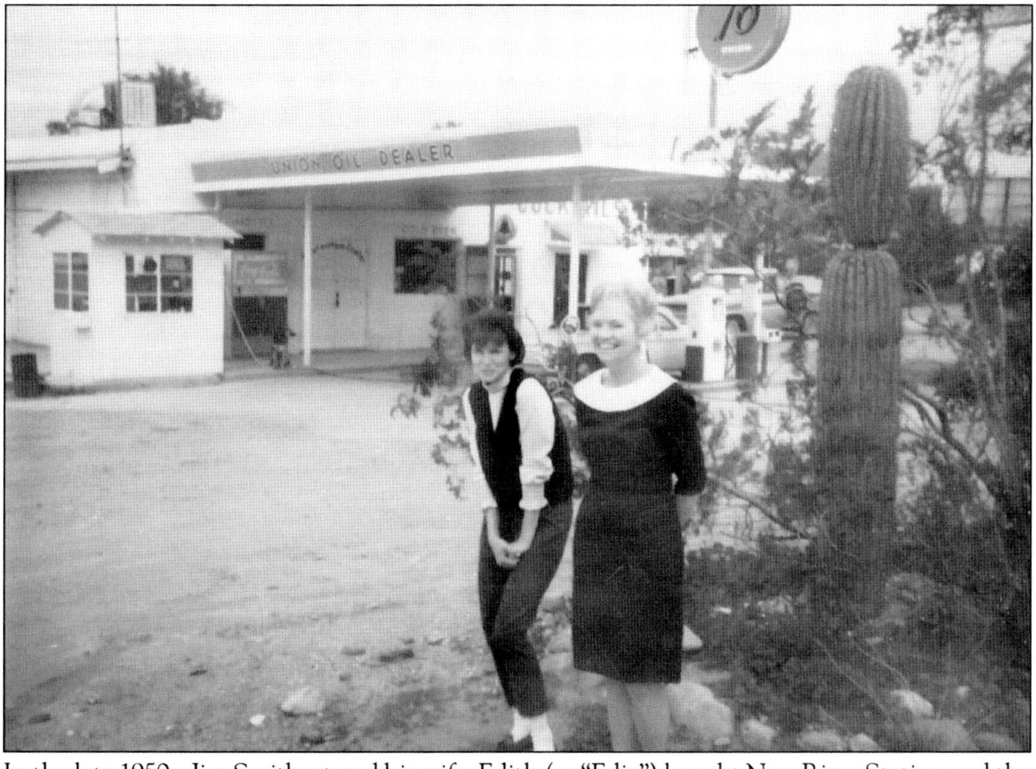

In the late 1950s, Jim Smithart and his wife, Edith (or "Edie") bought New River Station and the 20 acres it was situated upon. On the back of this photograph of Edie (right) and an unidentified friend, Edie had written, "This is our Station with a customer at the pumps. Isn't the place nice?" (Courtesy of Rene Faires.)

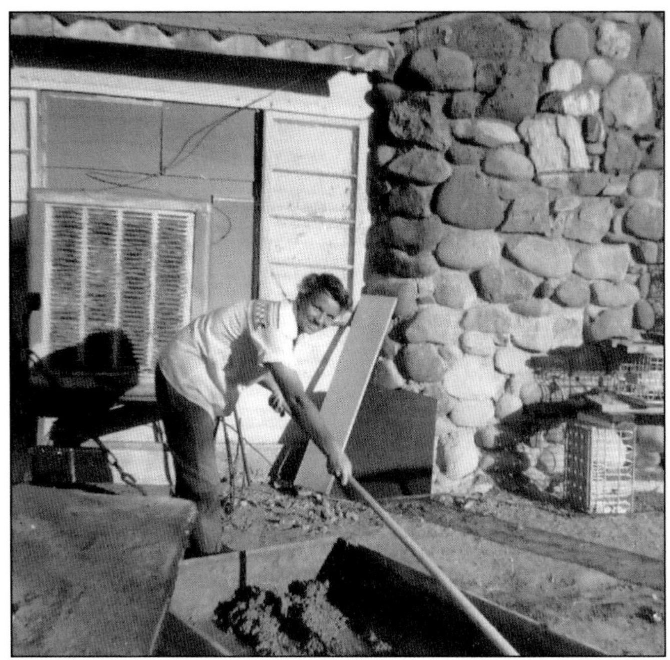

When Jim and Edie Smithart divorced, Edie bought out Jim's share of the business. The original Charles "Bones" Cable homestead had been divided many times and the property attached to the station was now but two acres. Edie ran and expanded the business and maintained the grounds on her own until marrying cowboy and rancher John Henry Cline of the T-Up T-Down Ranch. At left, Edie is hand-mixing concrete; below, she is doing yard work. When Edie passed away in 1993, her obituary noted that she would be remembered as an "honest, hard-working person who loved the community of New River." (Both, courtesy of Rene Faires.)

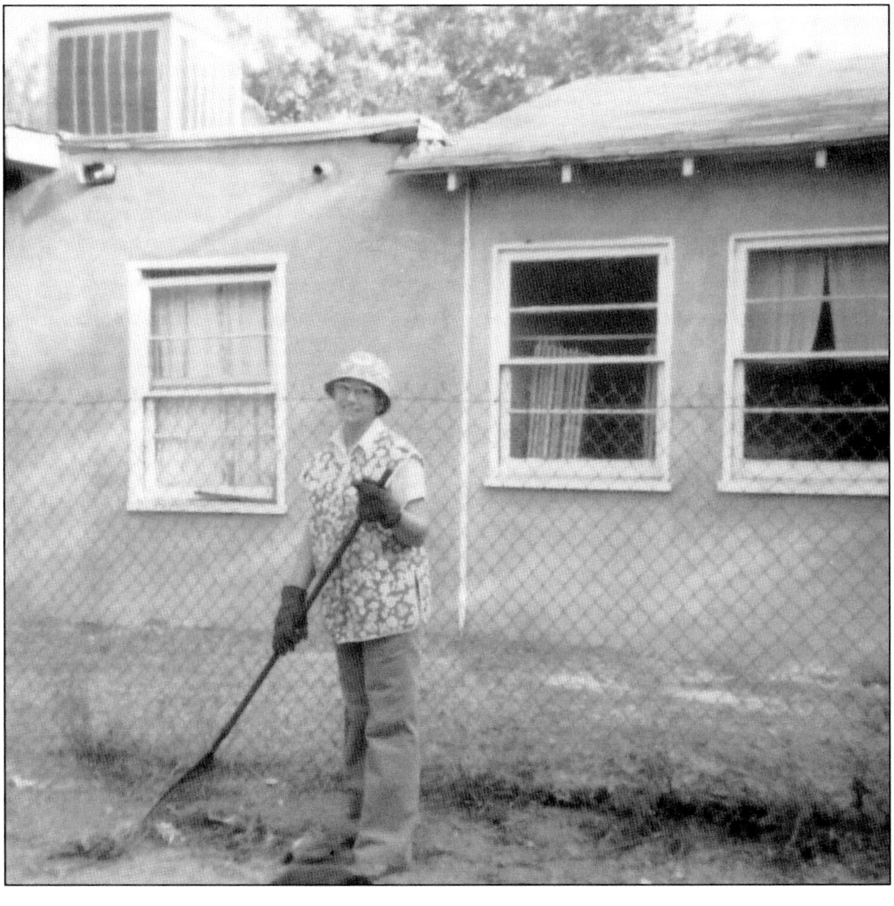

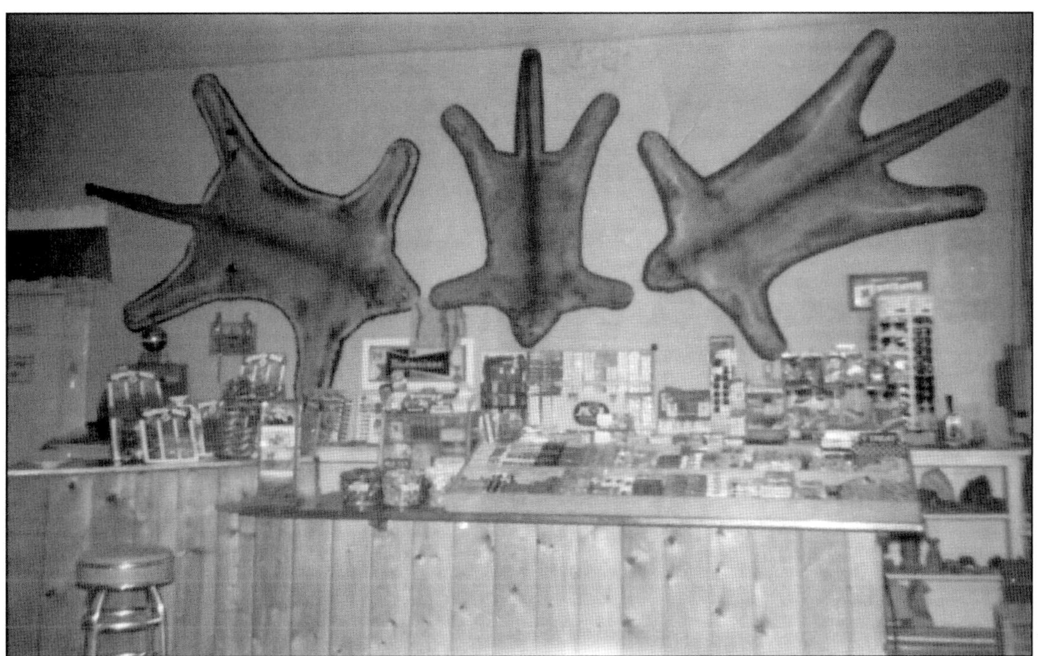

Edie Cline continued the labor of love of the station's previous owners, enlarging the original building into a café, bar, service station and general store. A newspaper clipping from 1984 describes Edie's schedule: she would open for breakfast at 7:00 a.m. and serve food until 6:00 p.m.; then the bar would open (with the help of additional employees) and remain open until one a.m. The photograph above shows some of the inventory. From the cigarette selection to the candy counter, snacks to sunglasses, the business carried many conveniences. Below is a better view of the bar. Complete with a mounted bear head, a neon "Pilsner A-1 Beer" sign suspended from the ceiling and a television set in the corner, the bar was a popular meeting place for local residents and cowboys. (Both, courtesy of Rene Faires.)

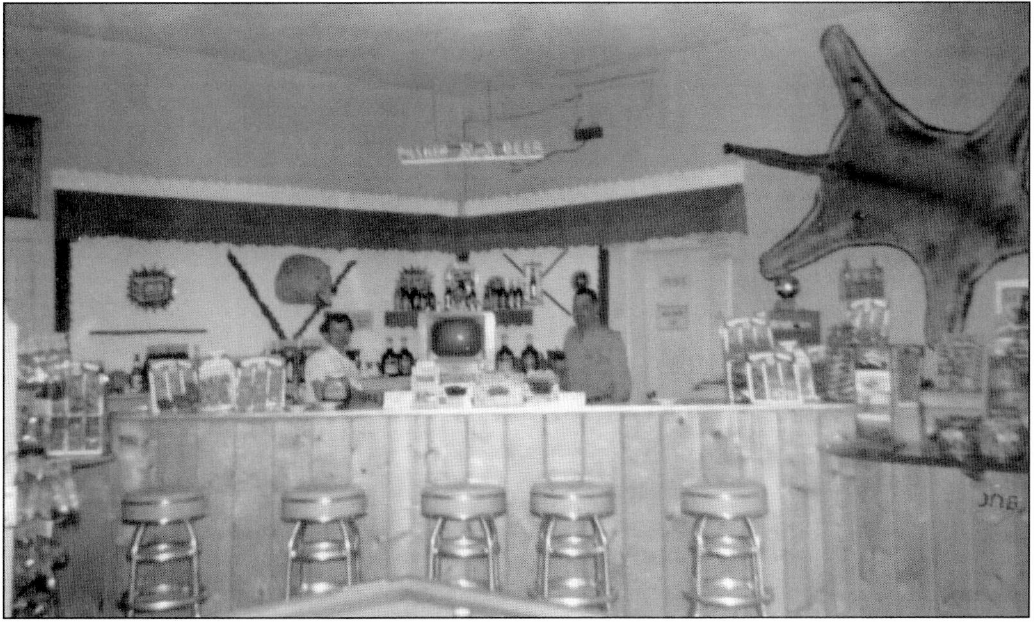

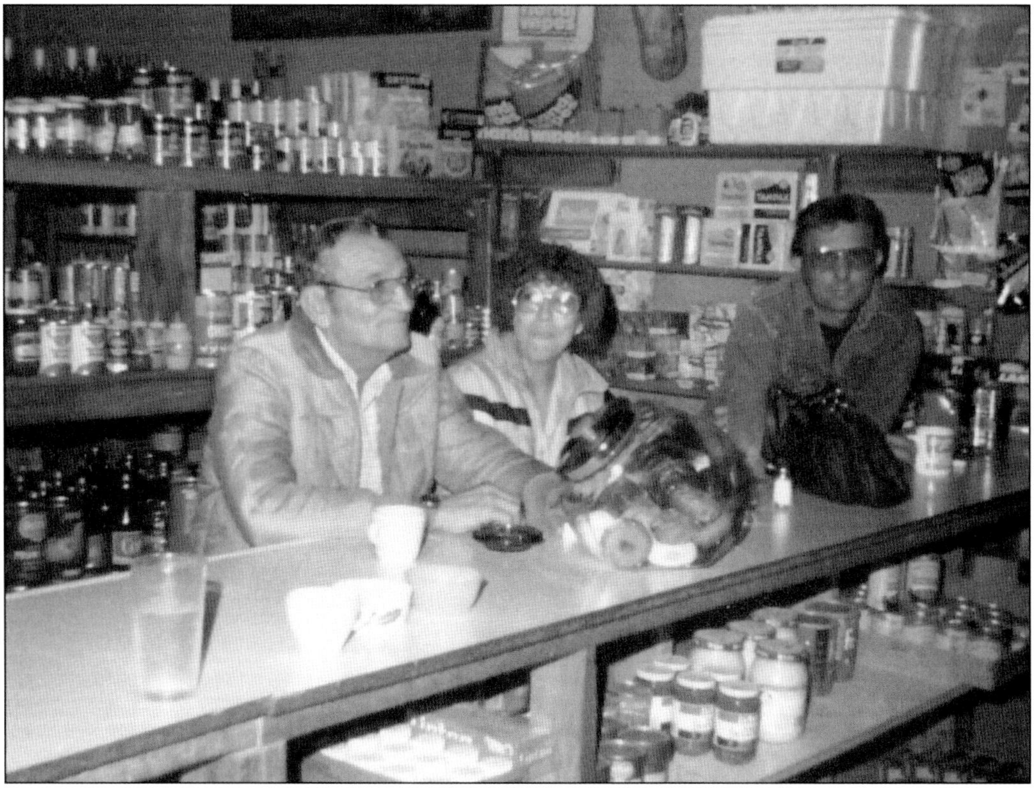

The general store and café section of the station stocked groceries and other essentials. Floyd Irwin (left) is joined at the counter by two unidentified friends. Even after supermarkets were introduced to Arizona, the nearest was many miles from New River. Locals depended on small markets and general stores for groceries, a cup of coffee, and those fresh doughnuts on the countertop. (Courtesy of Rene Faires.)

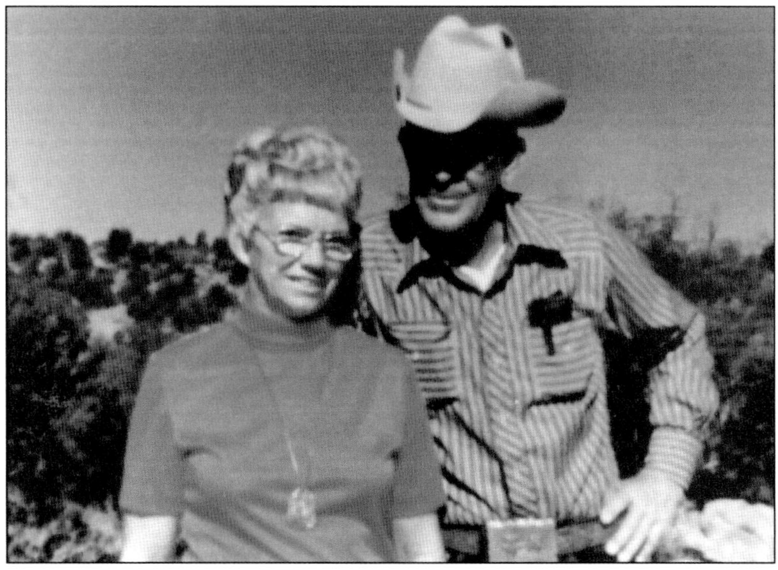

John and Edie Cline married in Flagstaff in September 1973 and—already longtime residents—lived for the rest of their lives along the banks of New River. Between the two of them, they represented the small business owner, cowboy, and rancher typical of the region. (Courtesy of Rene Faires)

Three

The T-Up T-Down Ranch

A Historic Cattle Ranch

Like the river, the T-Ranch—New River's largest, oldest ranch—has reshaped itself many times. In the 1870s, Charles Morton Mullen built a stagecoach stop, adobe house, and ranch on the banks of New River. His brand, the Triangle-Bar, was one of the county's earliest brands. Indians who once raided Mullen's ranch were later apprehended upriver by the cavalry. June Evans Bond, who lived in the old adobe ranch house as a child, remembers moveable wall blocks that served as defensive gunports against such attacks.

In 1886, Mullen sold the Triangle-Bar to Frank Tomlin Alkire, who in return sold the ranch in 1895 to Hosea Cline. Cline called his ranch the Flying Y. The nearest neighbor was Clarence B. Laird, 12 miles north. Laird, in partnership with W.W. "Billy" Cook (husband to Laird's sister Stella), owned the T-Up T-Down Ranch (variously called the T Down T Up, the T-T, the T-Evans, or simply the T Ranch); their brand was an upside-down *T* positioned above an upright *T*.

By 1924, Laird's outfit had accumulated considerable debt. Laird made a fortuitous arrangement with established rancher Dolph Evans and sons Claud, Gus, and Earl. In exchange for managing the ranch until eliminating all debt, they would receive a half interest in the outfit. With their oversight, the ranch blossomed, absorbing Hosea Cline's Flying Y; the X S Bar; and lease purchases on 75 sections along the Agua Fria. By 1941, it sprawled from Cave Creek to Lake Pleasant and south to Bell Road.

In 1943, the old adobe house burned to the ground. Gus and Earl pulled out, dispersing some holdings. In 1946, Laird died. Unable to hire cowboys due to the war's impact and hard pressed to manage the enterprise on his own, Claud Evans sold the ranch to Ray Cowden, Frank Armer, and Levi Reed. They allowed their hand, John Henry Cline, to buy in a little at a time from his $150 monthly wages. Cline ultimately owned 51 percent of the ranch, or 125,000 acres.

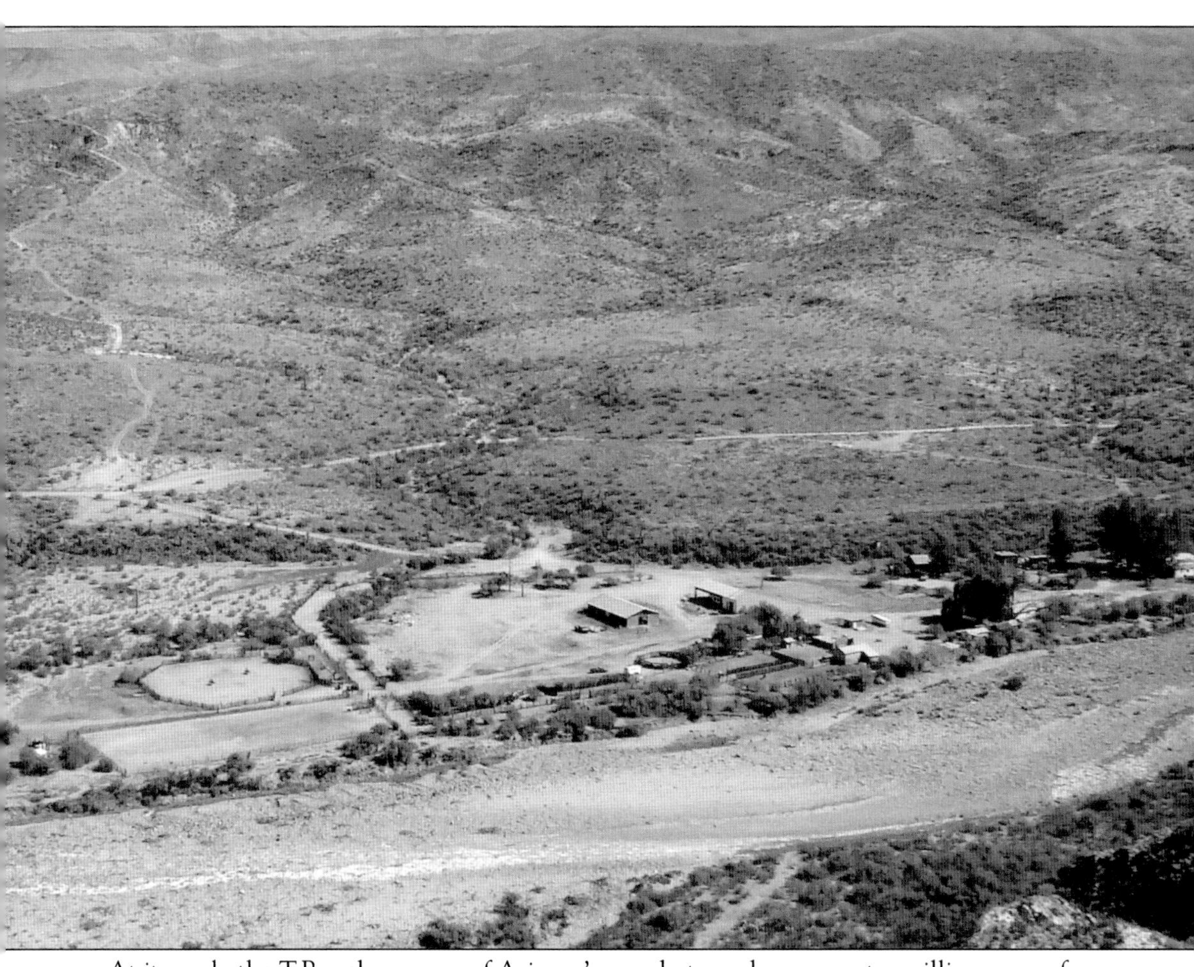

At its peak, the T-Ranch was one of Arizona's grandest ranches: a quarter million acres of range extending all the way south to Bell Road. The north side of the ranch was referred to as the "Forest Ranch" or the "Upper T." The lower T-Ranch was the "desert" side. The distinction was important to ranch management, even impacting cattle type. (Courtesy of Leon and Frances Lann Gee.)

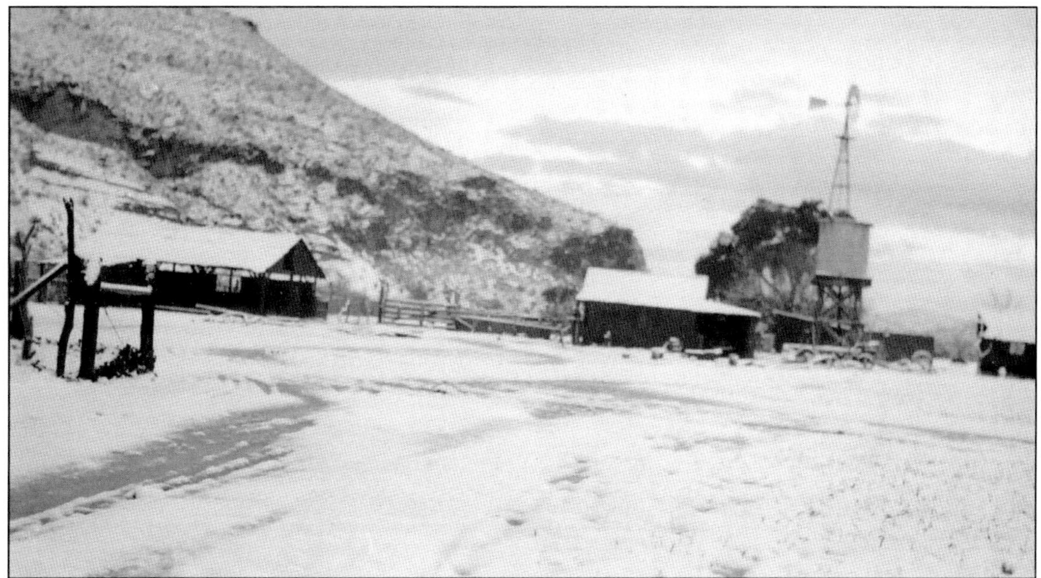

This photograph from a particularly harsh winter in the early 1930s shows the T-Up T-Down Ranch during a snowstorm. The view in this picture looks west to the water tower and the corrals. On the left side, one can see the corner of the front yard fence of the South House. Table Top Mountain (now Table Mesa) is in the background. (Courtesy of June Evans Bond.)

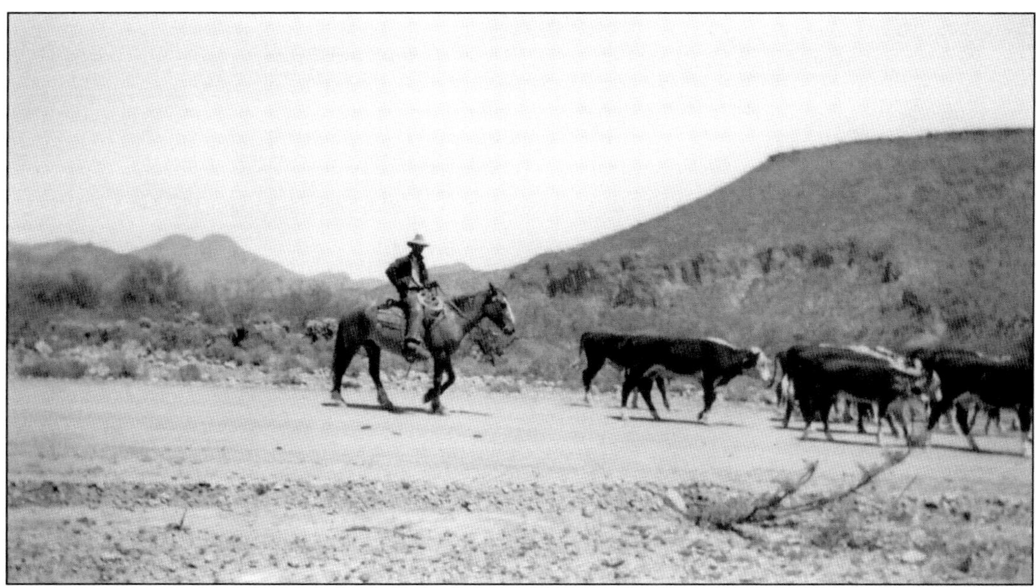

The following is inscribed on this 1940s photograph: "At the right is our old 'Flat Top' Mountain. The road, which looks better than it is, proceeds to the left, skirting the mountain, and the mesa on which the ranch horses and corral are located are just the other side of the old black sawed off crag. This is Claud Evans, driving the Herefords to round-up." (Courtesy of June Evans Bond.)

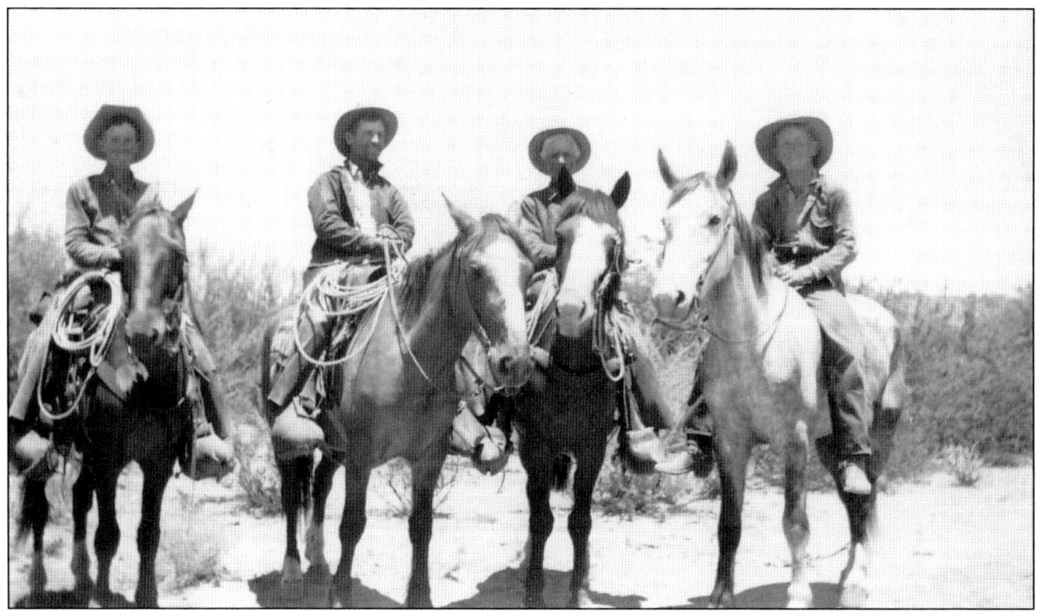

The T-Up T-Down Ranch was family-run and many of the cowboys were related by birth or marriage. From left to right, Jim Gibson, Claud Evans, Frank Wilson, and Bob Evans smile for this 1940 photograph. Wilson was said to be related to legendary gunfighter Pat Garrett; Jim Gibson was related to the Evans family. (Courtesy of June Evans Bond.)

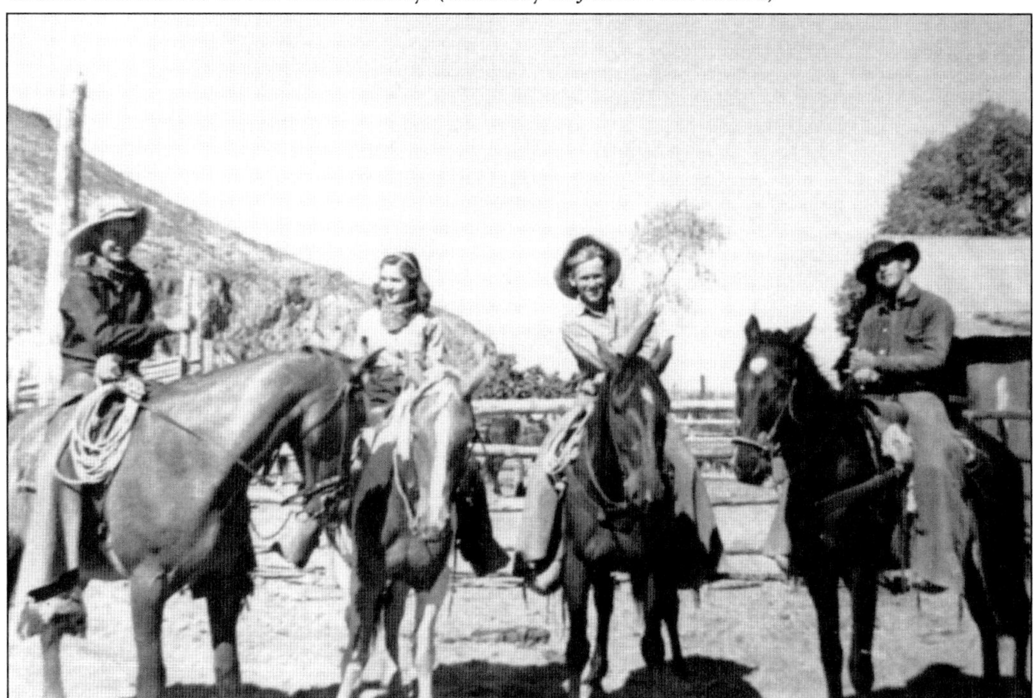

From left to right, Frank Bond, June Evans, Jim Evans, and Bob Evans stand in front of the stock corrals in 1940. Frank and June grew up together and later married. Looking at this photograph, June laughs, "Even then, I had my eyes on him." June's father, Claud Evans, owned the T-Ranch for many years. (Courtesy of June Evans Bond.)

Claud Evans bred a line of horses especially suited for the needs of the T-Ranch. As his foundation stud, Claud brought in a Morgan stallion (called Red Cloud after a famous sire) to breed to Arabian and Quarter-bred mares. Nimble in the rocks, they were suited to hot weather and comfortable to ride. Here, June Evans Bond trains a Red Cloud colt in 1942. (Courtesy of June Evans Bond.)

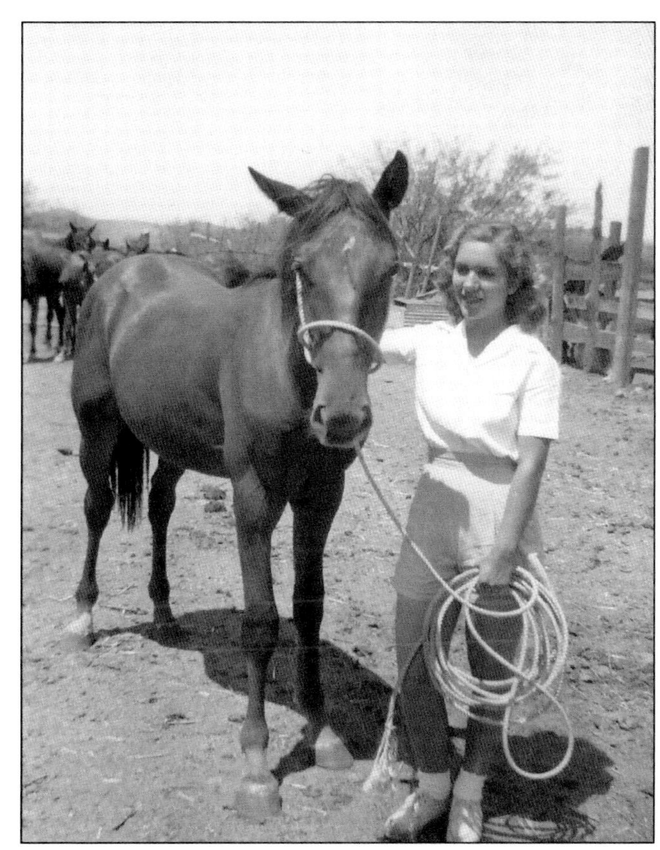

The "head of the river" was one of the most beautiful parts of the ranch. In this 1943 photograph, Claud Evans ponies a pack mule and range horse at the site. A true horseman, Claud cared greatly for his livestock, as evidenced by the superb condition of his horse and mule. June Evans Bond recalled him firing an otherwise outstanding cowboy for harshly treating livestock. (Courtesy of June Evans Bond.)

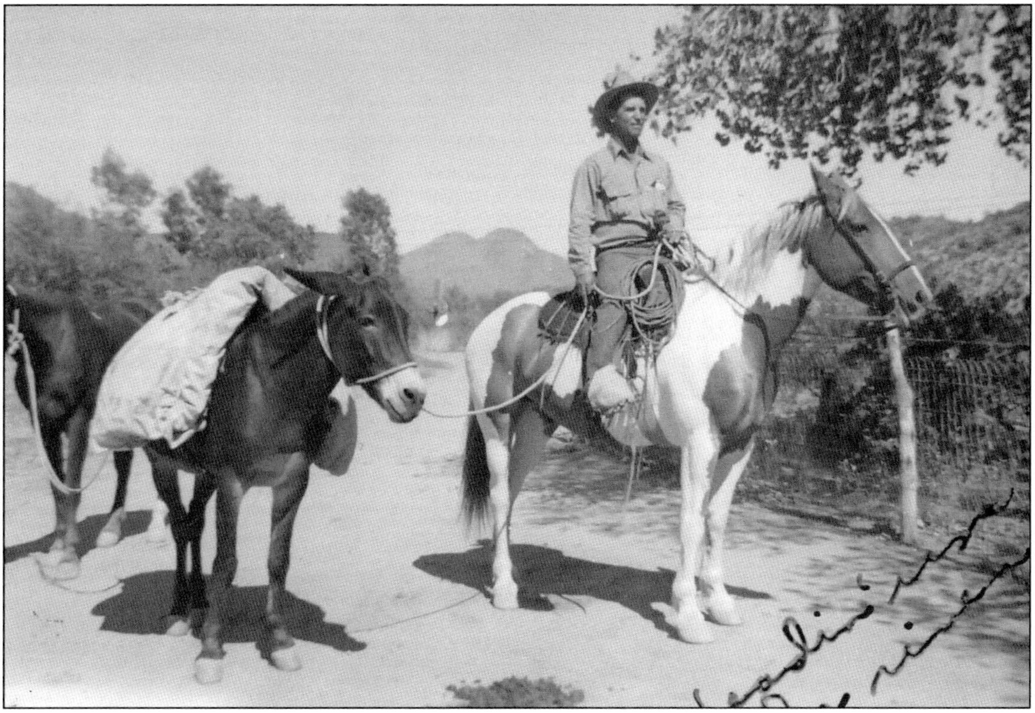

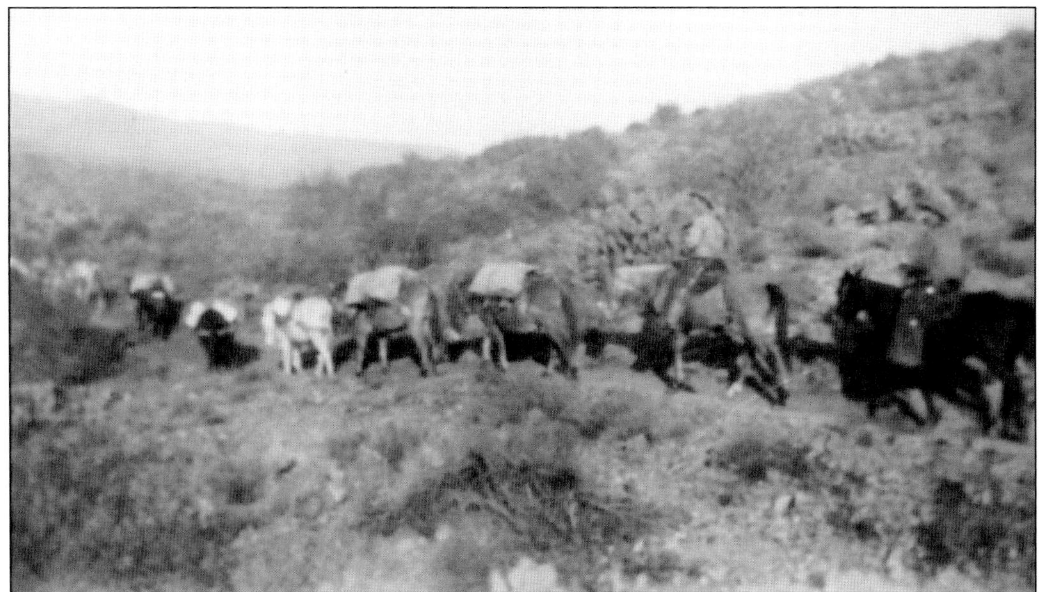

Burros and mules were essential to the ranch, packing supplies such as cattle salt to the remote parts of the range. Many of the burros lived for decades on the ranch. When Claud Evans sold the ranch, the new owners wanted different stock and sent all the livestock to auction, including Prieta, a 30-year-old burro who had spent her entire life on the ranch. (Courtesy of June Evans Bond.)

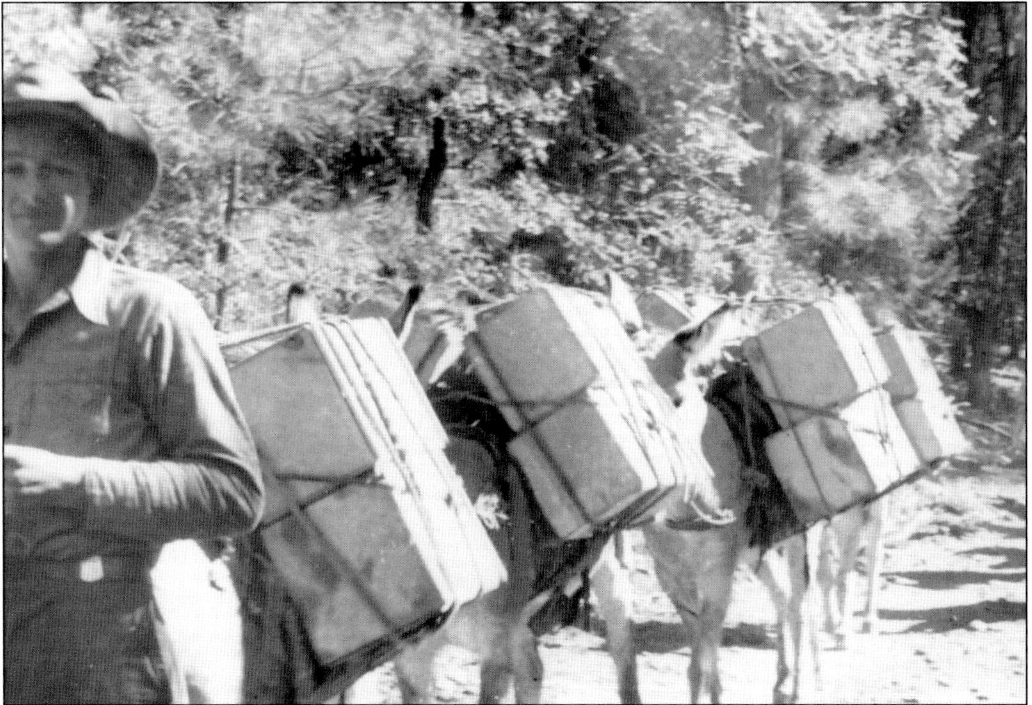

The squares packed onto these burros are salt blocks for the cattle. Each block is about 50 pounds. In this shot of the string returning from head of the river, the visitor at left complained that he only had his photograph taken once at the T-Ranch—and they did not even get all of his face. (Courtesy of June Evans Bond.)

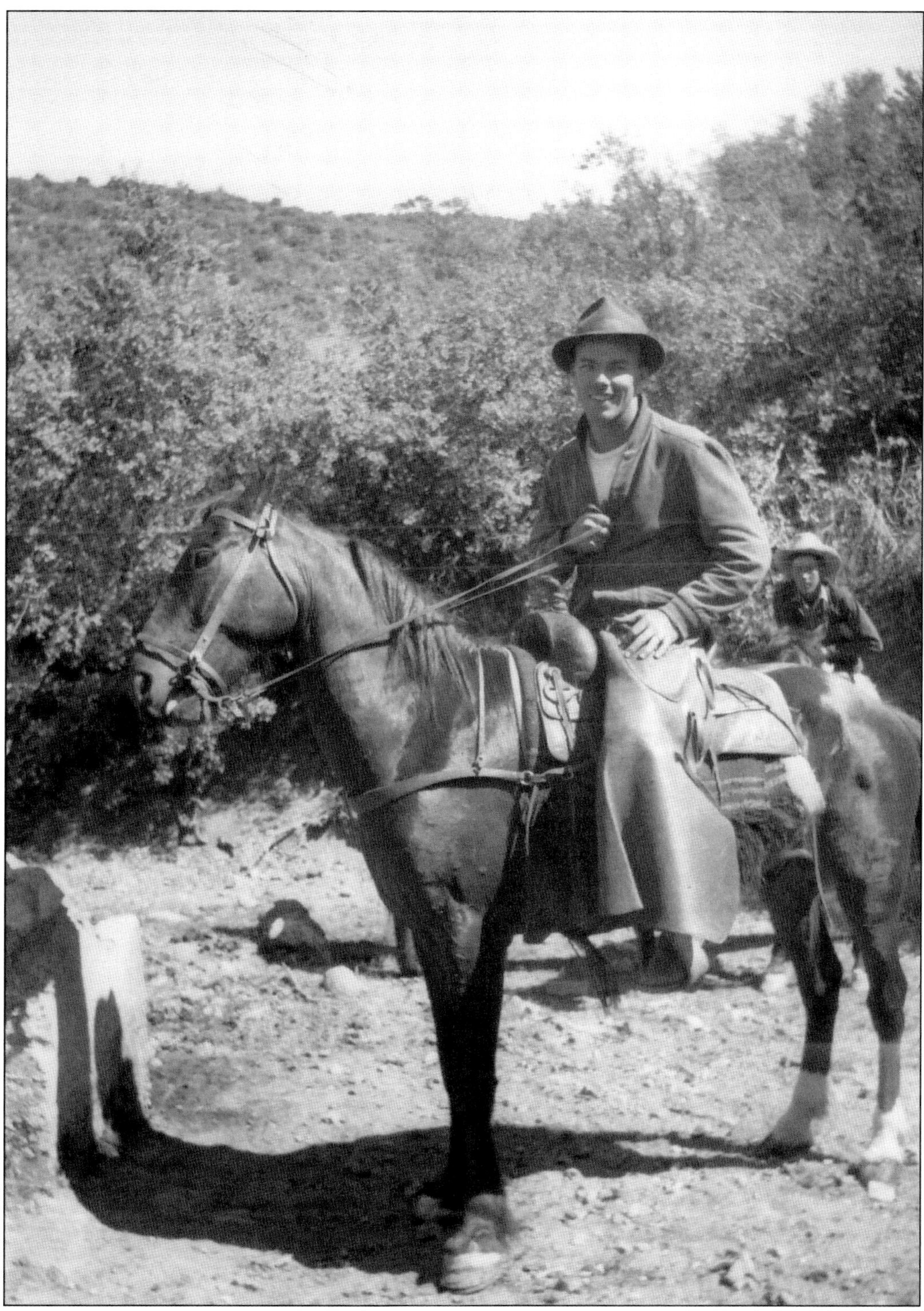

In this photograph from the early 1930s, a T-Ranch cowboy, possibly Cecil Anderson, poses near a concrete stock tank. The horse bears the distinct look of the Evans breeding: a nicely arched neck, the Morgan-type head, and legs built well forward. (Courtesy of June Evans Bond.)

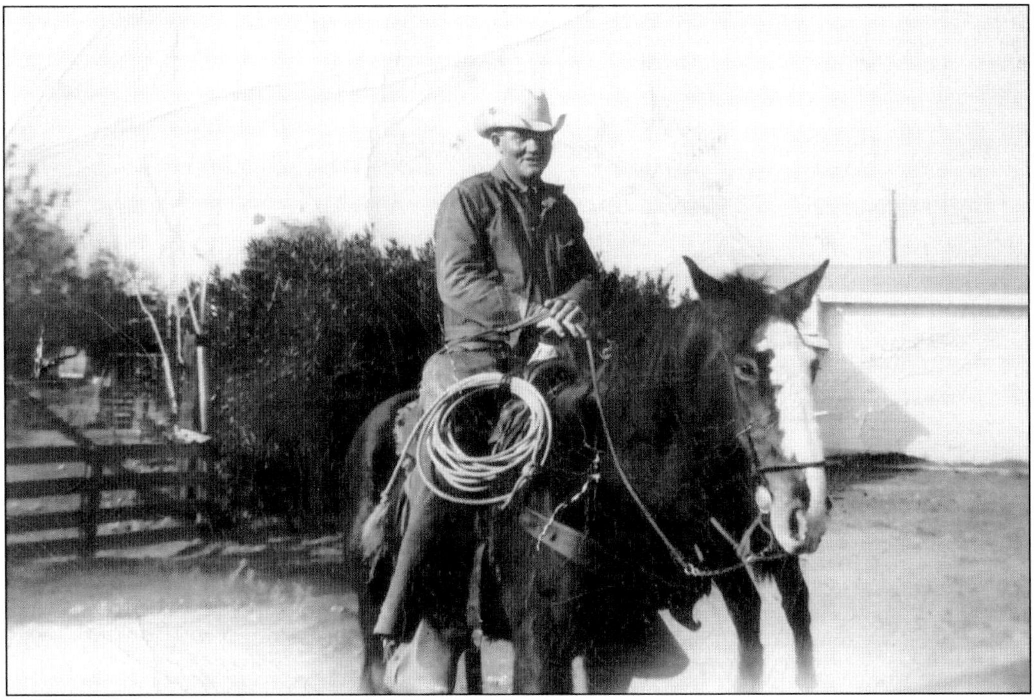

Burrel J. Lann was a cowboy's cowboy: tough as nails, hardworking, and capable. Burrel's son-in-law Leon Gee well recalls his ability to rope and handle the wild cows in the remote depths of the T-Ranch. Leon learned cowboying on the T-Ranch from Burrel, shown here in the mid-1950s. (Courtesy of Leon and Frances Lann Gee.)

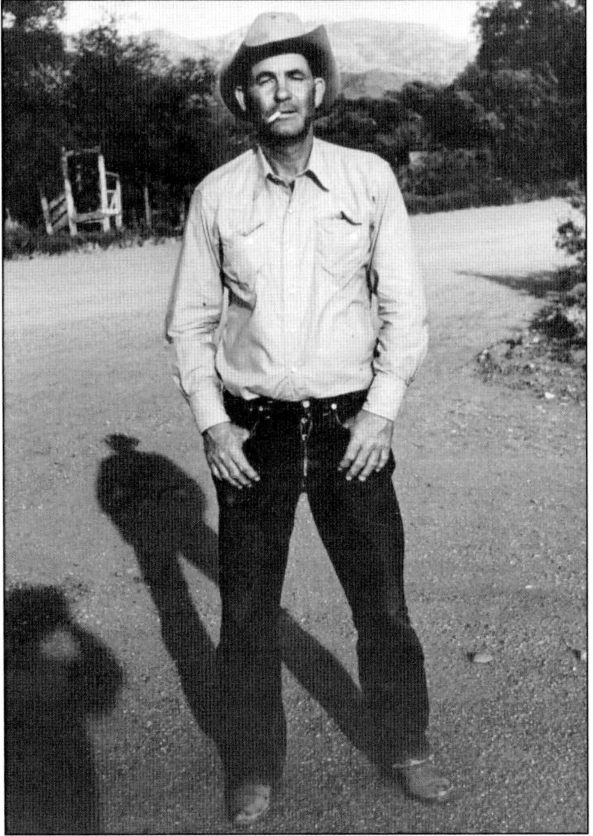

Many visitors to ranches in mid-20th-century Arizona were appropriately impressed by the cowboys they encountered. An unidentified tourist snapped this photograph of Burrel Lann in the Sunflower area, saying he wanted a picture of a "real cowboy." The photographer certainly found one. (Courtesy of Leon and Frances Lann Gee.)

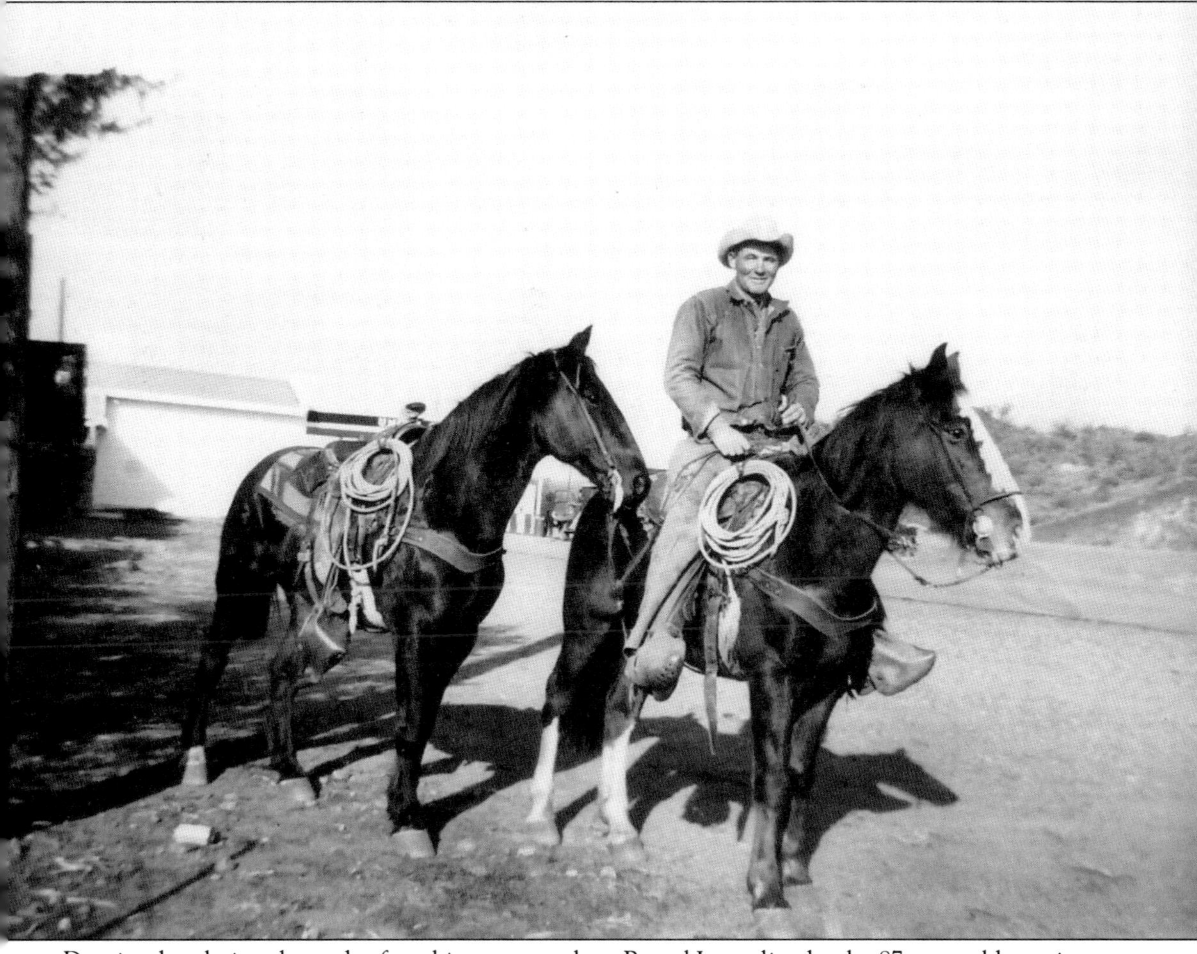

Despite the obvious hazards of working as a cowboy, Burrel Lann lived to be 87 years old, passing away in 1994. A handsome man with bright blue eyes, he mentored the young cowboys, including his sons, who had the privilege to learn cowboying from him. (Courtesy of June Evans Bond.)

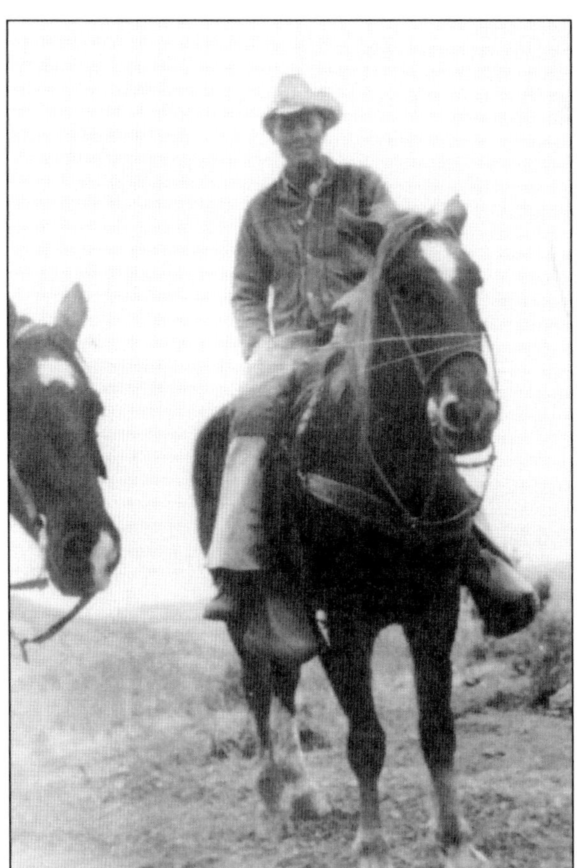

This image of Burrel Lann was taken in 1946, the year he arrived in New River from the Tonto Basin. John Cline also came from the Tonto Basin and began working on the T-Ranch that year. Cowboys had a unique kinship and a brotherhood of sorts, their lives overlapping through work, marriages, and, for many, rodeos. (Courtesy of Leon and Frances Lann Gee.)

Burrel J. Lann's status as a great cowboy is commemorated by the headstone on his grave at Cave Creek Cemetery. The brands of the outfits he owned and worked for are engraved on the stone. They include the "butcher hooks" brand from Burrel's Tonto Basin ranch and the "door key" brand from the Lann family ranch in Texas as well as New River–area ranches.

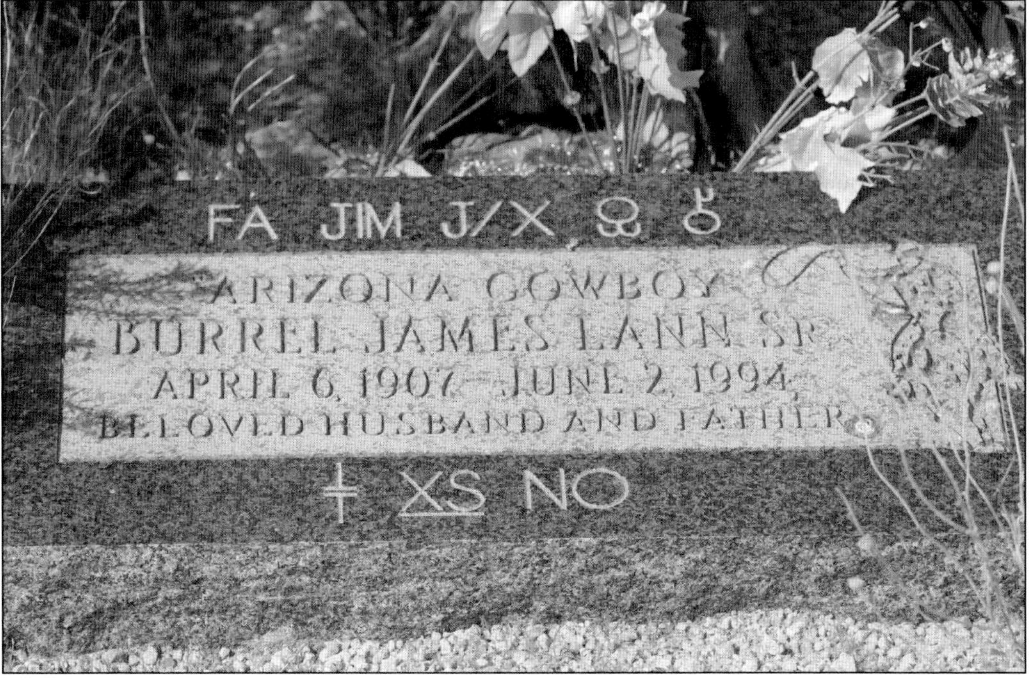

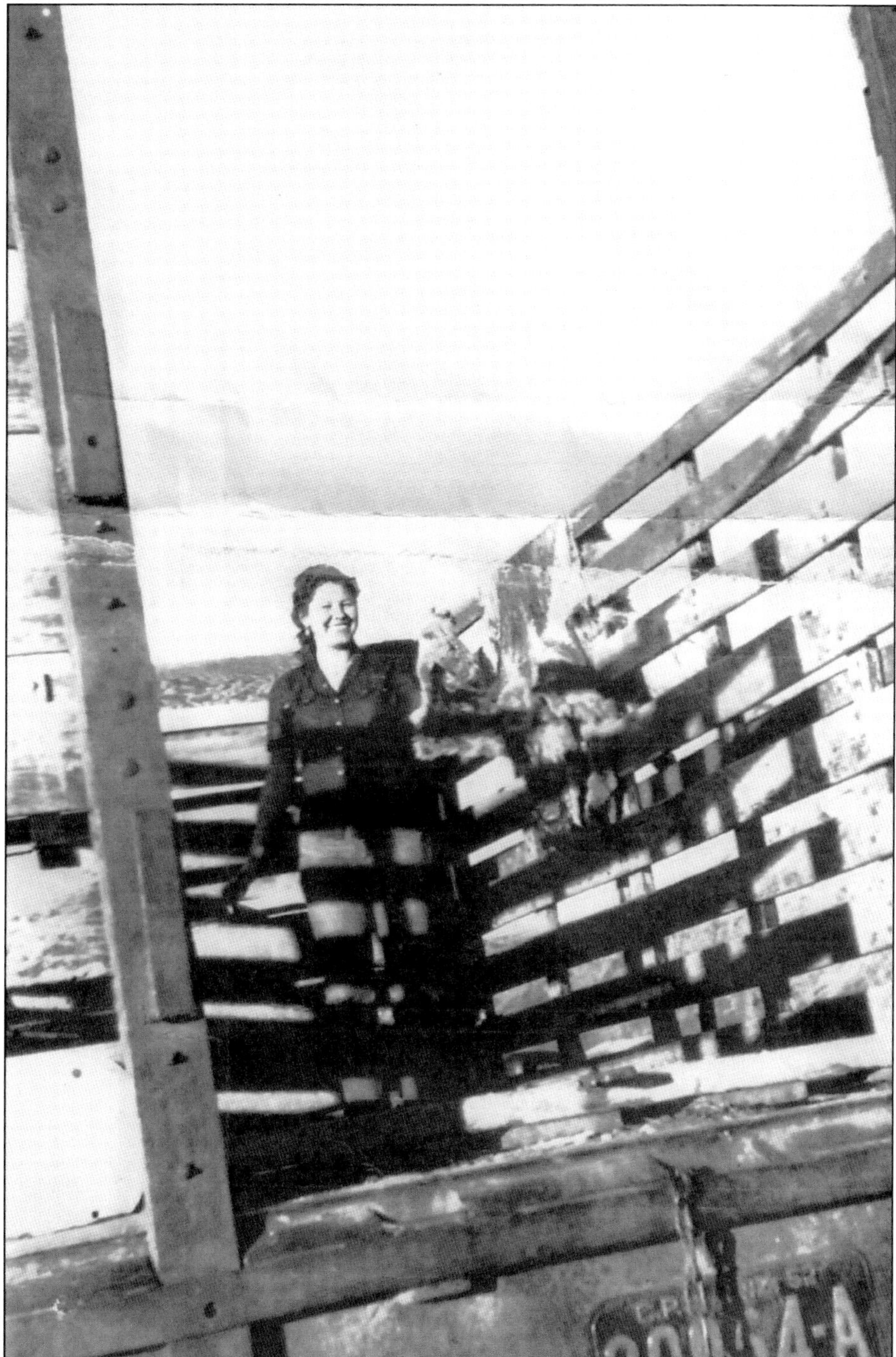

In this 1952 photograph, Burrel Lann's daughter Rosemary Pock stands next to the hides of mountain lions her father killed for the Cattleman's Association bounty. Mountain lions were a significant predator of cattle in the area. Cougars were not thrifty consumers; they would sometimes kill several cows at a time, eating nothing but the milk-filled udders and leaving the rest to waste. (Courtesy of Leon and Frances Lann Gee.)

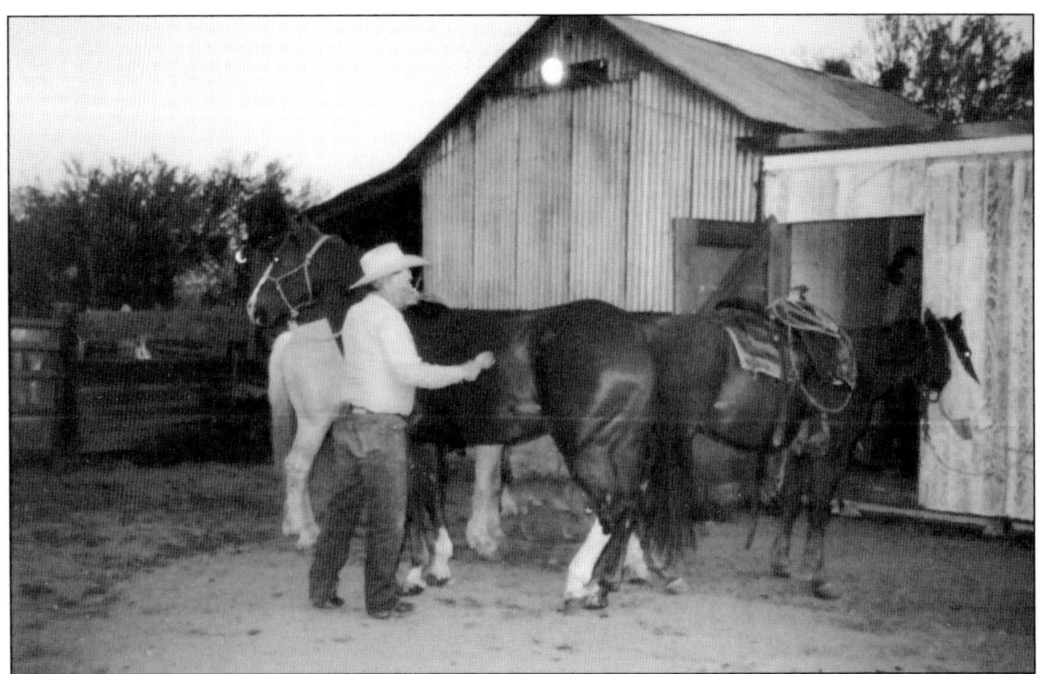

A cowboy's day often began before sunup; in the winter because days were short, and in the summer because the heat came early. Here, Don Pock curries his horse in front of the saddle barn at the T-Ranch. Note the nosebag on the horse at right, a time-efficient means of feeding grain while working. (Courtesy of Leon and Frances Lann Gee.)

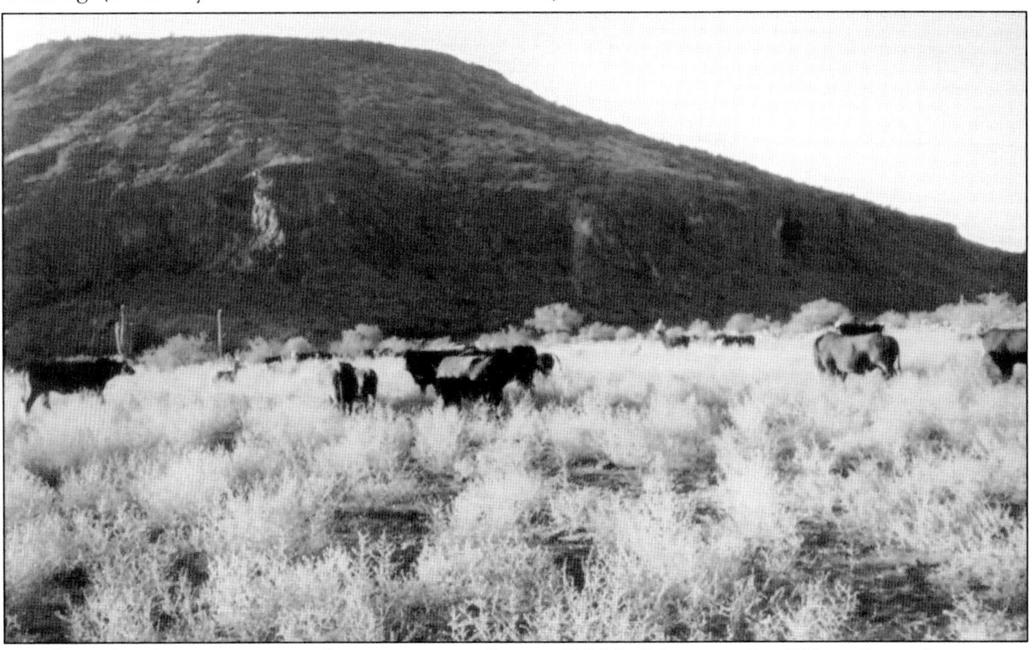

Cattle and at least one spotted goat graze in front of Table Mesa on the T-Ranch in this image from the 1950s. The cattle type varied over the years based on terrain and owner preference. Generally, Herefords ranged the forest side of the ranch, while heat-tolerant Brahmans were introduced in the desert side to the south. (Courtesy of Leon and Frances Lann Gee.)

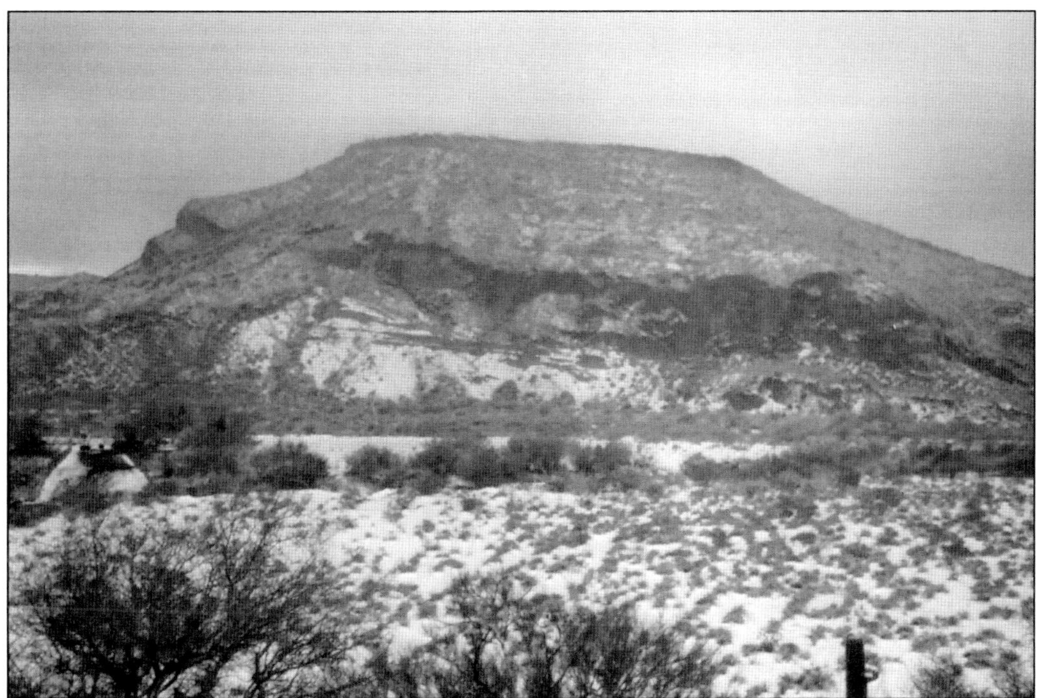

A rare sight, snow-covered Table Mesa provided a stunning backdrop for the ranch. Desert ranches required huge expanses of pasture to provide ample forage for the cattle, since each consumes an average of about 25 pounds per day. Area ranchers did not speak in term of "cattle per acre" but rather in "acres per head." (Courtesy of Leon and Frances Lann Gee.)

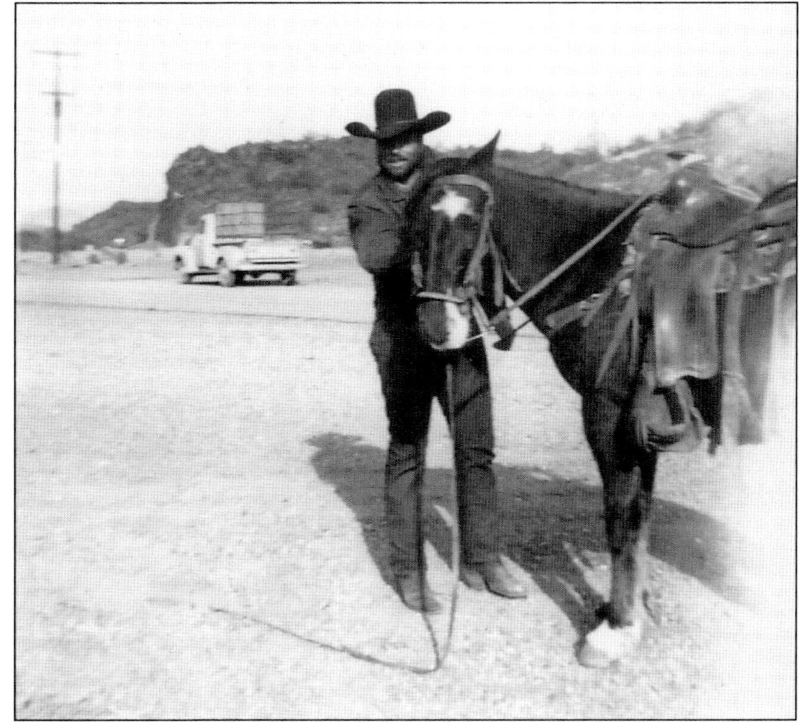

Local cowboy Casey Jack is shown here along the old Black Canyon road; the fact the road is paved indicates this is from the 1950s. Although not as often seen today, the working cowboys at the time used the tapaderos (stirrup covers) seen on Casey's saddle to prevent branches from snagging the stirrups in the thick brush. (Courtesy of June Evans Bond.)

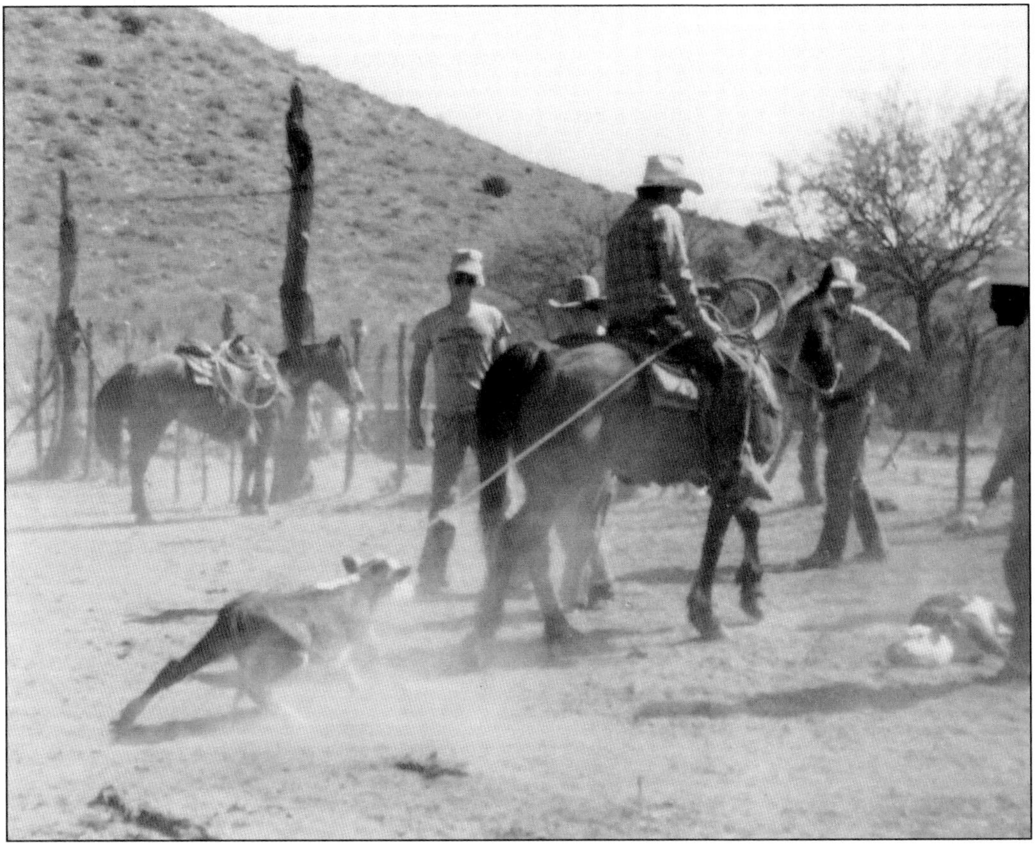

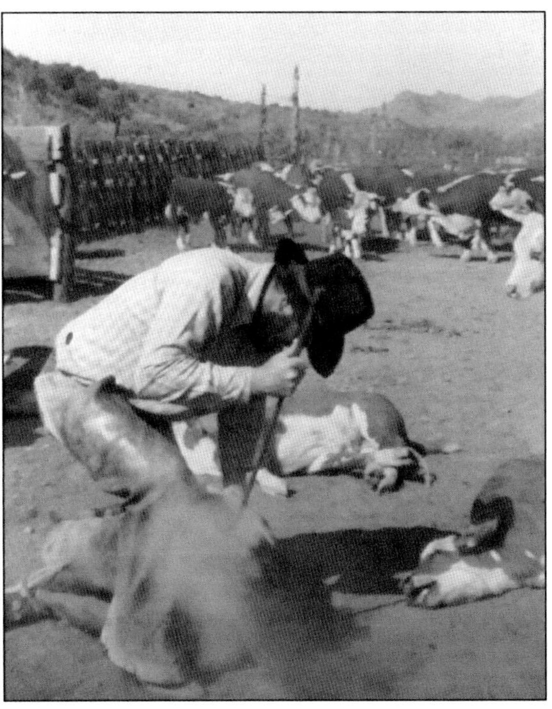

Branding day was a big event, often requiring additional temporary help. Calves and heifers would be gathered; unbranded calves would be branded and most bull calves would be castrated. Above, a T-Ranch cowboy drags a calf near the fire for branding. At left, the hot brand is being applied. The calf's legs are tied securely as others await attention. Note their watchful mothers standing nearby. These white-faced cattle are Herefords, a beef breed that dominated the Arizona range at the time. Prone to eye cancer, Herefords have since been replaced on most desert ranches. (Both, courtesy of Leon and Frances Lann Gee.)

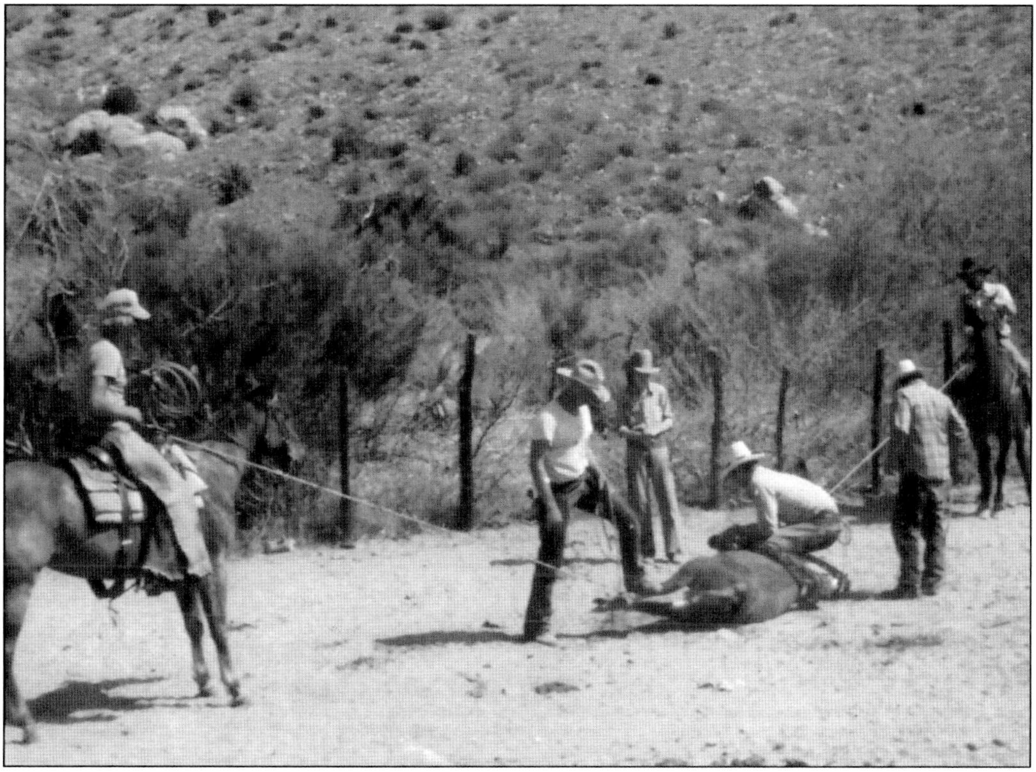

Above, one cowgirl assists in the branding activities. Note the tension on the rope and the position of the horse on the left's front legs. Roping horses are trained to maintain tension on the calf without direction from the rider, thus preventing the calf from freeing its back legs and escaping. Below, cowboys work cattle at the No. 32 windmill on the lower T-Ranch. Windmills were assigned section numbers and served as landmarks for ranch work. The No. 32 windmill was just southeast of Skunk Creek. In the background is a good view of Pyramid Peak, on the northeast corner of what is now the Circle Mountain Road and New River Road intersection. (Both, courtesy of Leon and Frances Gee.)

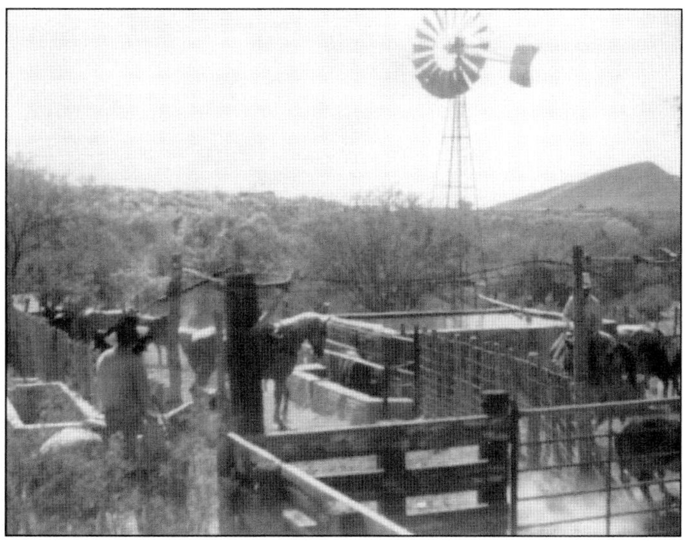

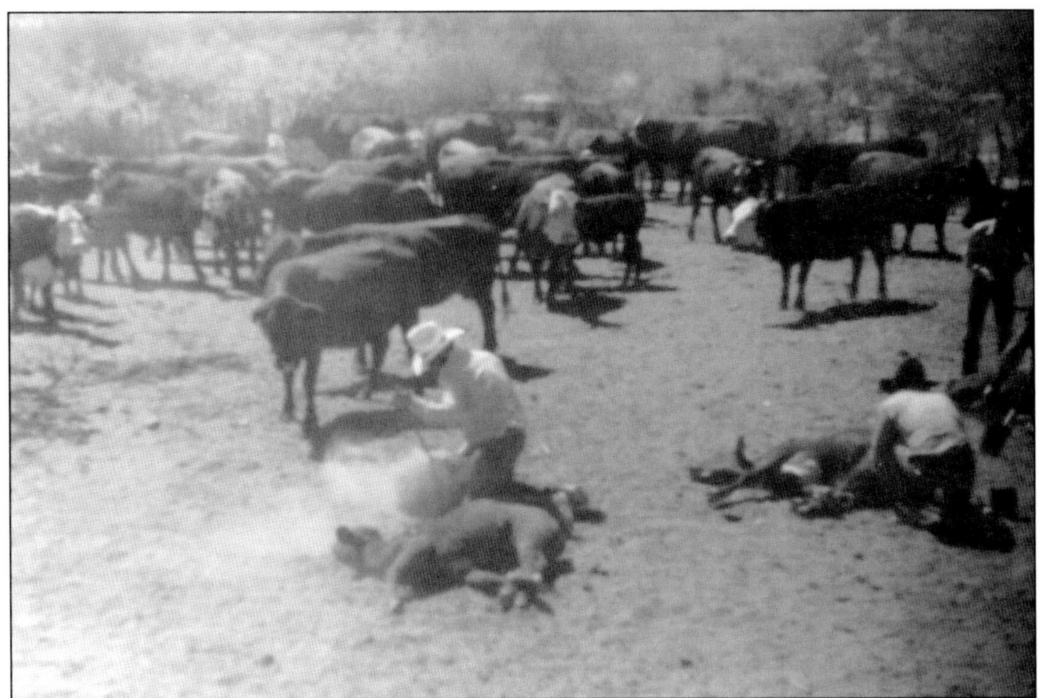

Above, while the cowboy on the left brands one calf, the cowboy on the right is castrating another. Calf castration was (and still is) a quick process involving little more than a sharp knife. The wound is left open to ensure proper drainage. The cattle here are a blended herd rather than just Herefords. Below, a calf struggles to its knees while the cowboys move in to subdue it. Calves are much stronger than they appear. Modern rodeo, a sport entirely descended from actual ranch work, has set maximum weight limits on calves for roping and bull-dogging to ensure fair competition. On actual beef ranches, cowboys handle larger, stronger stock. (Both, courtesy of Leon and Frances Gee.)

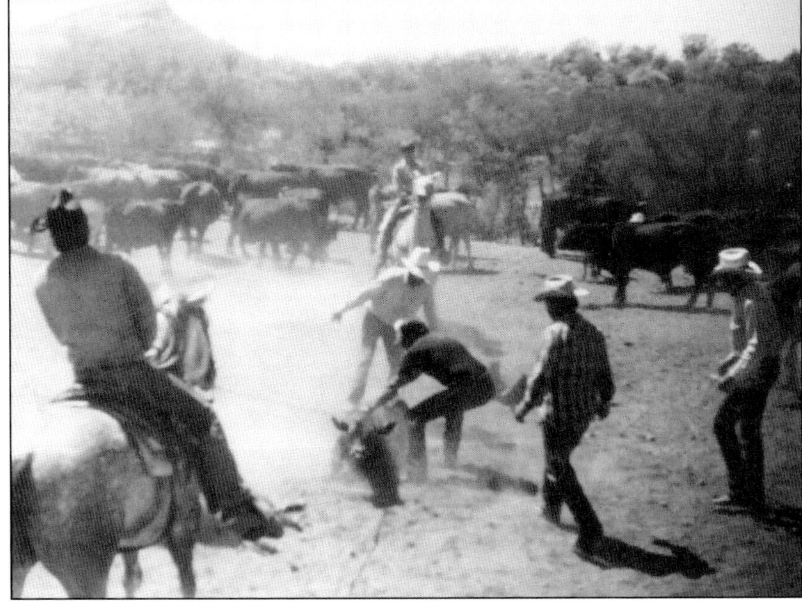

In 1946, John Henry Cline began working for Frank Armer, Ray Cowden, and Levi Reed, then owners of the T-Ranch. Early on, Cline committed to buying into the partnership from his $150 wages. John ultimately owned more than half of the ranch. At right, Cline and one of his hounds sit in front of a stone corral. Cline loved dogs, mules, and horses and could rarely be found without a dog close at hand. Below, Cline gives a lift to a speckled hound. Like many ranchers, he hunted mountain lions to protect his livestock and collect the bounty. Hounds were used to track the lions. (Both, courtesy of Rene Faires.)

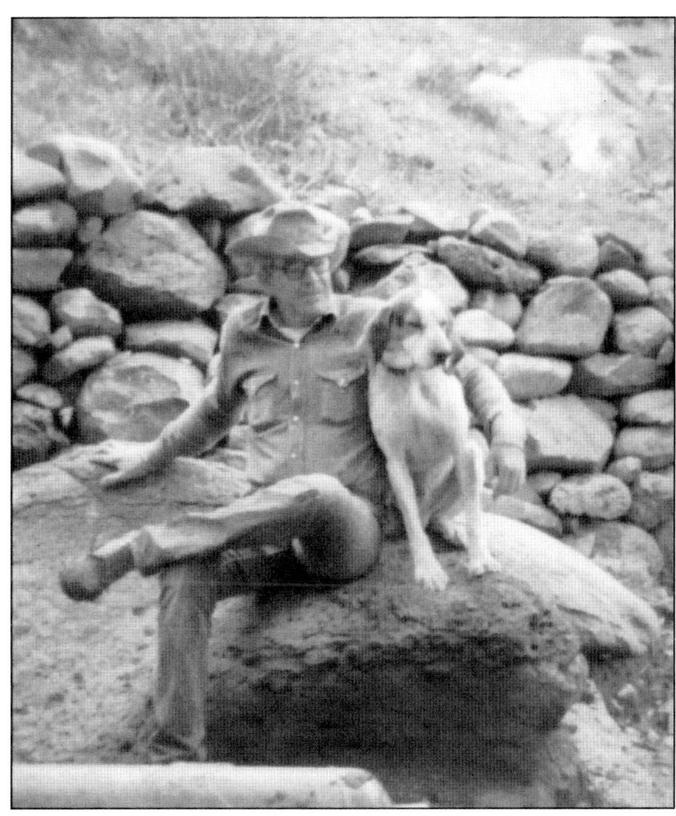

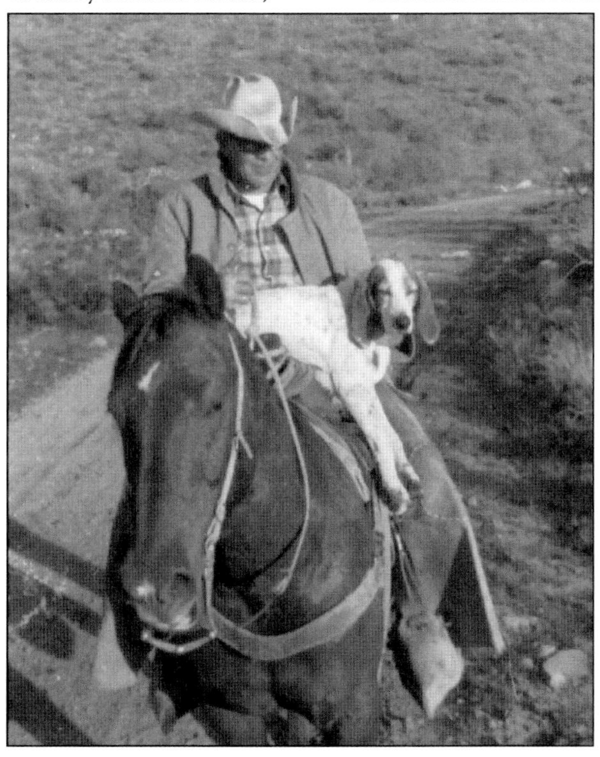

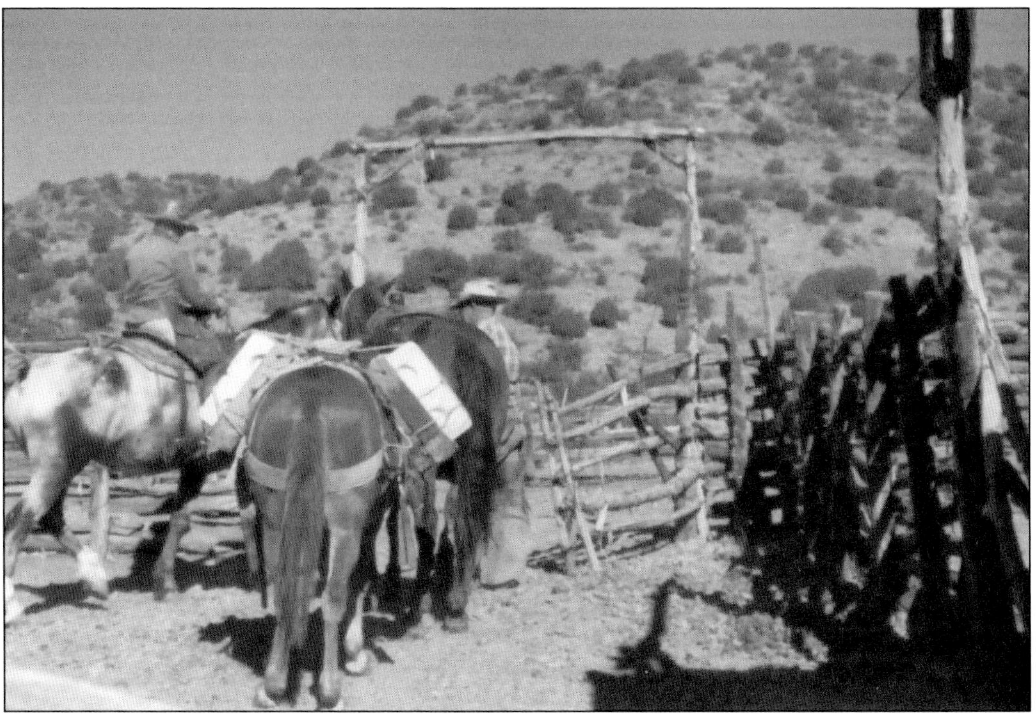

John Cline (right) prepares to deliver salt blocks to the cattle on the range. The blocks are evenly distributed on the mule's packs. Packing is a science all its own; even weight distribution is critical for the comfort and safety of the pack animal, the protection of the load, and the safety of the cowboy. (Courtesy of Rene Faires.)

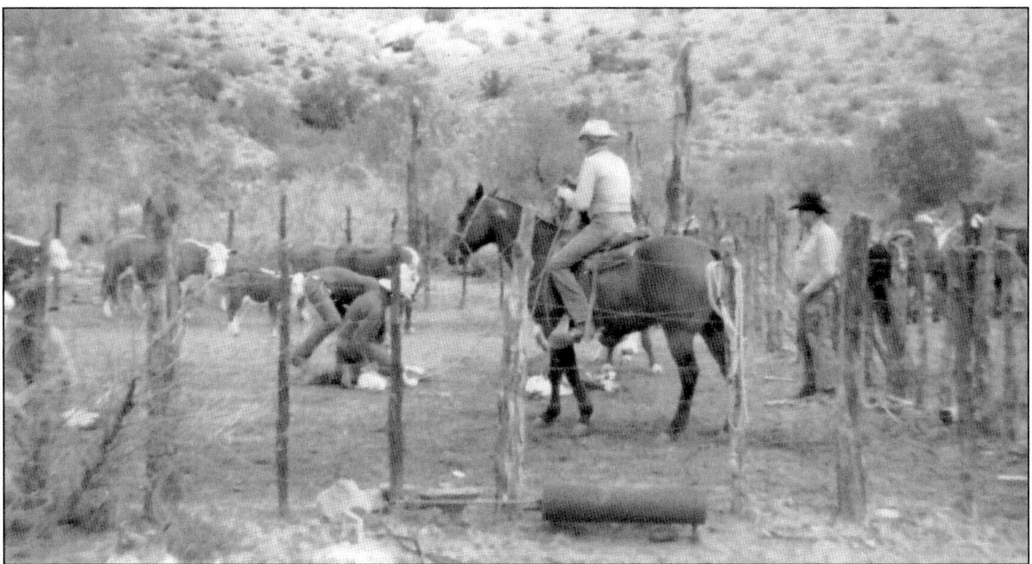

John Cline stood a lanky six foot two and his leggy frame shows in the bend of his knees in the saddle. Born in Punkin Center in 1913, a year after Arizona achieved statehood, John was a member of the famous Cline pioneer family in Tonto Basin. After his death in 1987, his body was returned to the area of his birth to be buried in the Cline Family Cemetery. (Courtesy of Rene Faires.)

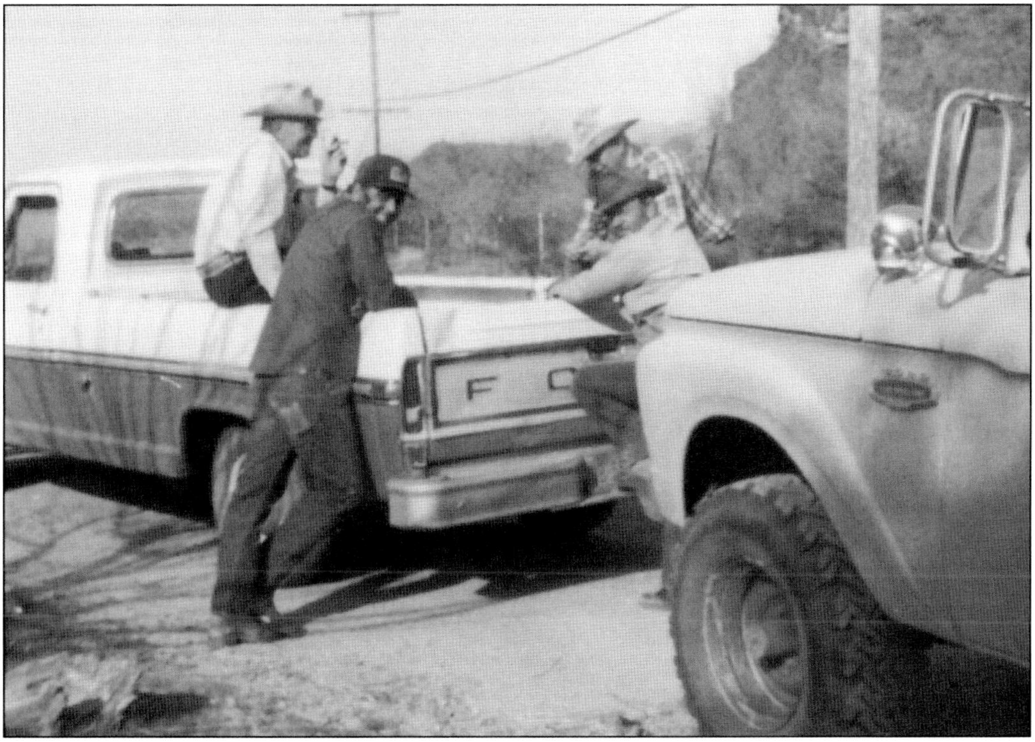

John Cline (left) joins three friends for a laugh and a smoke on the T-Ranch in the above photograph. Also shown are, from left to right, Bob Bolvin, Tom Riblin, and Rick Grant. Below, Cline (right) sits his horse in one of the T-Ranch stock corrals. A cowboy for life, even after retiring, Cline helped out on roundups as needed. Although he briefly lived with relatives in California, nearly his entire life was spent on ranches in either Tonto Basin or New River. He liked to say he had only gone "seventy miles in seventy years." The view below, looking to the north, was taken just north of Pepsi Cap Mountain. These Hereford cattle are in good condition, but drought and floods were a constant threat to the ranch. Frank Alkire, one of the earliest owners of the T-Ranch (then the Triangle-Bar), estimated that by the end of the drought of 1892–1898, seventy percent of the state's cattle had perished. (Both, courtesy of Rene Faires.)

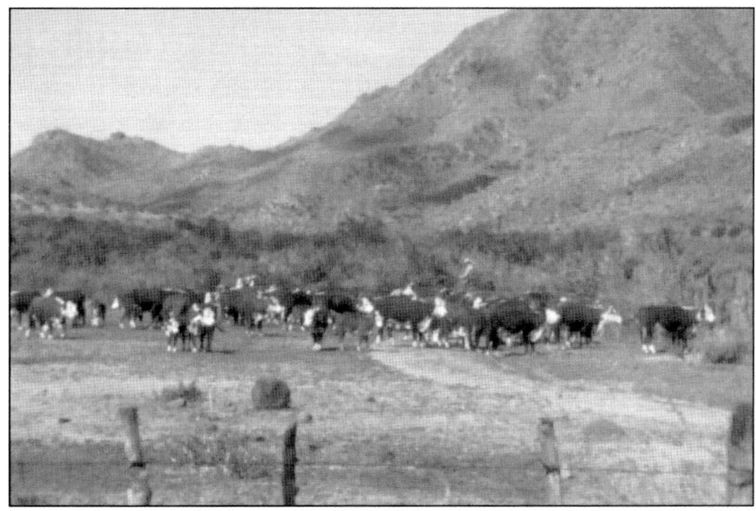

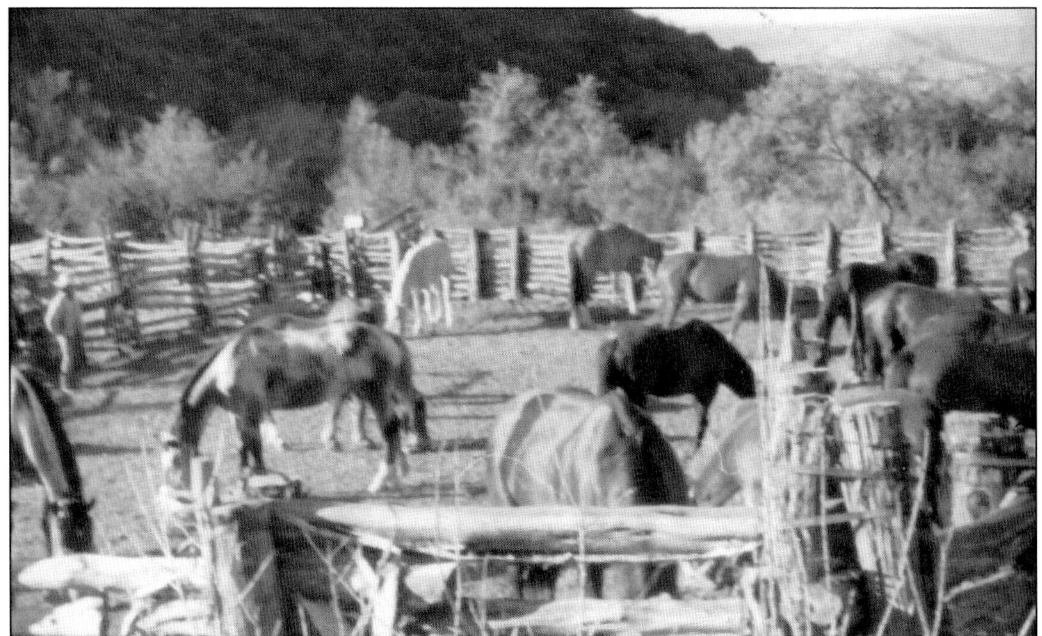

The remuda at the peak of the T-Ranch often required as many as 70 horses. A remuda is a ranch's saddle string, already broke to ride and maintained ready for work. These T-Ranch horses are visibly different in conformation and type from the horses once line-bred by Claud Evans. (Courtesy of Rene Faires.)

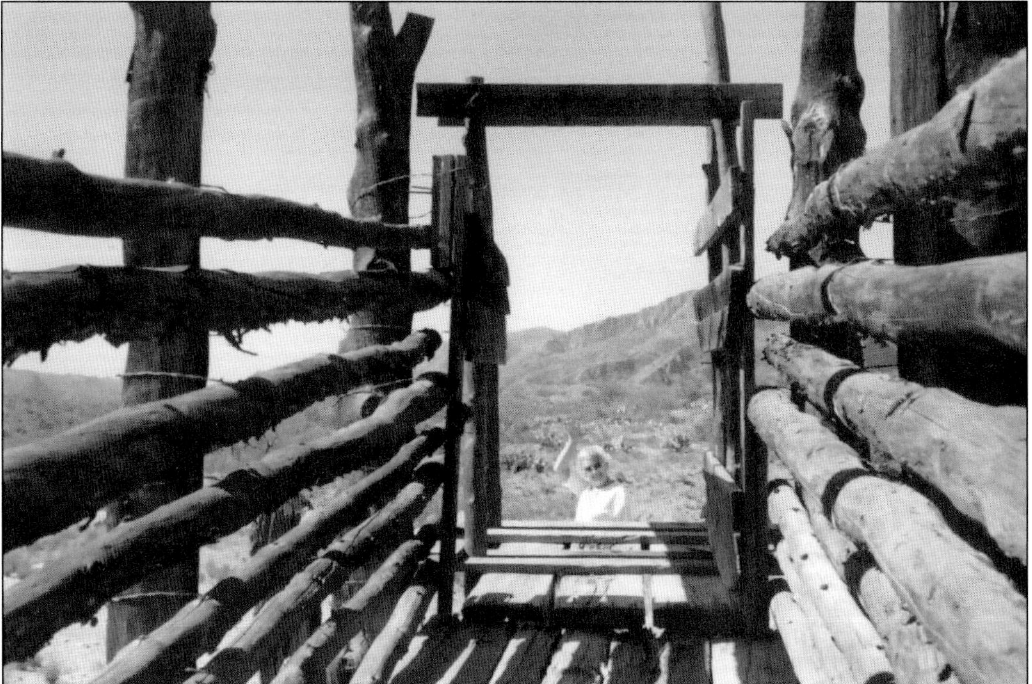

John Cline's second wife, Edie, waves here from a stock-loading chute on the upper T-Ranch. On the far left side of this photograph, with a view that looks south, is the steep peak used by the ancient Hohokams as a lookout and fortress. (Courtesy of Rene Faires.)

Four

The Homesteaders
The Heart of New River

Although cowboys and travelers were a constant presence in New River in the early 1900s, the community did not fully bloom until the arrival of the homesteaders of the 1920s and 1930s. The National Homestead Act of 1862 offered 160 acres of federally-owned land—a quarter section of land—to homesteaders who met specific criteria for eligibility and property improvements. The original act, as written, was unfeasible for most arid lands. Subsequent acts that revised the original requirements made Arizona more accessible for homesteaders. Still, the majority of homesteaders were ultimately unsuccessful in earning their land patents. Those who did were a rare breed of capable and persistent settlers. Of the 21,000 land patents issued in Arizona from 1870 to 1940, records indicate about 25 were granted in New River.

These 20th-century homesteaders proved up their lands while building the community around them. Most contributed in some way even as they built their own houses and often worked a full-time job "in town" (Phoenix) to make ends meet. Early school lessons and church services were conducted in the William Essary homestead on Fig Springs Road until a one-room schoolhouse was moved onto a donated part of Ernest and Sudie Essary's property. Homesteaders such as Doris Avis and Boyd "Pappy" Sears shuttled kids to classes in improvised school buses. Mildred Donham, from a homestead just north of the school, served as teacher for several years, while her husband, Paul, was the Sunday school director. Bob Stewart, who raised pigs on his property, also ran a small local store. Jerry Jacka Sr. and his wife, Rose, ran a sheep-watering business in addition to running a café and providing quarters for guests. Small in number but seemingly unlimited in energy and dedication, the homesteaders were New River's forefathers and founders.

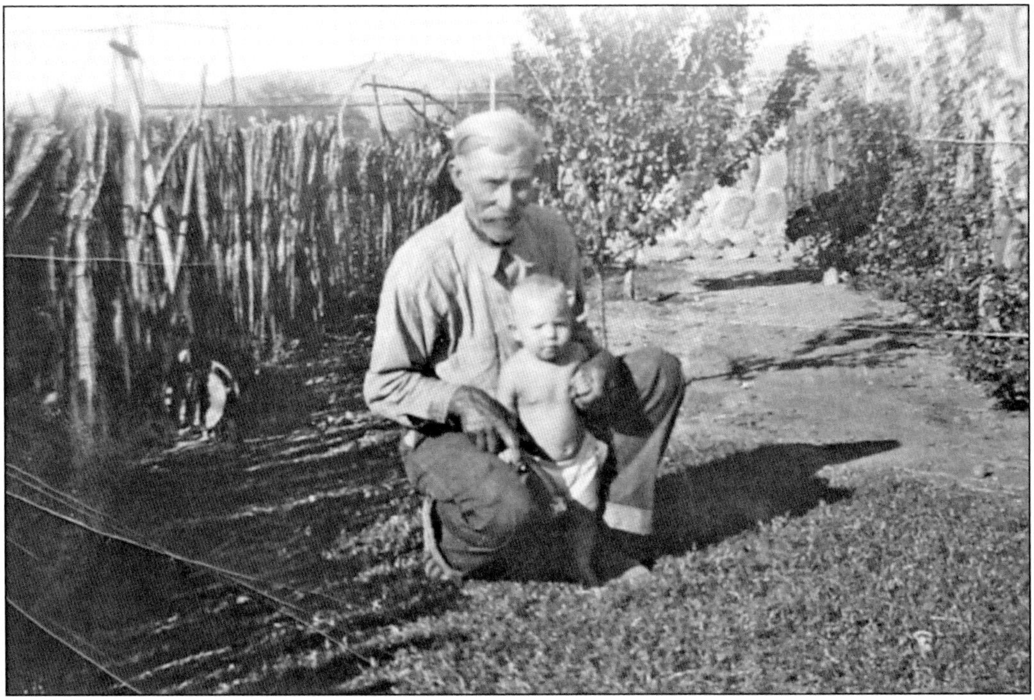

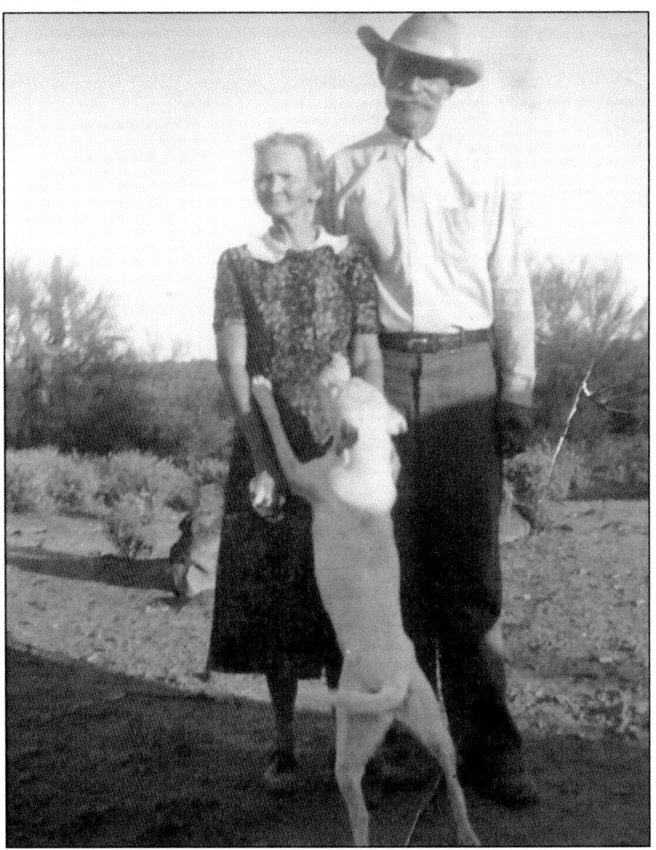

Amos Lafayette "Fate" Essary lived an extraordinary life. Born in Texas in the late 1870s, he married Della in 1903 and they moved to southern Arizona to homestead in Rucker Canyon, near Douglas. In addition to ranching, Fate served as a Cochise County deputy before bringing his family to the Phoenix area to provide a better education for their children. He is shown above with his granddaughter Lois in 1935. At left, he and Della, shown with the family dog Jack, look every bit the strong, capable pioneer couple that they were. Fate died in January 1949; Della survived him by only a year. (Both, courtesy of Jerry D. Jacka and Lois Essary Jacka.)

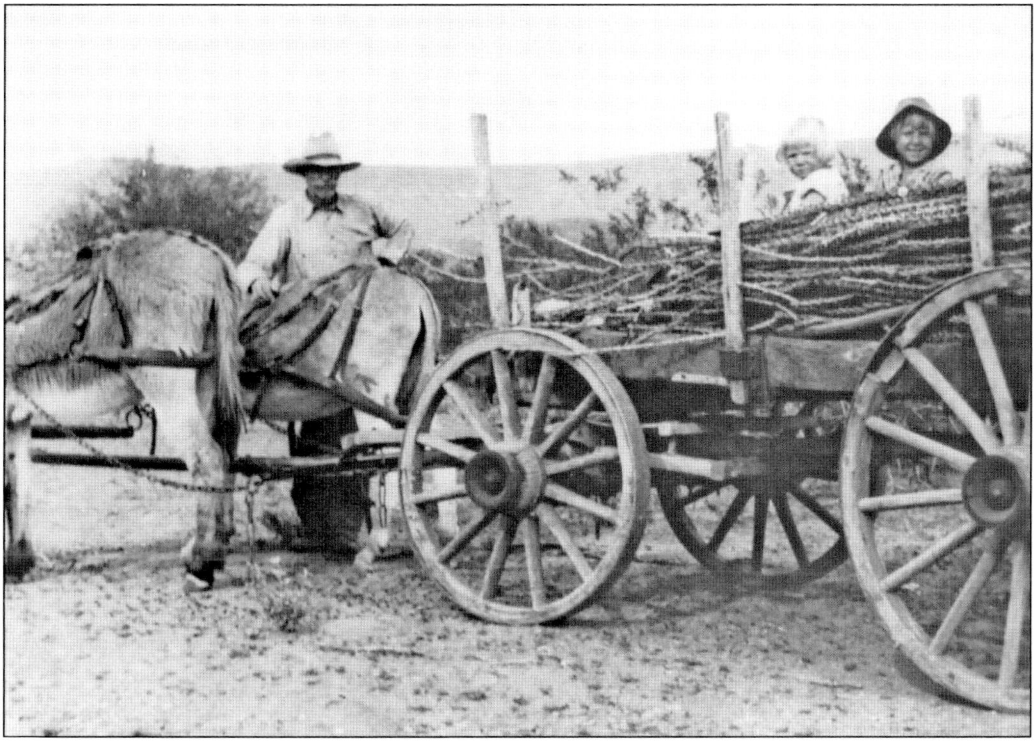

Fate Essary and his wife, Della, came to New River by wagon during the Great Depression. Initially, they lived off the land, camping and trapping. The spiny branches in front of Fate's granddaughters Pauline (center) and Barbara are ocotillo branches. Used as fencing, ocotillo branches sprout leaves with each rain. (Courtesy of Jerry D. Jacka and Lois Essary Jacka.)

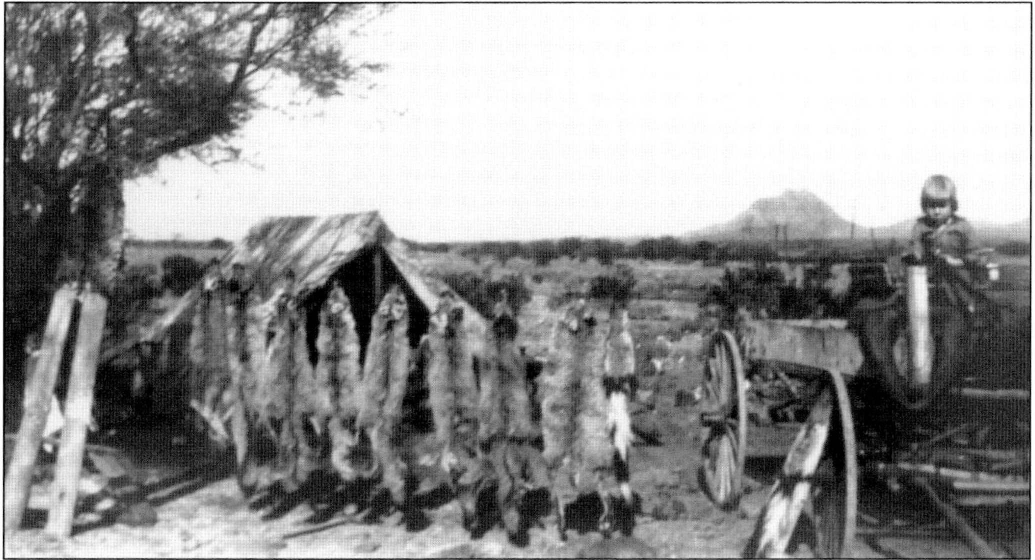

Three-year-old Barbara Essary and her sisters often visited grandfather Fate Essary's trapping camps. The pelts shown here would be sold. In the background is the south face of Gavilan Peak. This camp is at Cline Tank, named after early rancher Hosea Cline, near what is now Anthem. (Courtesy of Jerry D. Jacka and Lois Essary Jacka.)

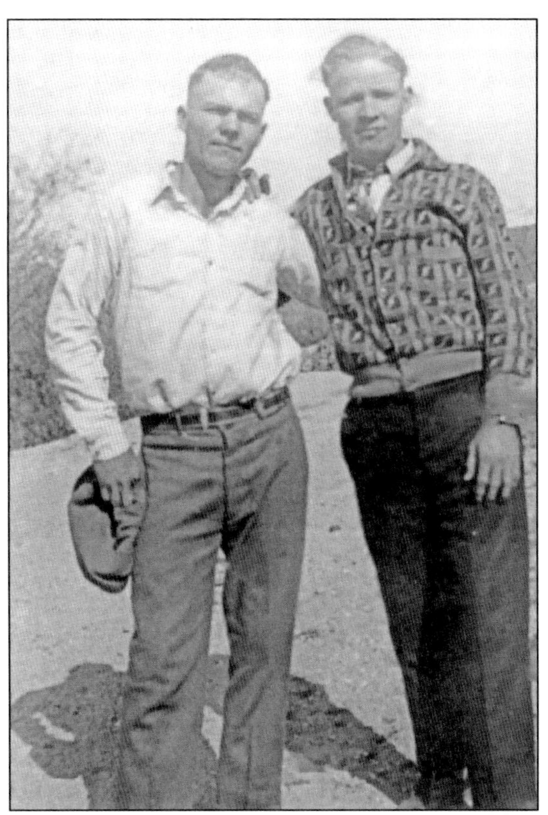

Cousins Ernest Essary (left) and Bill Essary settled near each other on New River homesteads with their wives, Sudie and Rowena. Bill and Rowena hosted the first New River school classes in their living room. Later, Ernest and Sudie donated the land on which New River's first one-room schoolhouse would be placed. (Courtesy of Jerry D. Jacka and Lois Essary Jacka.)

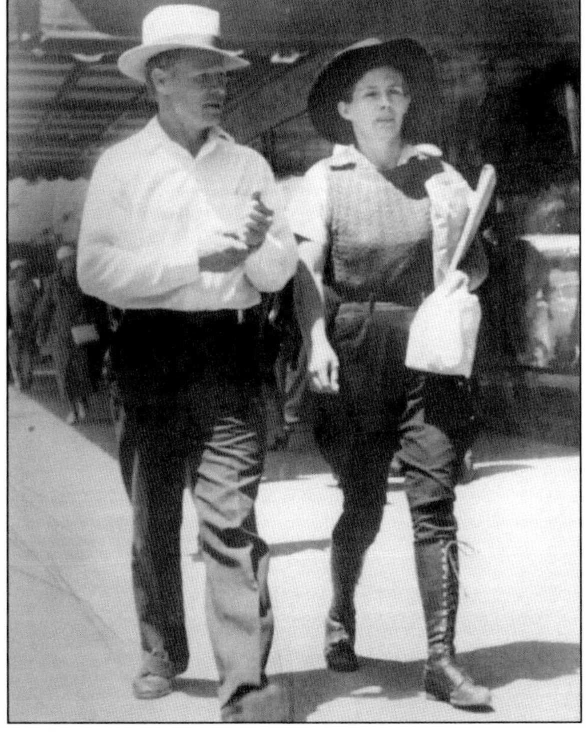

Homesteaders Bill and Rowena Essary were part of a family that contributed tremendously to the settlement of New River. Rowena's family, the Grays, moved to Phoenix from Missouri when Rowena was 15. Four years later, she met and within just two months married Bill Essary. They moved to New River when homestead lands became available. (Courtesy of Jerry D. Jacka and Lois Essary Jacka.)

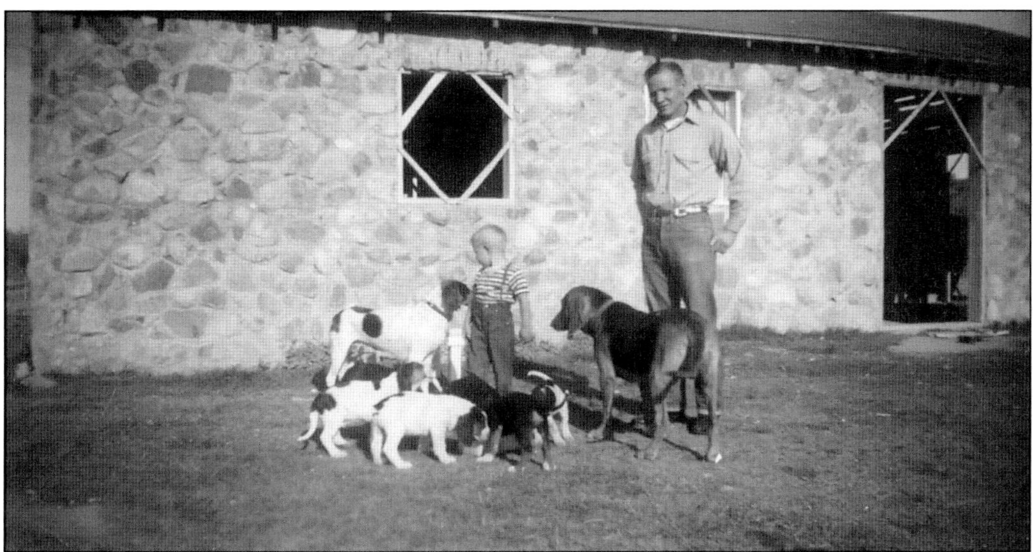

Hounds were popular on many ranches and homesteads not as pets but as hunting dogs. Bill Essary and his son Gary kept this pack of hounds. They are standing in front of the third stone house Bill built in New River, still under construction in this photograph from the early 1950s. (Courtesy of Jerry D. Jacka and Lois Essary Jacka.)

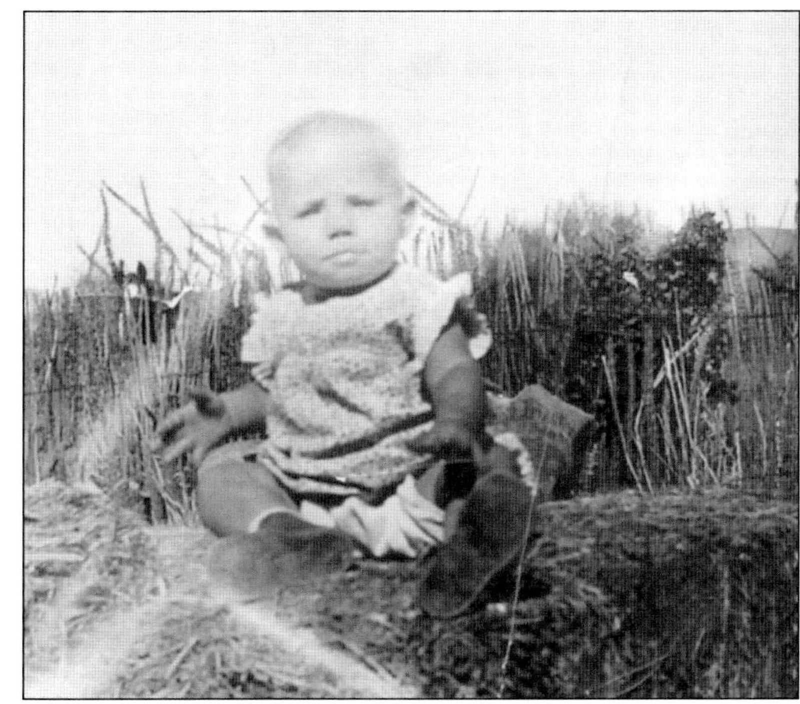

In this 1935 photograph, Lois Essary perches in front of the ocotillo branch fence at the Essary homestead, watched over by one of the family's horses. The community was still small at the time, numbering not much over a dozen families. (Courtesy of Jerry D. Jacka and Lois Essary Jacka.)

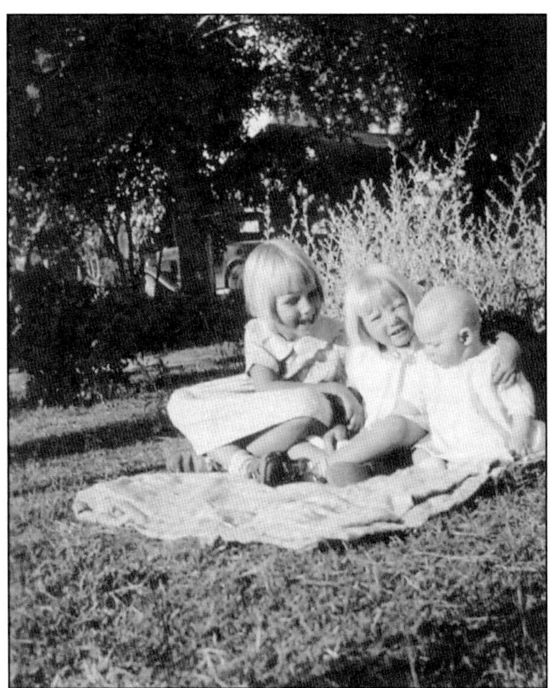

The Essary sisters—from left to right, Barbara, Pauline, and Lois—enjoyed a freedom unimaginable to youngsters today. Few homes even had locks; those families that did rarely used them. Certainly, the homestead lifestyle had its own hazards. Scorpion bites and close calls with snakes were common, but the youngsters grew up independent and capable, largely unafraid of the violent threats today's parents fear for their children. (Courtesy of Jerry D. Jacka and Lois Essary Jacka.)

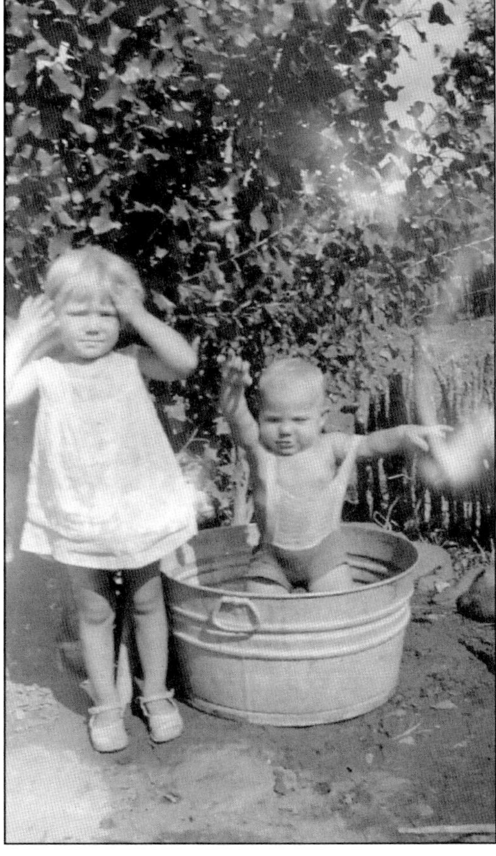

The reliable old metal washtub was essential equipment on a homestead. It could be used to wash clothes, water a thirsty animal, or bathe children. Pauline (left) and Lois Essary used it outdoors to cool off in the summer heat as well as to wash up in the kitchen by the warmth of the stove. (Courtesy of Jerry D. Jacka and Lois Essary Jacka.)

The three fair-haired Essary sisters are celebrating Lois Essary's first birthday on December 9, 1935, in front of the homestead. Barbara (standing) is seven and Pauline (right), four. Sadly, no trace of the beautiful, hand-built Essary house that was so much a part of New River's early community remains at the old homestead site. (Courtesy of Jerry D. Jacka and Lois Essary Jacka.)

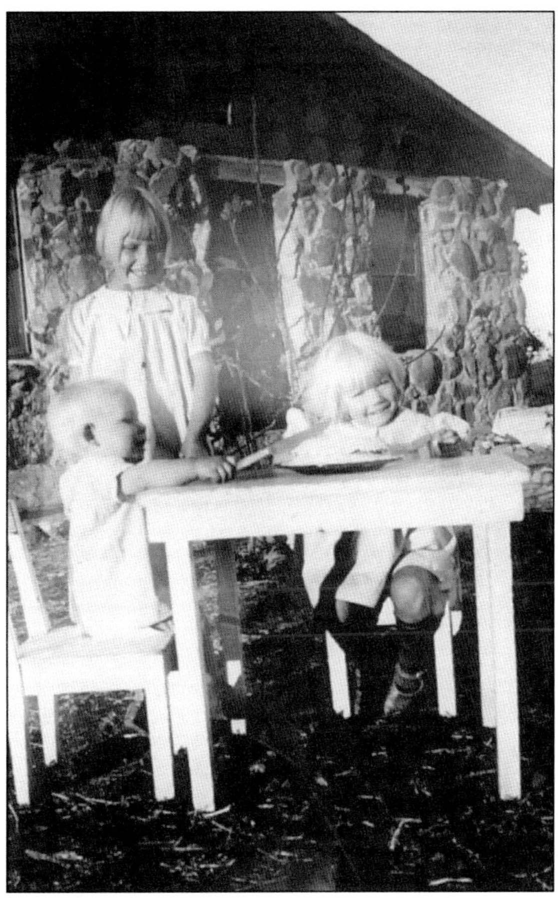

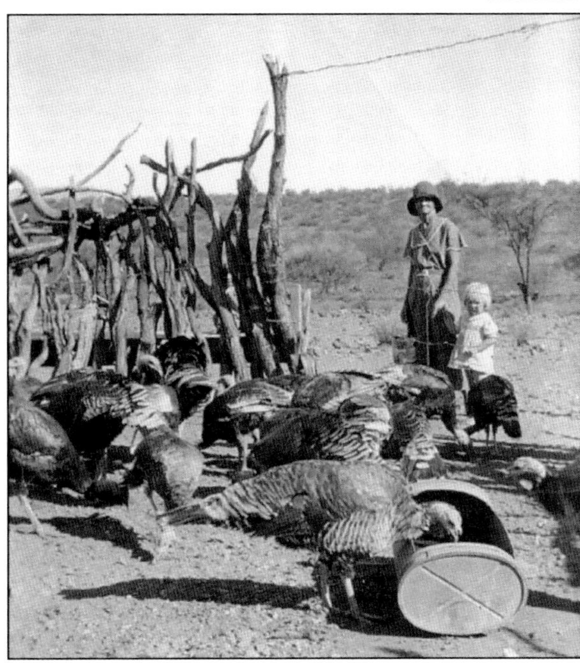

Della Essary, accompanied here by her granddaughter Pauline in 1934, raised turkeys at the Essary homestead. The turkeys could be relied upon to sound the alarm when rattlesnakes approached. Della caught and sold the live snakes to the Evans Reptile Gardens on East Van Buren. New River residents often had a "reptile garden" in their own backyards. (Courtesy of Jerry D. Jacka and Lois Essary Jacka.)

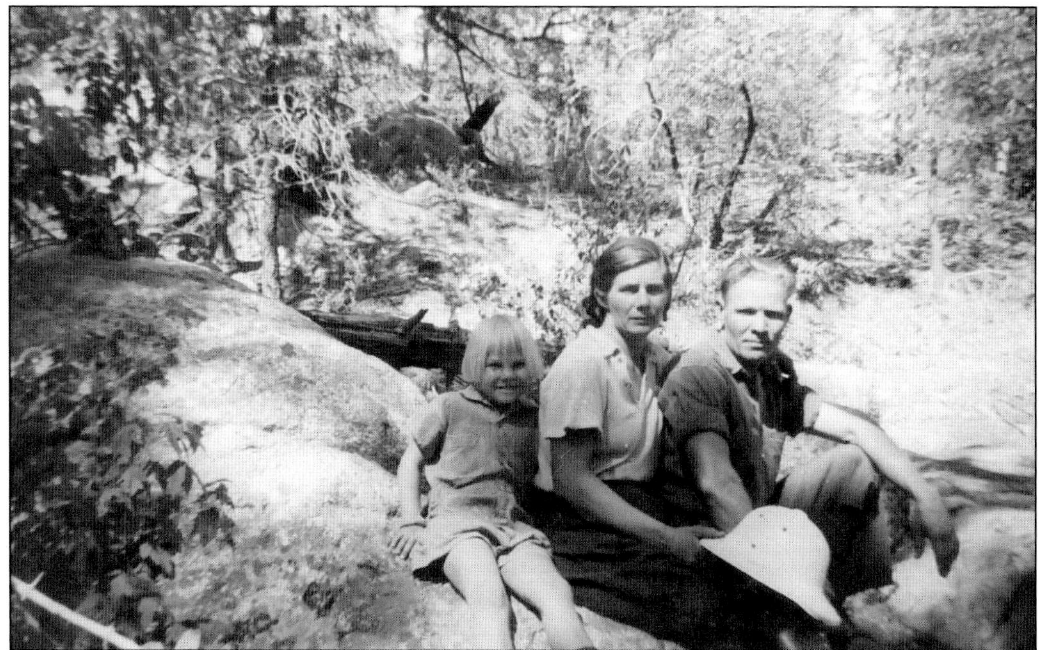

Many of the homesteaders cherished the land around them even as they dealt with the daily challenges it presented in the form of climate, thorny plants, and venomous creatures. Rowena, Bill, and young Lois Essary are pictured here on a 1940 hike in the desert foothills. (Courtesy of Jerry D. Jacka and Lois Essary Jacka.)

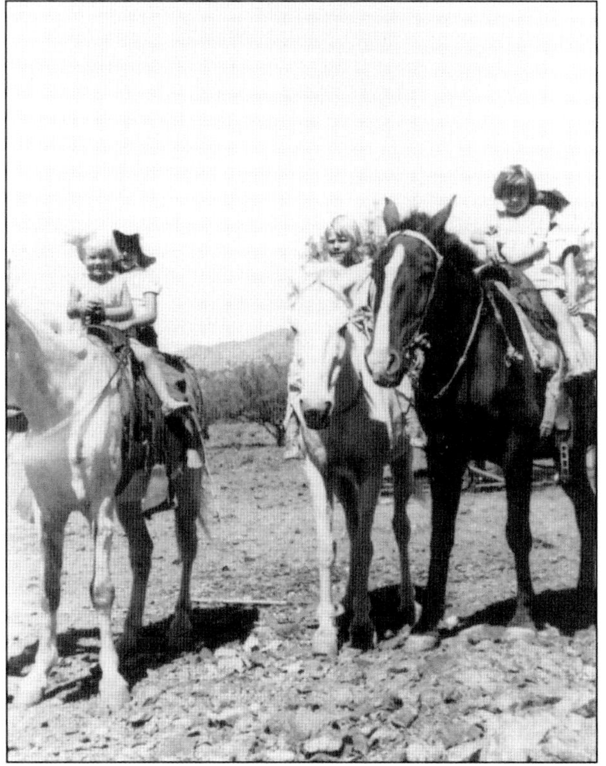

The daughters of homesteaders were a close-knit bunch. From left to right, Pauline Essary, Jean Stewart, Barbara Essary, Pat Donham, and Lorene Stewart enjoy one of the area's most popular activities, then and now: horseback riding. Pat Donham's mother, Mildred, became New River's schoolteacher in 1936. The Stewart girls' father, Bob, owned area stores. (Courtesy of Jerry D. Jacka and Lois Essary Jacka.)

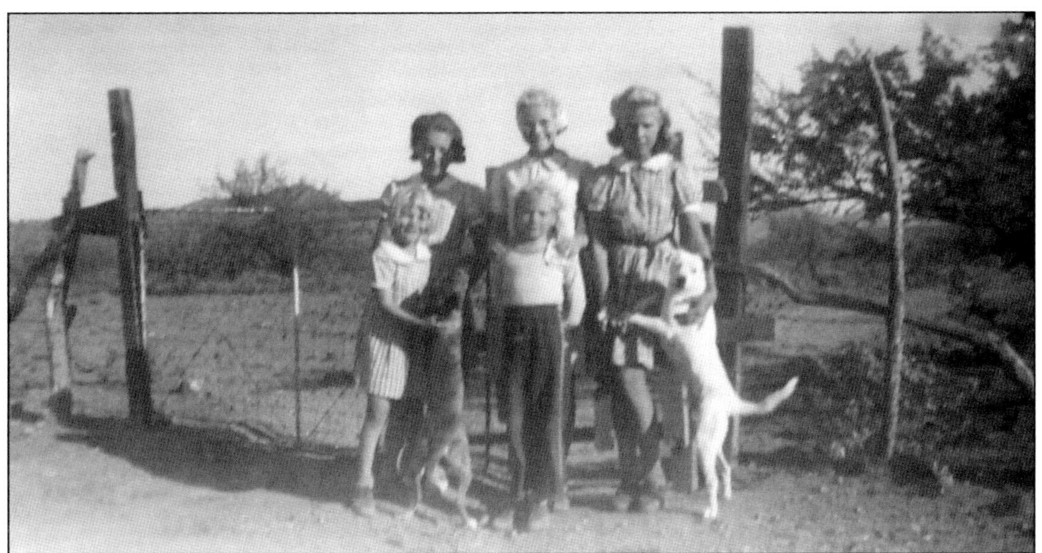

From left to right, Pat Donham, Lily Millage (the Essary girls' cousin), and Barbara Essary stand behind Lois (left) and Pauline Essary. Constant companions Tigie (left) and Jack join the girls here in 1941. Dogs were cherished members of most homestead families, even welcome at the one-room schoolhouse. (Courtesy of Jerry D. Jacka and Lois Essary Jacka.)

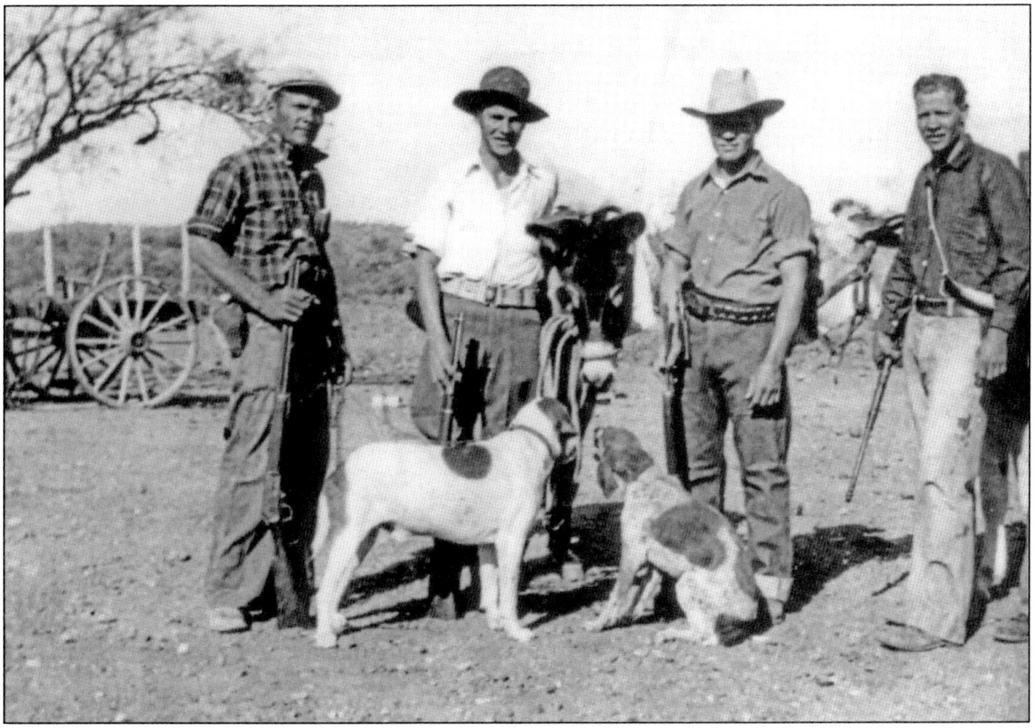

New River's wildlife afforded ample opportunities for hunting. From left to right, Ernest Essary, his brother-in-law R. L. "Buddy" Stephensen, Bill Essary, and Bill's brother Amos Essary pose with their hounds and pack burros prior to leaving for a deer hunt. Around 1950, Stephensen and his wife, Helen, also moved to New River. Note the powder horn slung around Amos's neck. (Courtesy of Jerry D. Jacka and Lois Essary Jacka.)

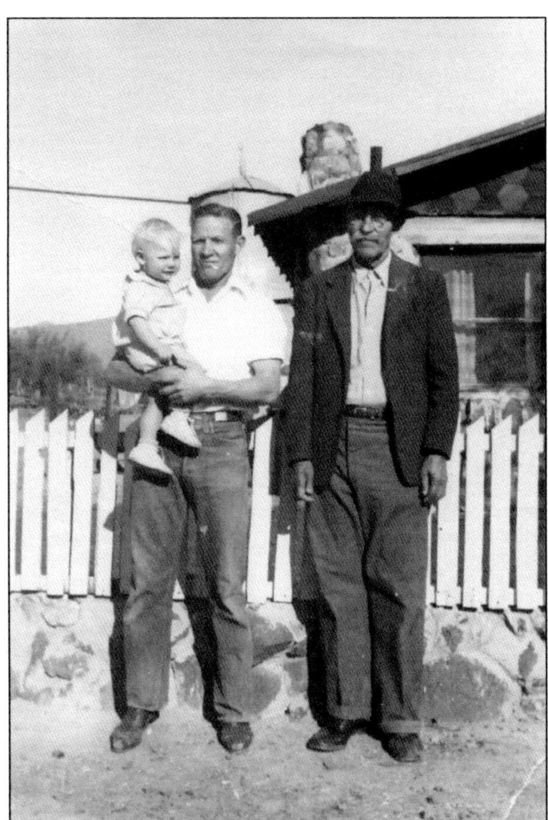

In 1947, three generations of Essary men pose in front of the Essary homestead: Gary (left), Bill (center), and Fate Essary. All three lived on New River homesteads for much of their lives. Gary grew up to marry Sharon Avis, the daughter of homesteaders. The Avis property was farther north, along the Black Canyon road. (Courtesy of Jerry D. Jacka and Lois Essary Jacka.)

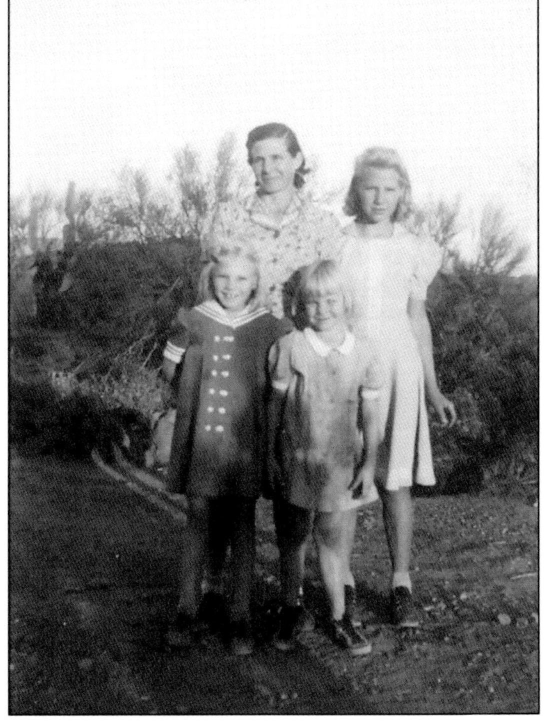

Rowena Essary raised three beautiful daughters on the Essary homestead. From left to right are (first row) Pauline and Lois; (second row) Rowena and Barbara. Rowena's family, the Grays, moved to Arizona from Missouri in 1923. Shopkeepers and merchants, they owned businesses and property in Phoenix. (Courtesy of Jerry D. Jacka and Lois Essary Jacka.)

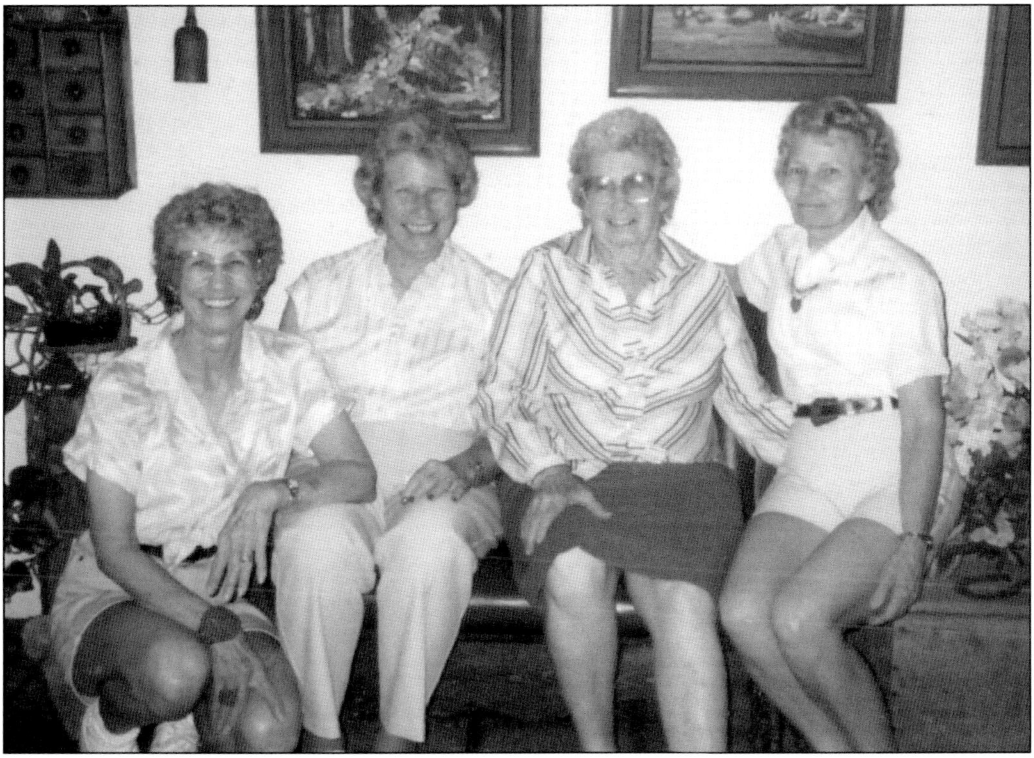

Decades of life, loss, joy, and sorrow later, the Essary daughters are pictured together again with their mother Rowena in the 1990s. From left to right are Lois, Barbara, Rowena, and Pauline. In 1987, as a tribute to her parents' 60th anniversary, Pauline wrote and published a book about the family's homestead called *Land of Our Own*. (Courtesy of Jerry D. Jacka and Lois Essary Jacka.)

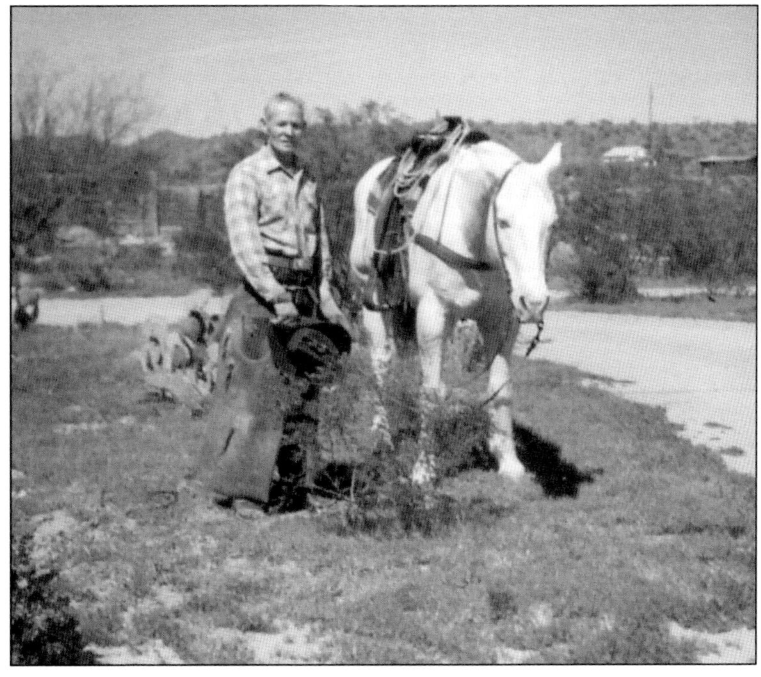

By the 1950s, houses sprouted like tumbleweeds from the New River desert, as can be seen on the ridge behind Bill Essary. Bill lived in his third hand-built stone house until his death at age 88 in 1992. His wife, Rowena, lived to be 94, passing away in April 2003. (Courtesy of Jerry D. Jacka and Lois Essary Jacka.)

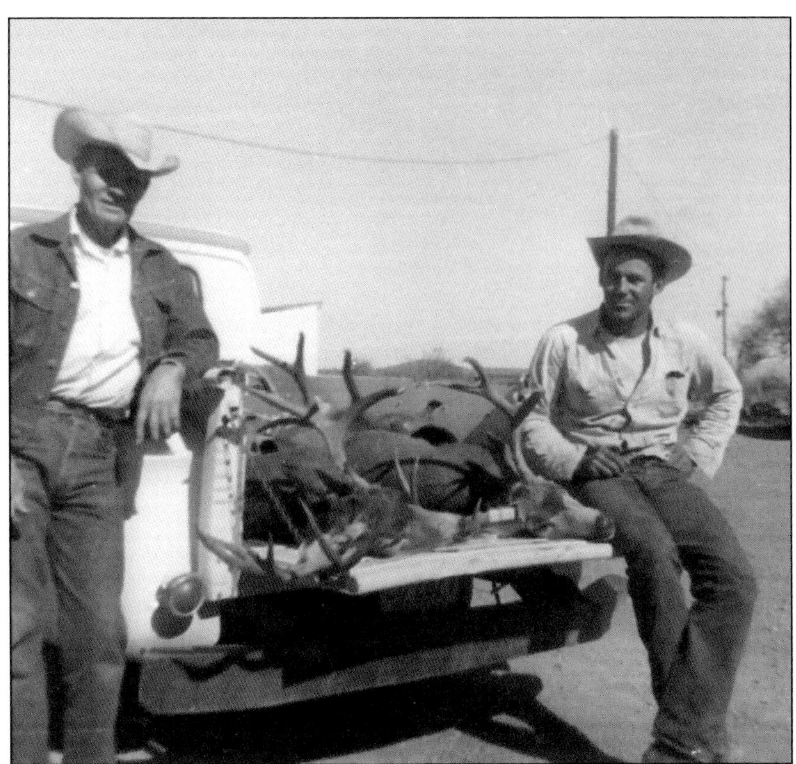

New River has long been a hunter's paradise. From doves to deer, area wildlife offered the local outdoorsmen abundant game opportunities. Bill Essary and his son-in-law and Pauline's husband, Jim McMains, had a successful mule deer hunt in 1961. Note the western saddle in the truck bed behind the deer. (Courtesy of Jerry D. Jacka and Lois Essary Jacka.)

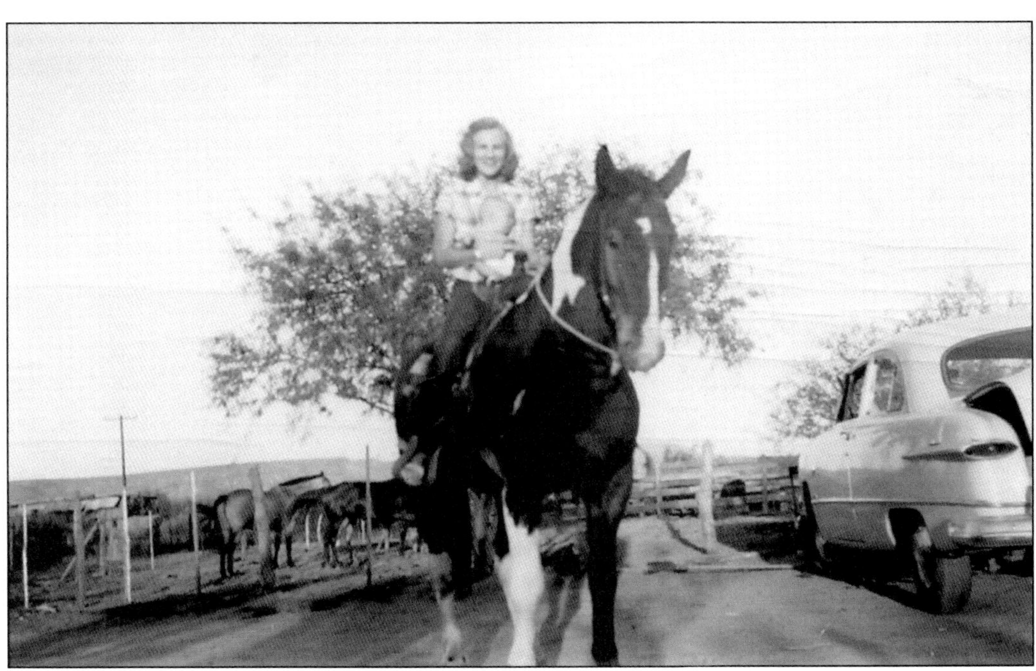

Shown here in 1952 on the flashy pinto Timber, Lois Essary introduces a member of a new generation of New River natives to horseback riding before she can even crawl. The baby, Cherie McMains, is the one-week-old daughter of Lois's sister Pauline. (Courtesy of Jerry D. Jacka and Lois Essary Jacka.)

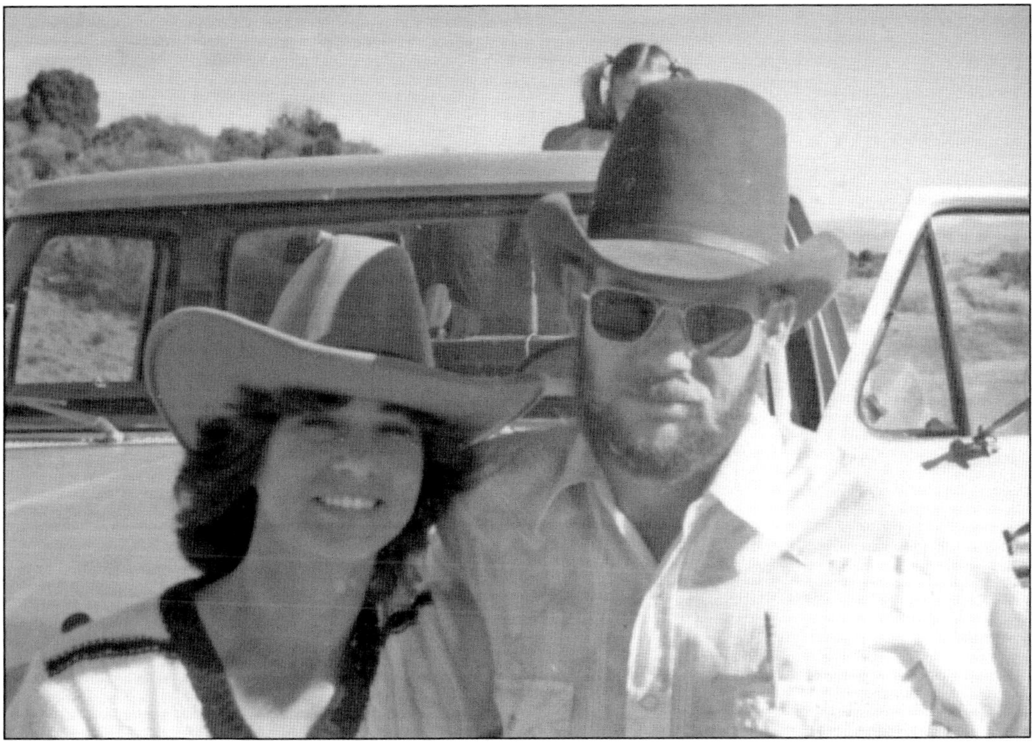

Among the many New River natives who married within the community were Gary Essary and Sharon Avis, both the children of homesteaders. Growing up together, they died together at the age of 36. Along with their young daughters Misty and Gina, the couple was tragically killed in a 1982 boating accident on Lake Mohave. (Courtesy of Jerry D. Jacka and Lois Essary Jacka.)

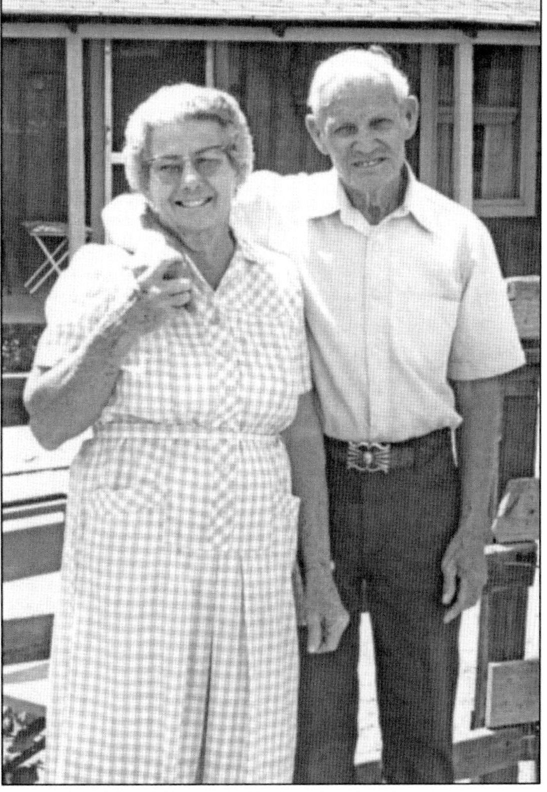

Of the original homesteaders, only Bill and Rowena Essary (shown here) and Rose and Jerry Jacka Sr. lived until the end in their New River homes. Their long lives spanned wars, political assassinations, and the advent of computers and atomic bombs. Locally, they saw the arrival of telephones, electrical service, and air-conditioning. As bridges were built and roads paved, their once oft-isolated community had become less remote. (Courtesy of Jerry D. Jacka and Lois Essary Jacka.)

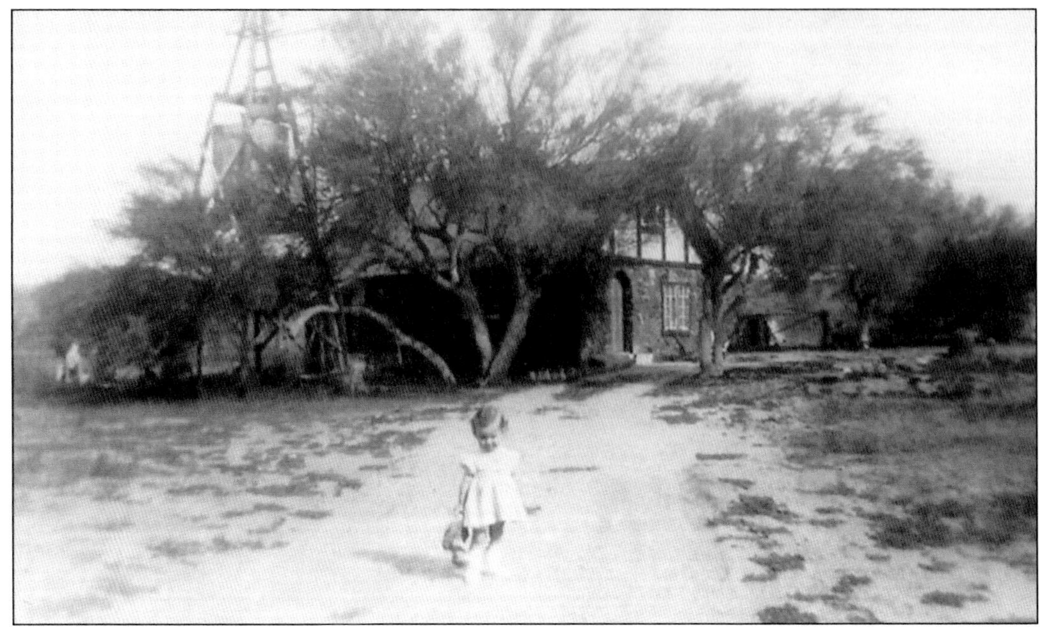

Judy Donham's parents, Paul and Mildred, homesteaded land that is now the area of Fifteenth Avenue and New River Road. They received their land patent for their 160.9 acres on May 9, 1935. The beautiful stone house has since been incorporated into a larger home. (Courtesy of Jerry D. Jacka and Lois Essary Jacka.)

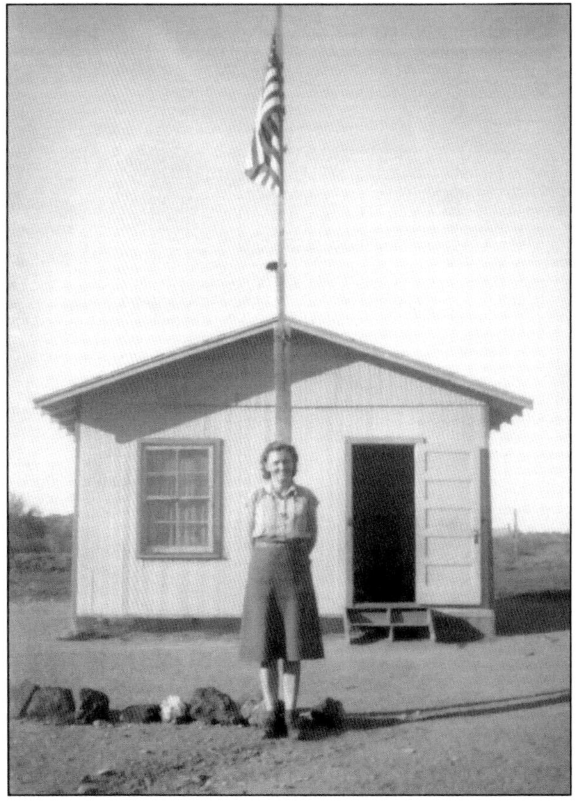

Mildred Donham was the much-loved teacher of New River's one-room schoolhouse from 1936 to 1944. Her husband, Paul Donham, along with the Essary men, brought the schoolhouse from Cave Creek on a flatbed truck. The school stood at the corner of Fig Springs and New River Roads, not far from the Donham house. (Courtesy of Jerry D. Jacka and Lois Essary Jacka.)

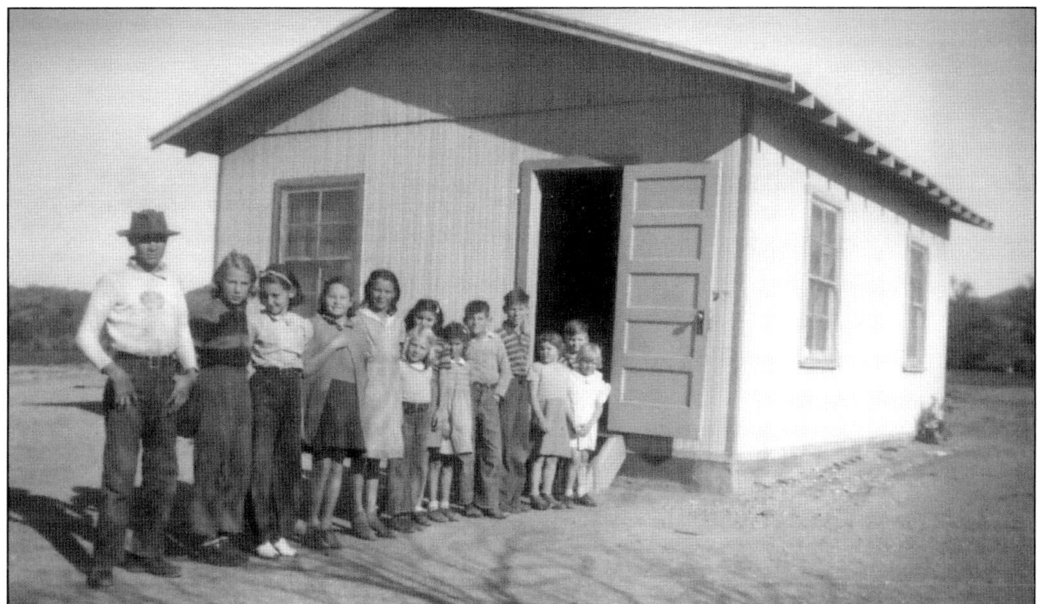

The children of the multigrade one-room school excelled academically. Here, from left to right, are the 1940–1941 students: Lloyd Moore, Barbara Essary, Pat Donham, Charlynn Moore, Lorene Stewart, Pauline Essary, Jean Stewart, Juanita Stewart, Hal Moore, Bobby Sears, Mary Lou Moore, Lois Essary, and Jerry Jacka. The latter two students began dating in high school and remain married today. (Courtesy of Jerry D. Jacka and Lois Essary Jacka.)

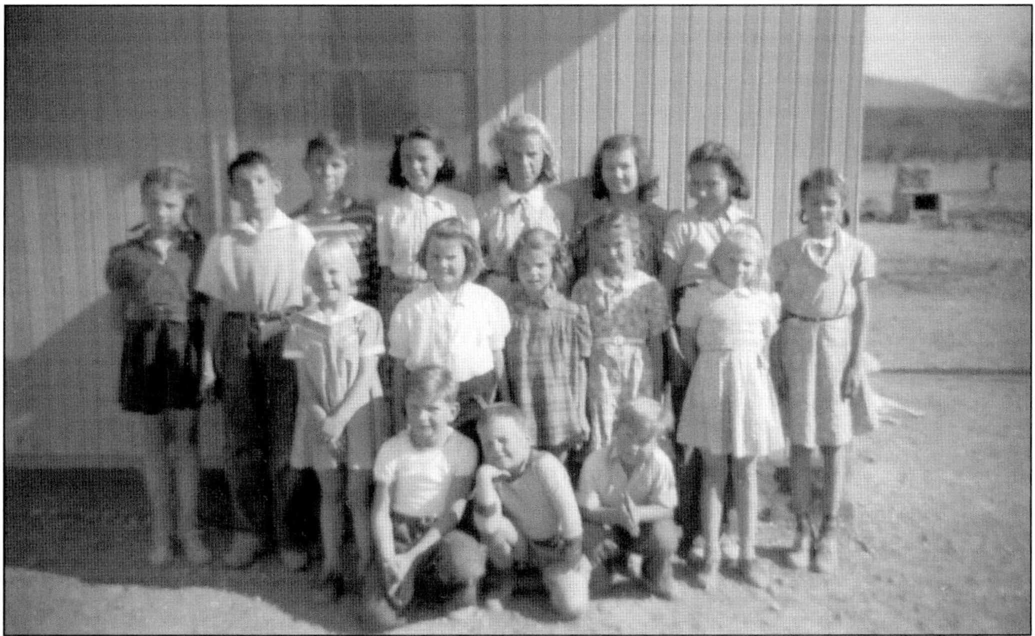

The 1941–1942 class included new faces. Pictured from left to right are (first row) Jerry D. Jacka, Pete Halle (of Wrangler's Roost), and an unidentified boy; (second row) Lois Essary, Mary Lou Moore, Thelma Avis, Juanita Stewart, Pauline Essary, and Jean Stewart; (third row) Nita Avis, Hal Moore, Bobby Sears, Lorene Stewart, Barbara Essary, Charlynn Moore, and Pat Donham. (Courtesy of Jerry D. Jacka and Lois Essary Jacka.)

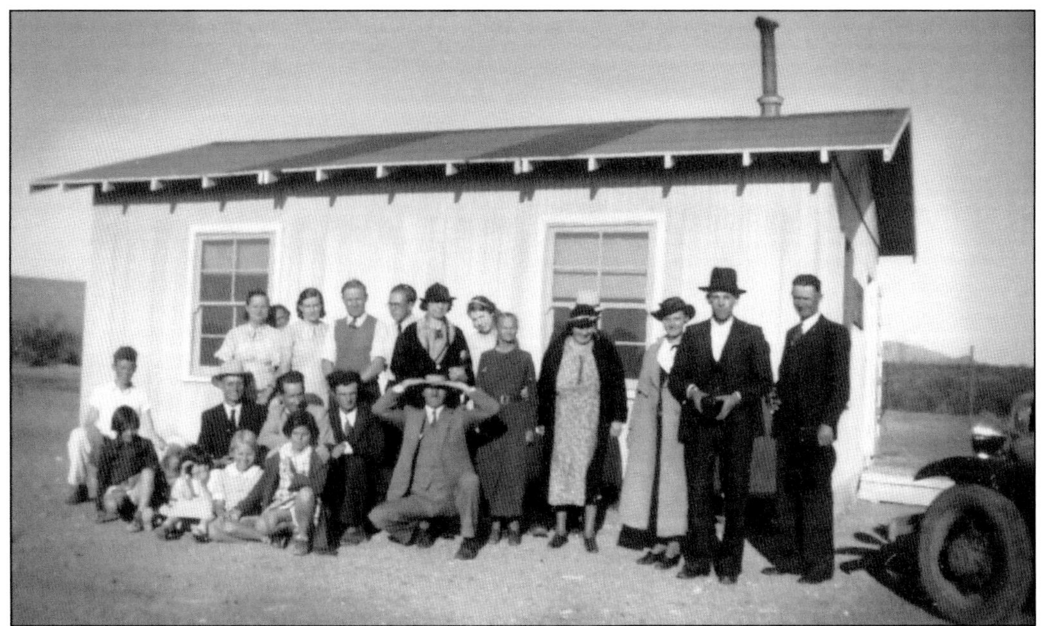

The schoolhouse hosted church services until the New River Bible Chapel was built a short distance south in 1959. The church, sanctioned by the American Sunday School Union, was the only church for many years until the Assembly Church arrived, followed in 1970 by the Latter-day Saints. Della Essary is at center of this photograph from the 1930s. (Courtesy of Jerry D. Jacka and Lois Essary Jacka.)

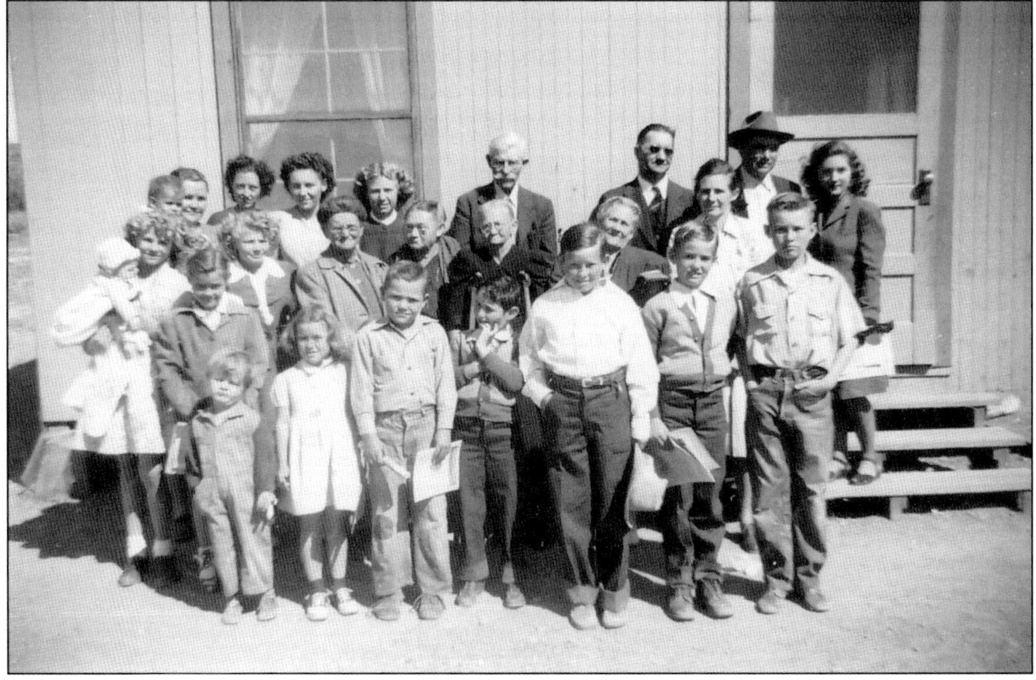

This 1947 image of the New River Sunday School, still held in the one-room schoolhouse, includes June Evans Bond standing on the steps in the back row at the far right. Della Essary, with her husband standing directly behind her, is again at center. (Courtesy of June Evans Bond.)

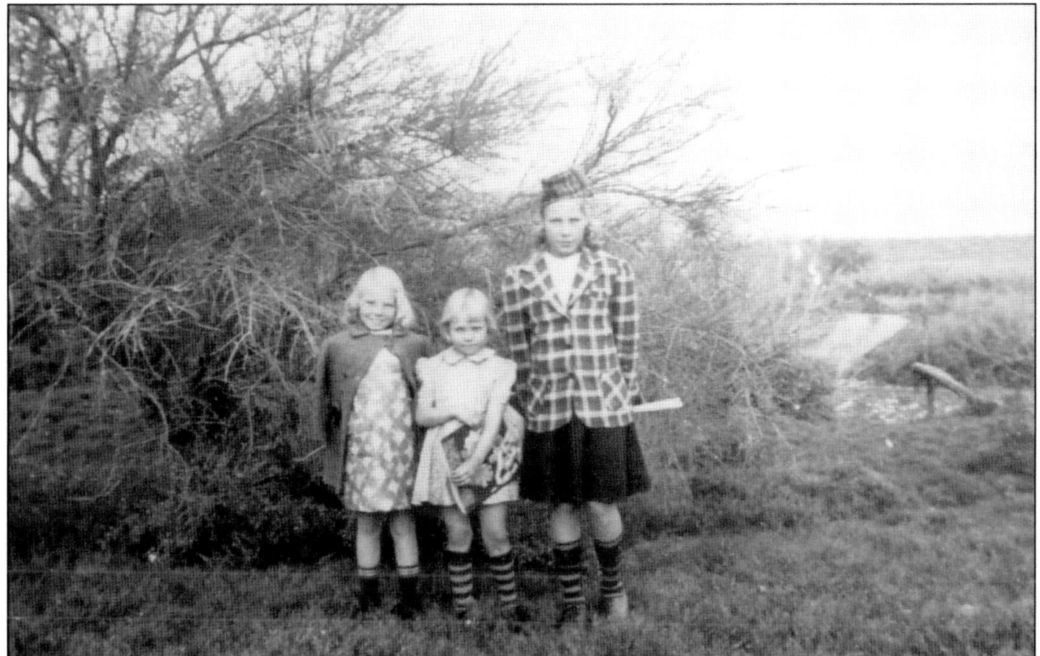

The church was an important part of New River life, and the Essary family rarely missed services. One's Sunday best meant dresses (and often hats) for the girls and women. Here, Pauline (left), Lois (center), and Barbara Essary sport their church clothes in the 1940s. The creek behind them, normally dry, is flowing rapidly. (Courtesy of Jerry D. Jacka and Lois Essary Jacka.)

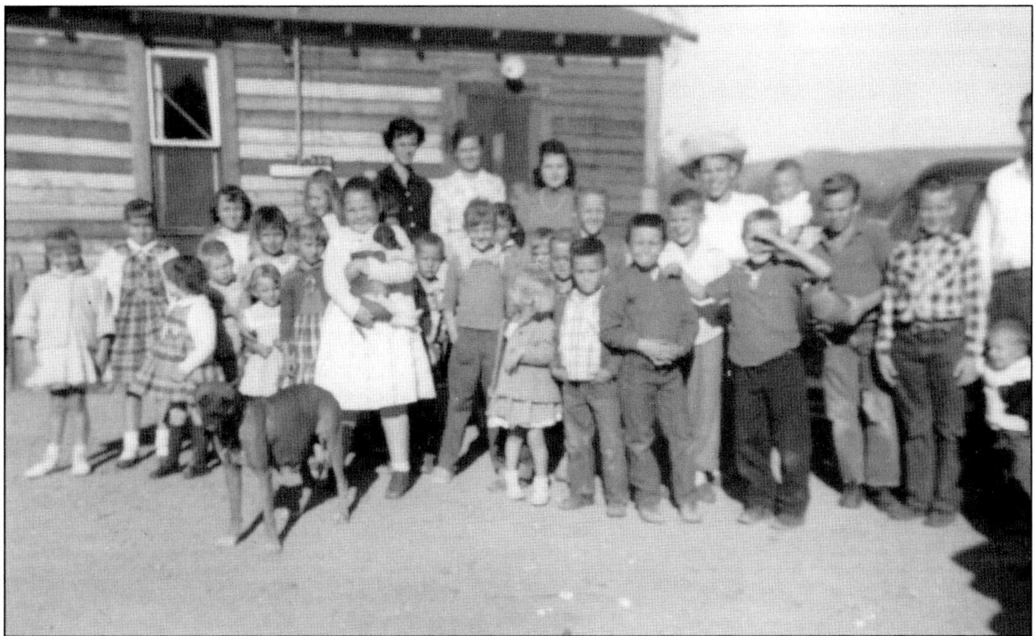

The community celebrated important occasions together with large gatherings. Dances, parties, and church services were all part of New River's tightly woven social fabric. In this image, families congregate at the Rye home to properly acknowledge a birthday. The Rye family lived in New River for seven years before moving to Oklahoma. (Courtesy of June Evans Bond.)

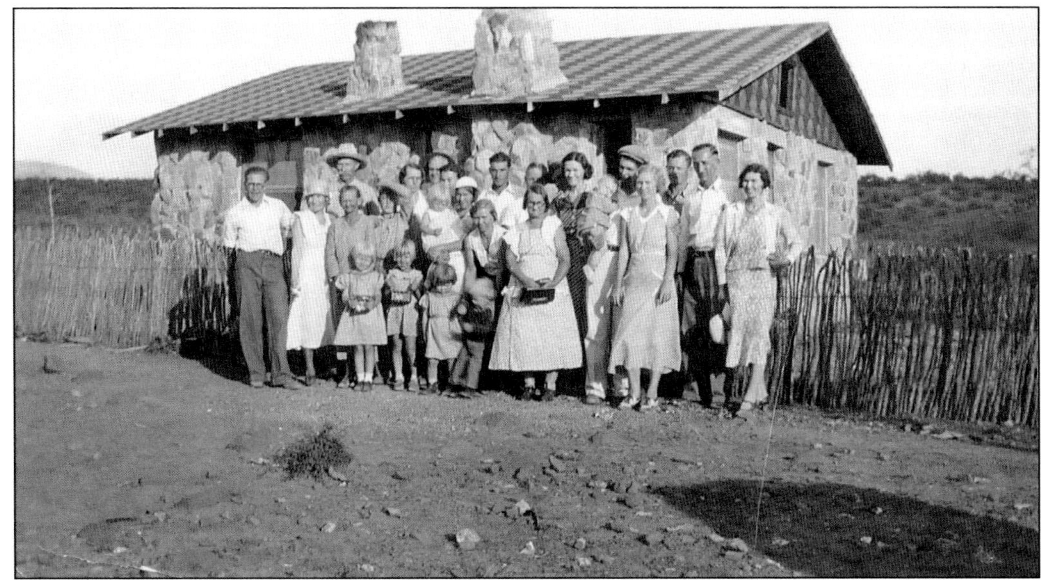

Holidays at the homesteads were also big events to be celebrated in the company of friends and family. The Essary homestead hosted this gathering on Easter 1934. Della Essary is easily recognizable in front of her granddaughters toward the left side; her husband, Fate, stands behind her. (Courtesy of Jerry D. Jacka and Lois Essary Jacka.)

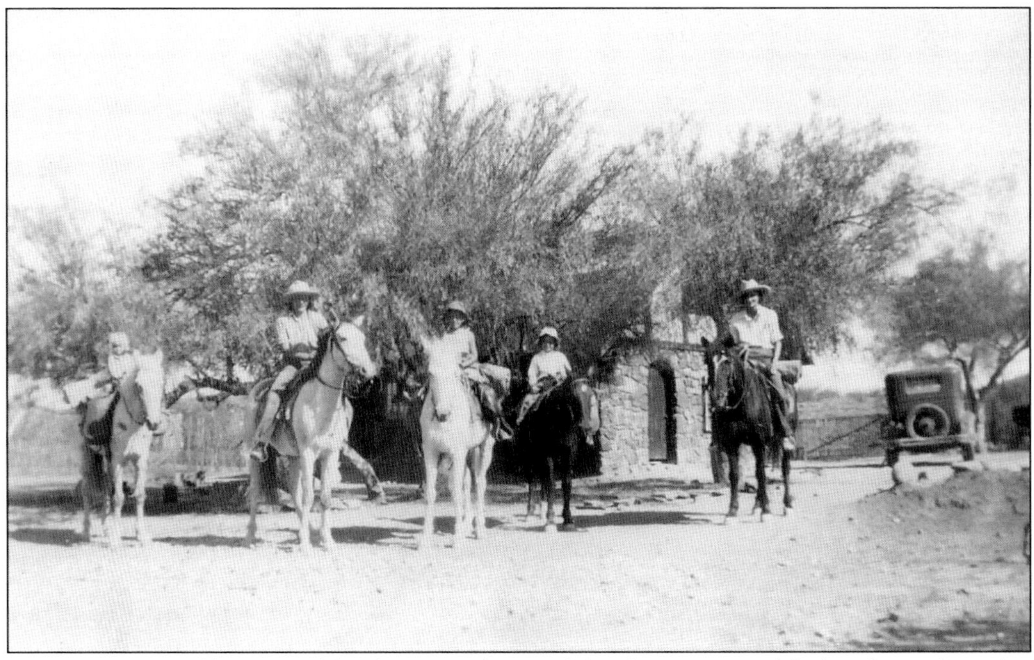

Two generations of homestead families—mothers and daughters—are saddled up for a ride in this photograph from the 1930s. From left to right, Pauline Essary, Rowena Essary, Barbara Essary, Pat Donham, and Mildred Donham line up in front of the Donham homestead. A bedroll tied onto the rear of each saddle indicates a long ride ahead. (Courtesy of Jerry D. Jacka and Lois Essary Jacka.)

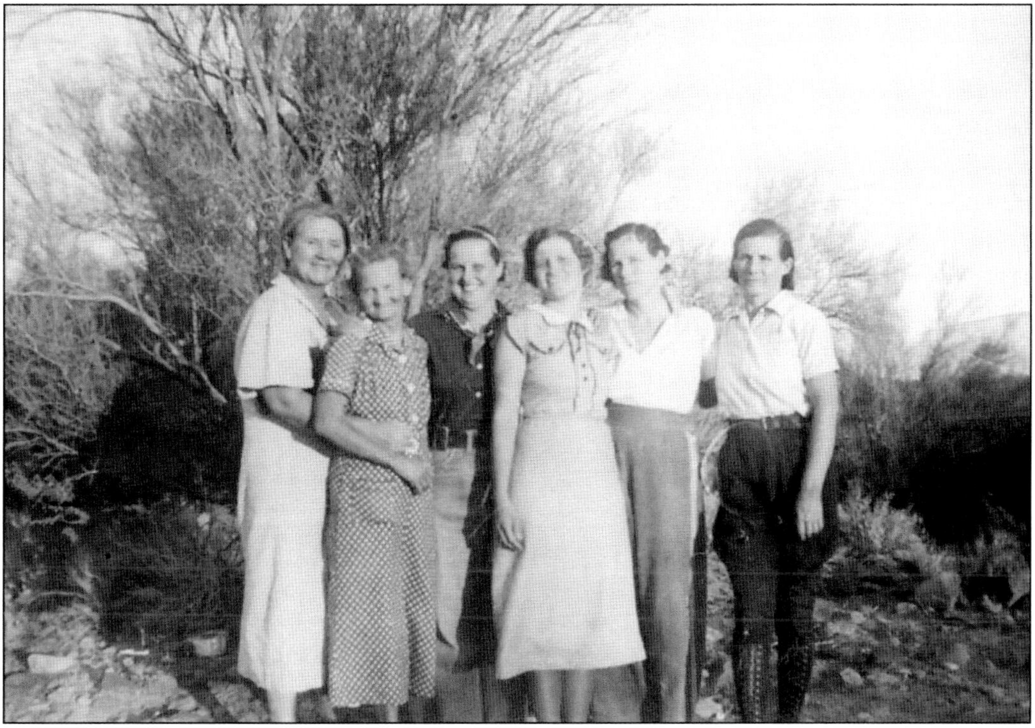

Both the warmth and the grit required of New River's homestead women are reflected in their faces. From left to right, Maude Kuykendall, Della Essary, Opal Farrar, Maggie Cox (Rowena's sister-in-law, visiting), Sudie Essary, and Rowena Essary pose around 1934. The Kuykendalls homesteaded a property north of the L.C. Beverly Ranch, now the Spear-S Ranch. (Courtesy of Jerry D. Jacka and Lois Essary Jacka.)

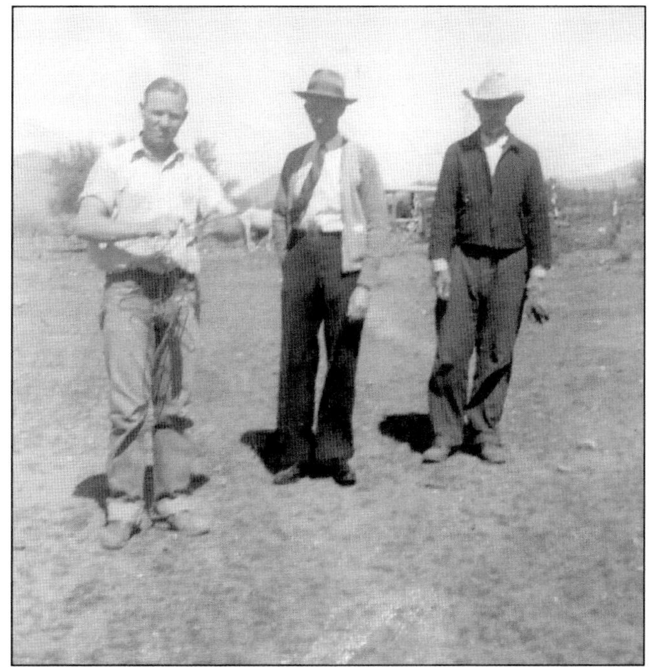

Bill Essary and his father, Fate Essary, flank Roy Farrar in this 1942 photograph. Farrar, a disabled veteran of World War I, and his wife, Opal, homesteaded along the old Black Canyon stagecoach road just north of New River Road near today's Roadrunner Saloon. (Courtesy of Jerry D. Jacka and Lois Essary Jacka.)

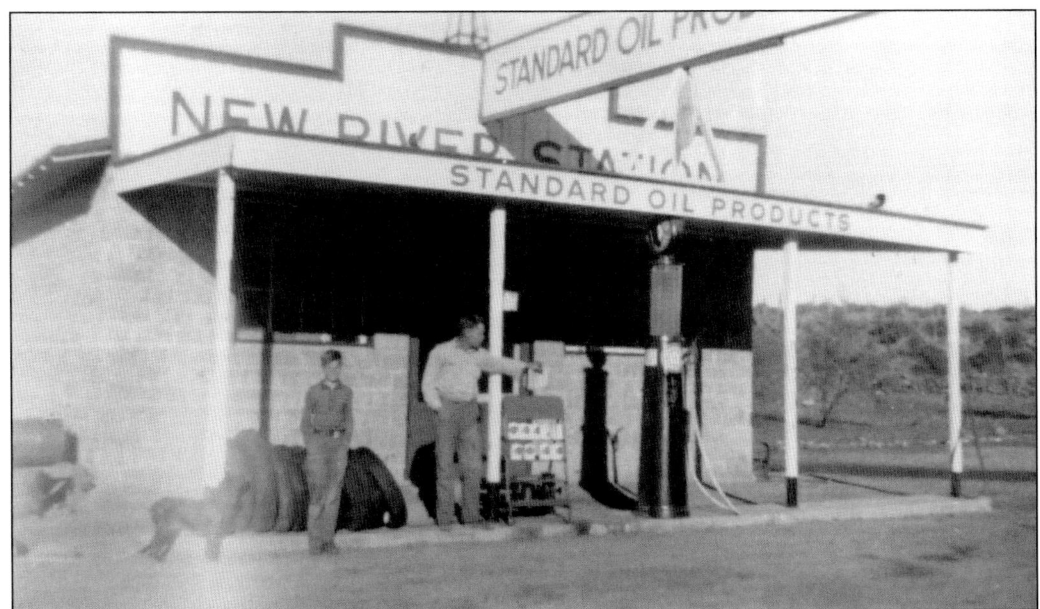

Like many homesteaders, Boyd "Pappy" Sears filled several community roles. Sears ran New River Station when it was a general store. He also drove New River teens to Glendale High School in the 1940s. June Evans Bond describes him as the "best" bus driver, as he was hard of hearing, and when kids became loud, he turned his hearing aid off. (Courtesy of Jerry D. Jacka and Lois Essary Jacka.)

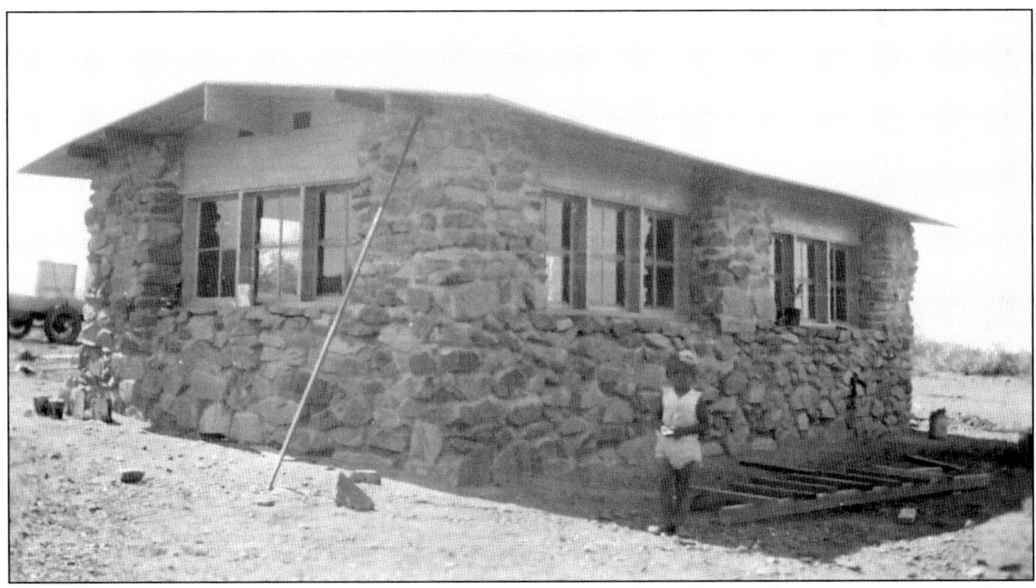

The one-room Mayer homestead, built in the 1930s, stood in the southernmost section of the New River area. Within just a few years, Fred and Blanche Mayer returned to Illinois. Today, the stone house is gone; the site, near Anthem Way and the freeway, is part of the master-planned community of Anthem. (Courtesy of Jerry D. Jacka and Lois Essary Jacka.)

Jerry D. Jacka recalls that in the 1940s, several families who would greatly involved in the community moved in. Among these were the Rolstons. Bud Rolston drove kids to high school—a 40-mile one-way trip—using a repurposed Army truck as a bus. Here, Nihla Rolston (left), Lois Essary (center), and Nelle Rolston pose at the Essary homestead in 1945. (Courtesy of Jerry D. Jacka and Lois Essary Jacka.)

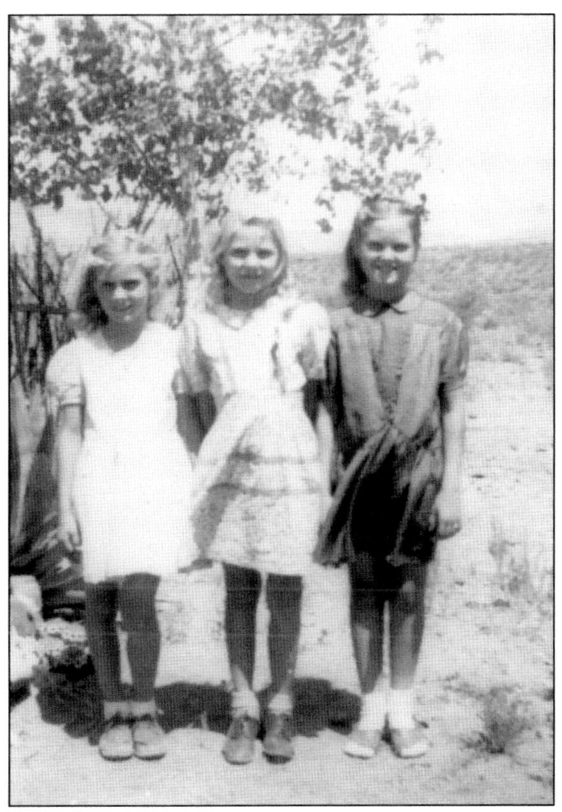

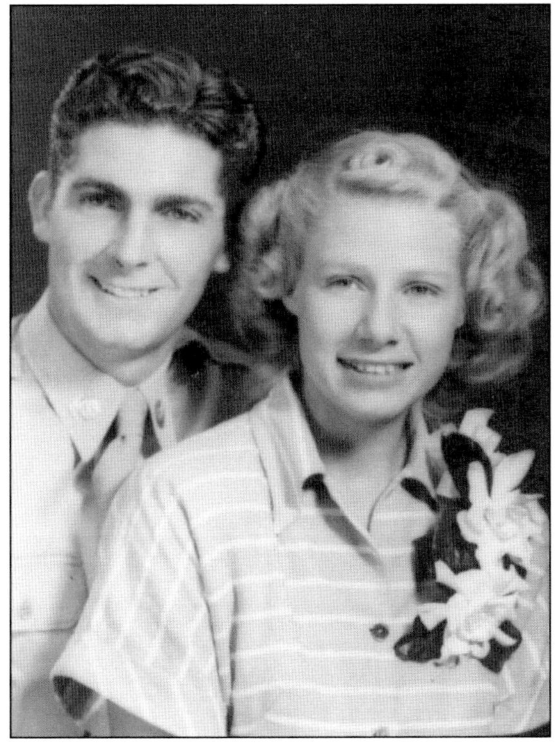

Barbara Essary married Loyal Rolston on September 11, 1948. They stayed in New River for many years, buying the Bruce King homestead in 1953. The King homestead was on Fig Springs Road east of the Essary homesteads. Later, Barbara and Loyal moved to California, where the Rolston family had roots. (Courtesy of Jerry D. Jacka and Lois Essary Jacka.)

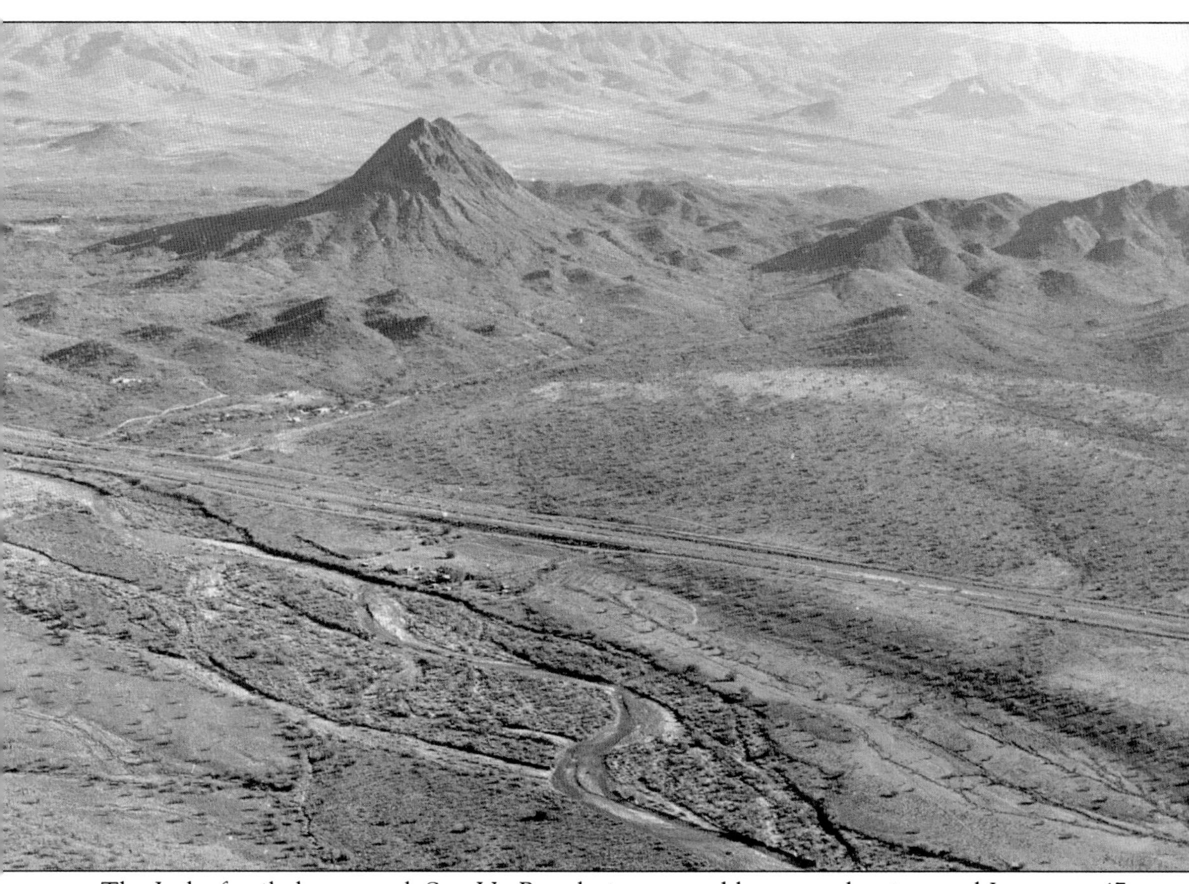

The Jacka family homestead, Sun-Up Ranch, is centered between the river and Interstate 17 in this aerial view looking northeast toward Gavilan Peak. Locals often called Gavilan "Twin Buttes." The best-preserved of New River's homesteads, Sun-Up is still owned by the Jacka family. Since 1988, it has been listed in the National Register of Historic Places. (Courtesy of Jerry D. Jacka and Lois Essary Jacka.)

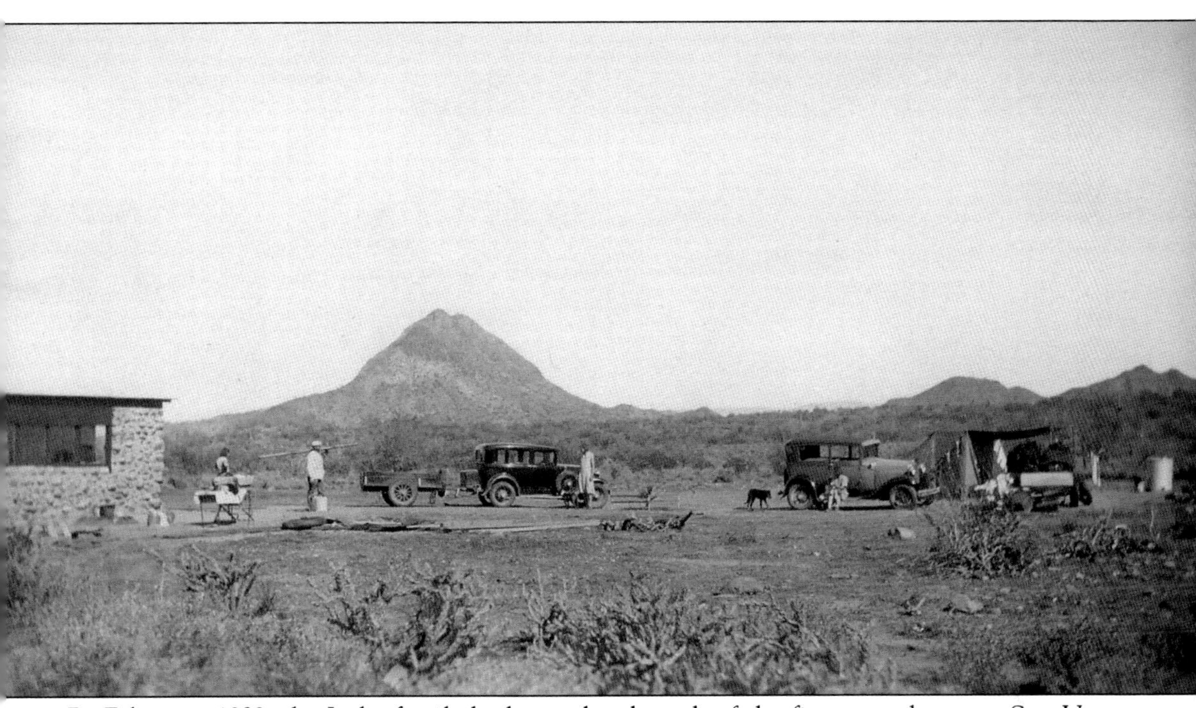

By February, 1932, the Jacka family had completed much of the first stone house at Sun-Up Ranch. Jerry Jacka Sr. and Rose Jacka (center) are flanked by Rose's sister Josephine Kubes (left) and neighbor Blanche Mayer (right). Mayer's family lived on the homestead to their south. (From the book *Sun-Up Ranch: An Arizona Desert Homestead* by Jerry D. Jacka.)

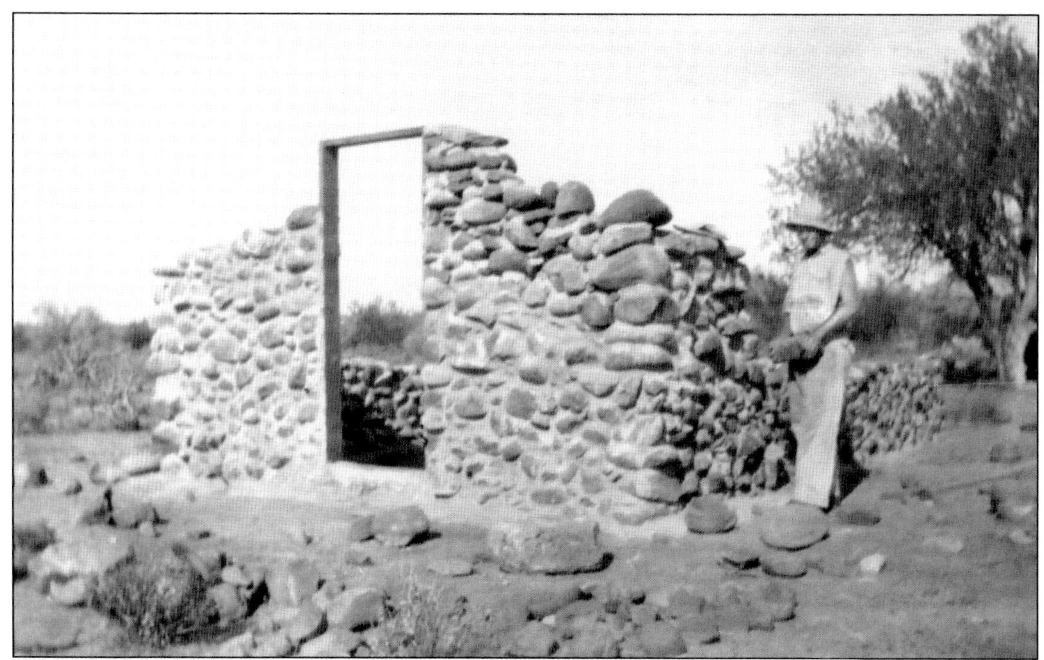

Built by the homesteaders' own hands, New River's early houses were uniquely personal. As they were generally constructed of the ubiquitous New River rock, it is no coincidence that they seem to be part of the land from which they have emerged. Jerry Jacka Sr. fitted each rock carefully into place to build the walls of each Sun-Up structure. (From the book *Sun-Up Ranch: An Arizona Desert Homestead* by Jerry D. Jacka.)

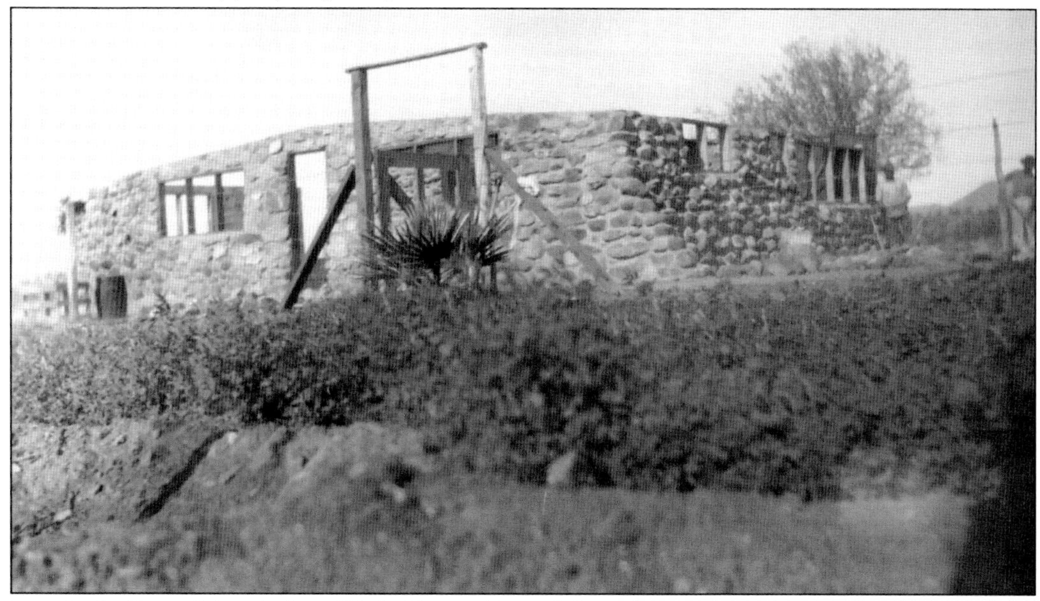

Jerry Jacka Sr. and family friend Bob Slusser (far right) work by the nearly completed walls of the Sun-Up Ranch house in this 1933 photograph. Slusser, one of many who moved to Arizona's dry climate for health reasons, lived with the Jackas, helping build the structures. Slusser later lived in the smaller Sun-Up cabin. (From the book *Sun-Up Ranch: An Arizona Desert Homestead* by Jerry D. Jacka.)

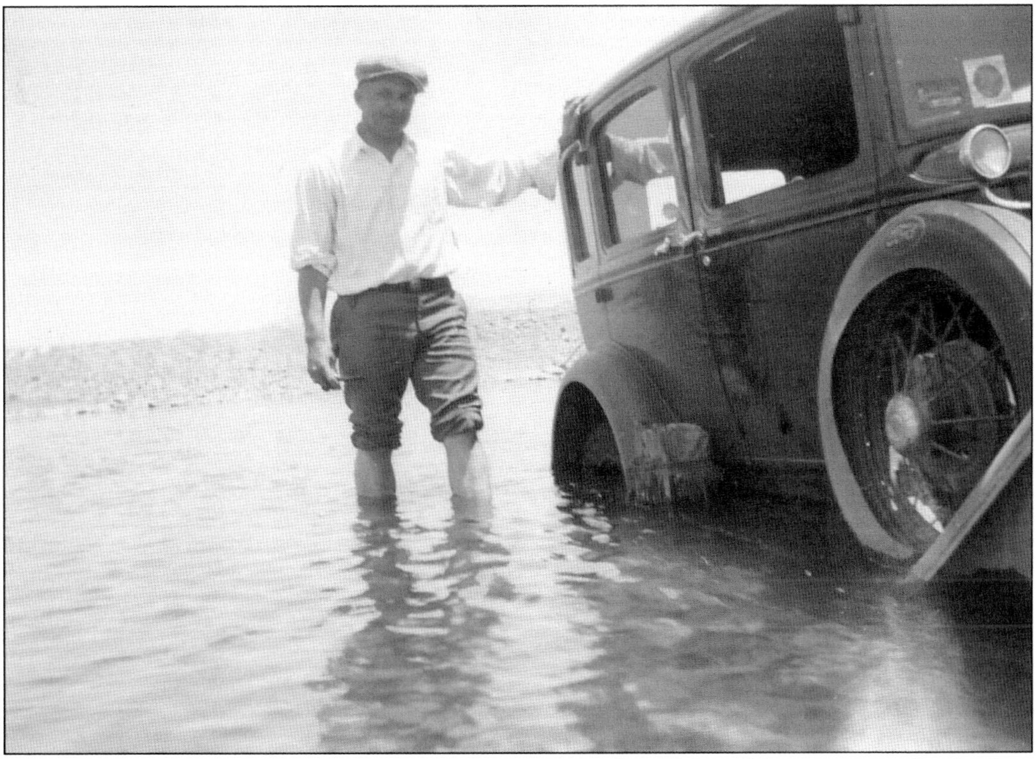

When the rains came, normally dry washes and creeks flowed forcefully. Homesteaders had no bridges and forded often dangerous waters. Nearby Dead Man Wash is named for an incident in the 1920s in which a man drowned while attempting to cross in his Model T. Here, Jerry Jacka Sr. is shown on Black Canyon road at Skunk Creek around 1930. (Courtesy of Jerry D. Jacka and Lois Essary Jacka.)

The logistics of managing water in the desert were critical to the homesteaders. The Jackas settled by the river, assuming it would ensure shallow groundwater. To their dismay, their first well had to be drilled over 200 feet deep. In 1938, they brought in this metal tank, one of three they relied on for water storage. (Courtesy of Jerry D. Jacka and Lois Essary Jacka.)

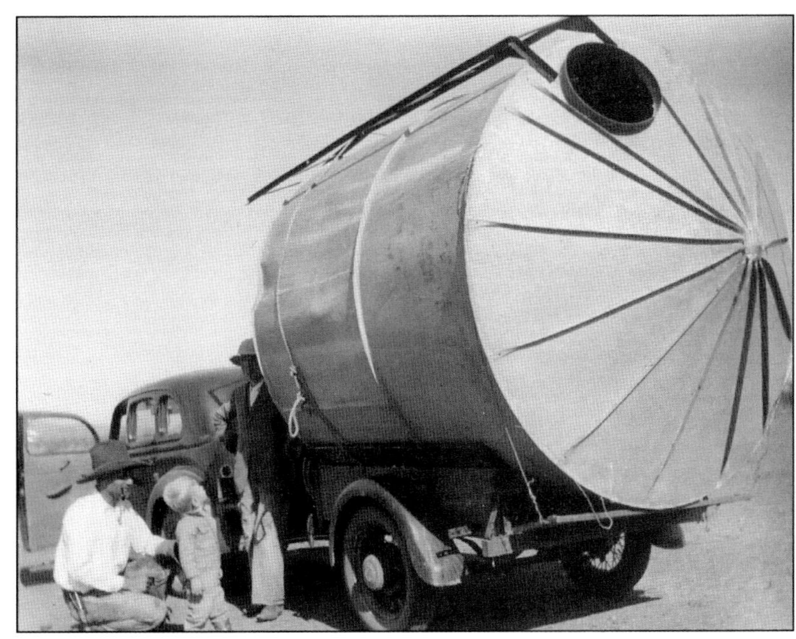

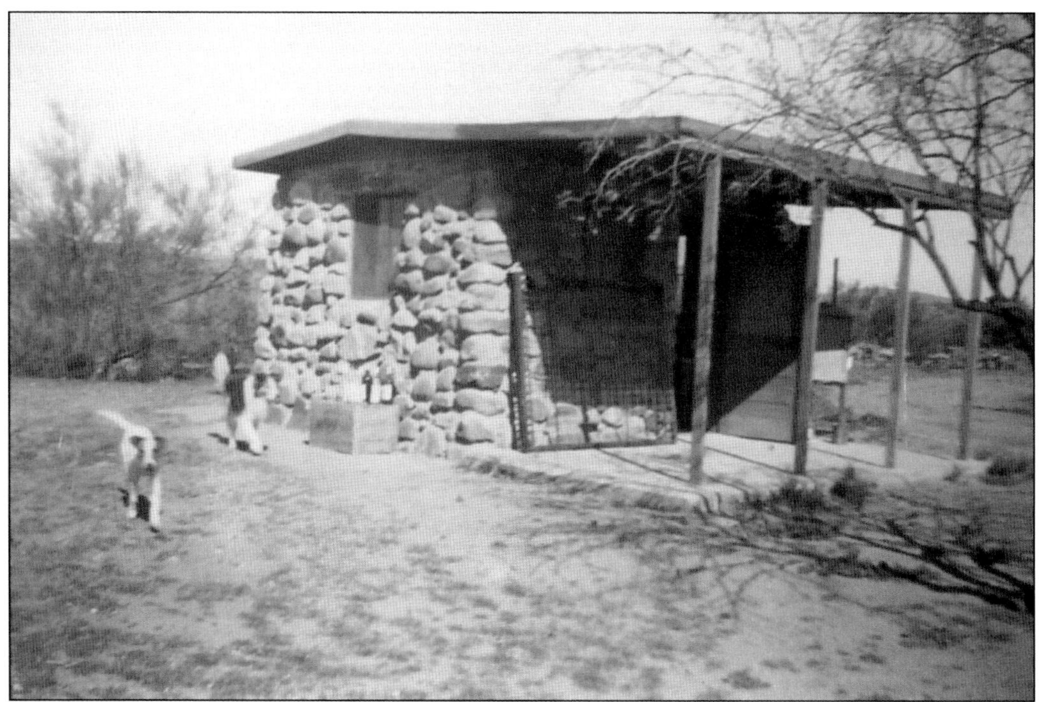

The caretaker's cabin at Sun-Up Ranch was the smaller of two stone cabins the Jackas built in addition to the main house. This cabin, which is 11 by 14 feet with an 8-foot front porch, had neither plumbing nor electricity. Air-cooled and sun-heated, it shared a two-holer outhouse with the larger guest cabin nearby. (From the book *Sun-Up Ranch: An Arizona Desert Homestead* by Jerry D. Jacka.)

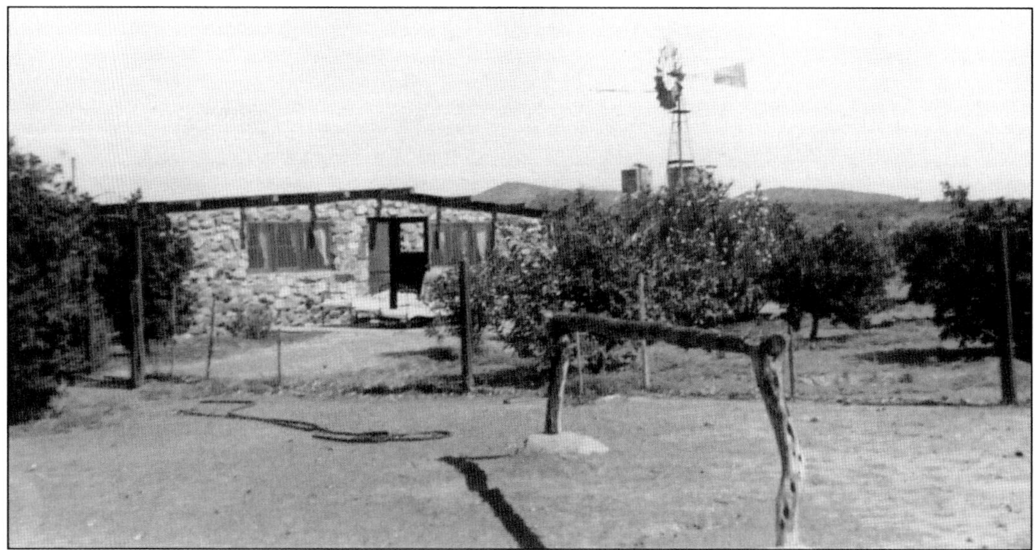

By the late 1930s, the Sun-Up fruit trees were thriving. Rose Jacka loved to garden and nurtured her plants. Today, the orchard continues to produce abundant citrus. To the left of the house, concealed by the trees, was the traditional sleeping porch (also called an "Arizona room"). Desert-dwellers relied on these screened rooms to sleep in during hot weather. (Courtesy of Jerry D. Jacka and Lois Essary Jacka.)

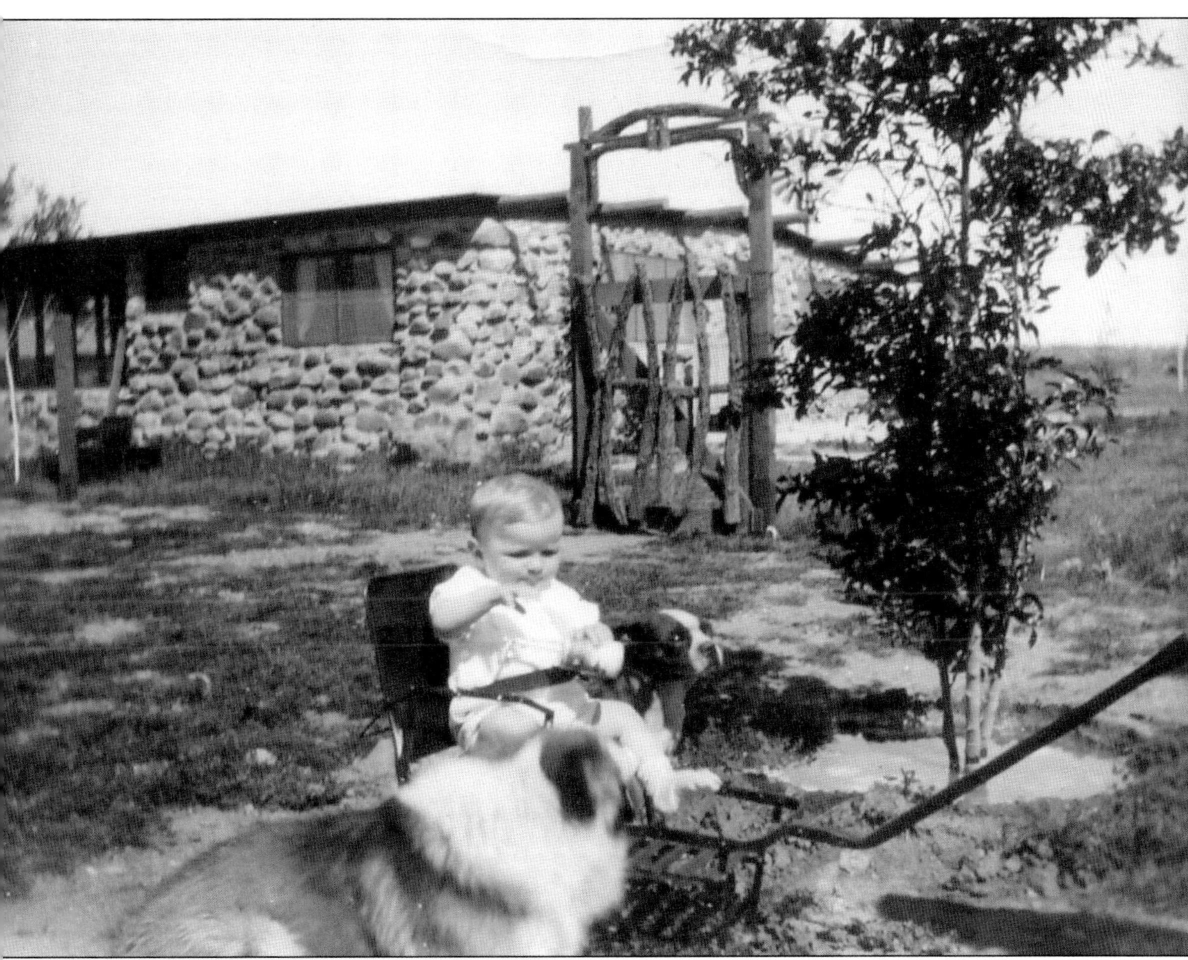

By 1935, the Jacka family had not only finished the ranch house, but were now tending their active baby boy as well. Watched over by canine companions Donnie and Do-Do, Jerry D. Jacka sits beside one of the saplings in what grew to be a lush orchard. The accent pieces on the gate in the photograph are dried cholla cactus branches. (Courtesy of Jerry D. Jacka and Lois Essary Jacka.)

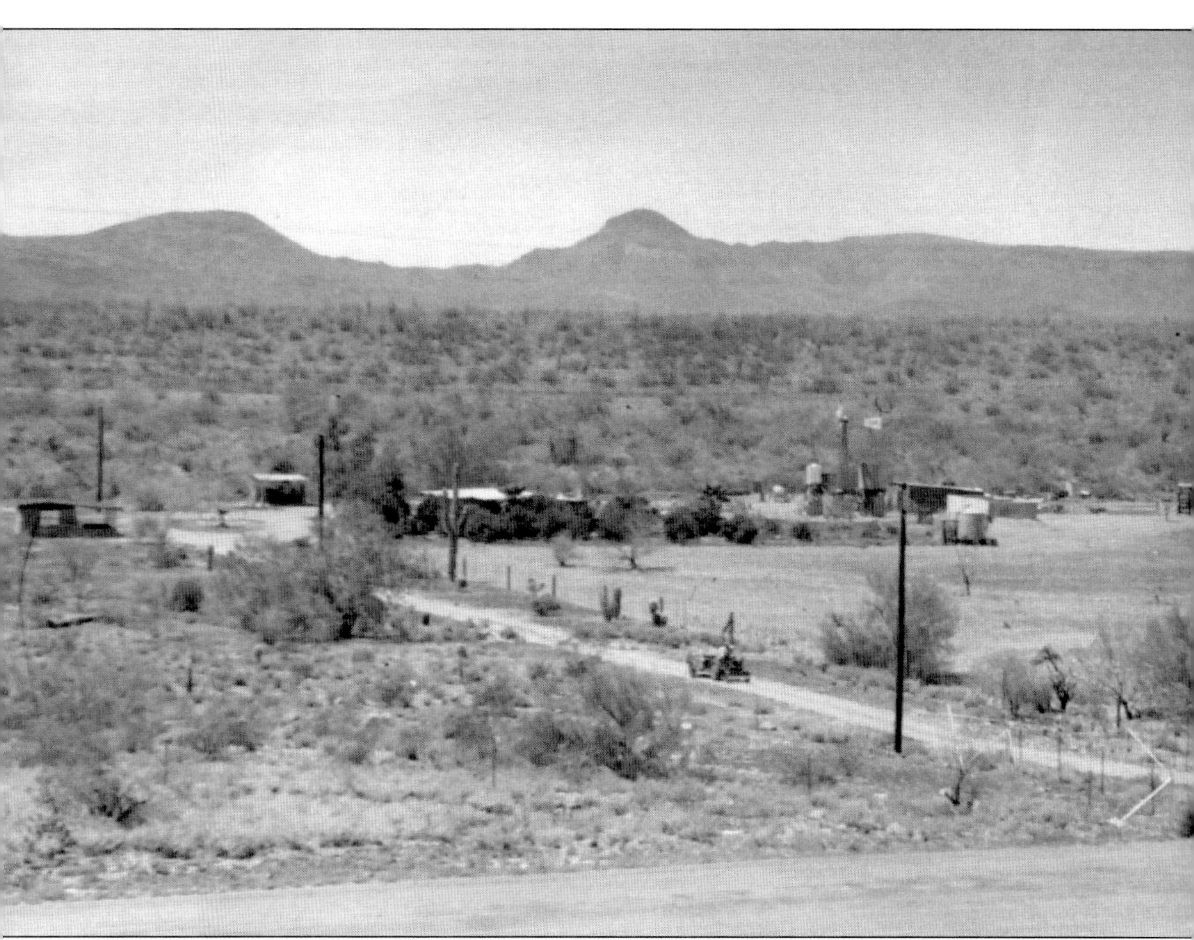

Looking westward in the direction of what is now Lake Pleasant, in the late 1940s, Sun-Up Ranch did not yet have the stand of aged saguaros now lining the driveway. When freeway construction began, crews made a practice of simply bulldozing native plants. Loving the land as they did, the Jackas moved many saguaros. (From the book *Sun-Up Ranch: An Arizona Desert Homestead* by Jerry D. Jacka.)

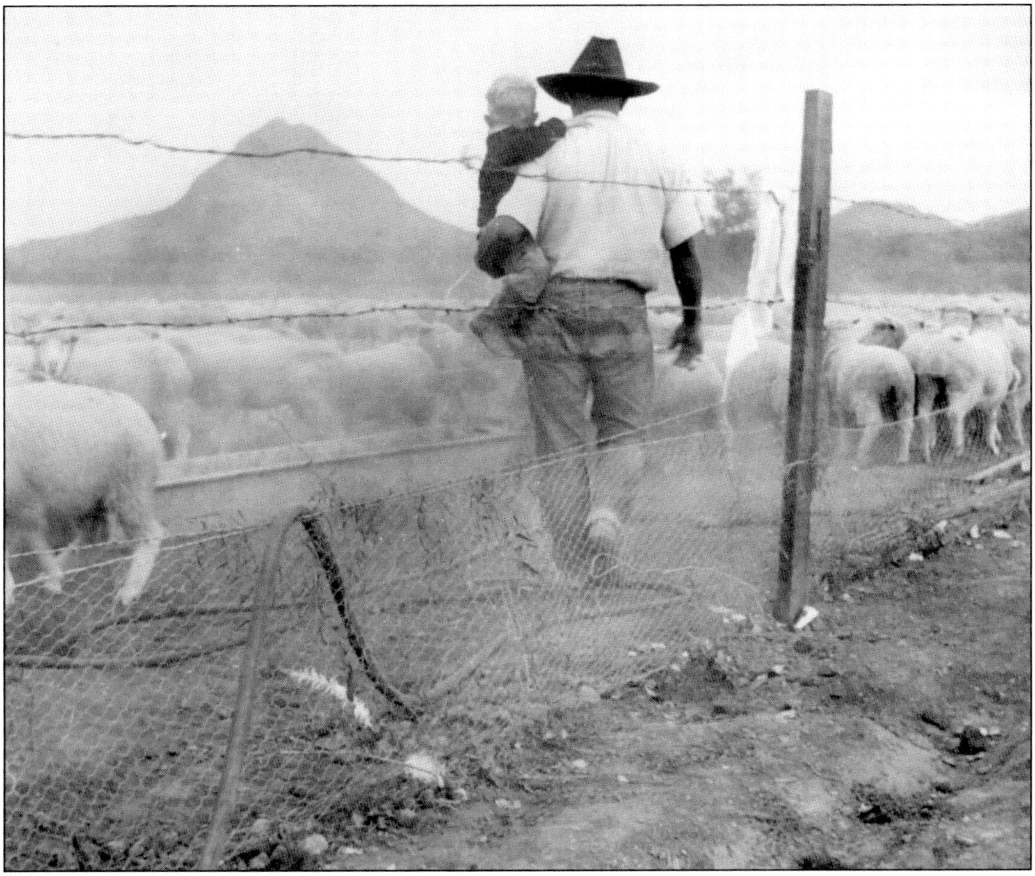

In the 1930s and 1940s, sheep drovers often herded huge flocks of sheep to and from seasonal pastures in northern Arizona along the Black Canyon Livestock Driveway. In 1939, an estimated 215,000 sheep were driven along that trail. Herders, aided by burro packtrains, camped along the way and sometimes stayed at the Sun-Up. Jerry Jacka Sr. arranged to water the sheep at a penny a head and constructed a holding pen for the thirsty animals. The sheep ranchers worked with Jacka to install the metal troughs shown in the photograph above. Jerry Jacka Sr. is shown carrying his son through a vast flock. (Both, courtesy of Jerry D. Jacka and Lois Essary Jacka.)

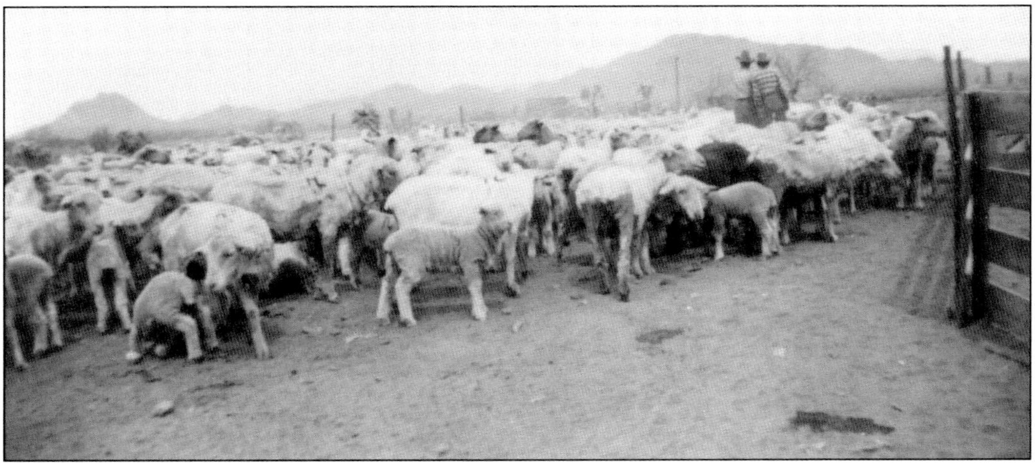

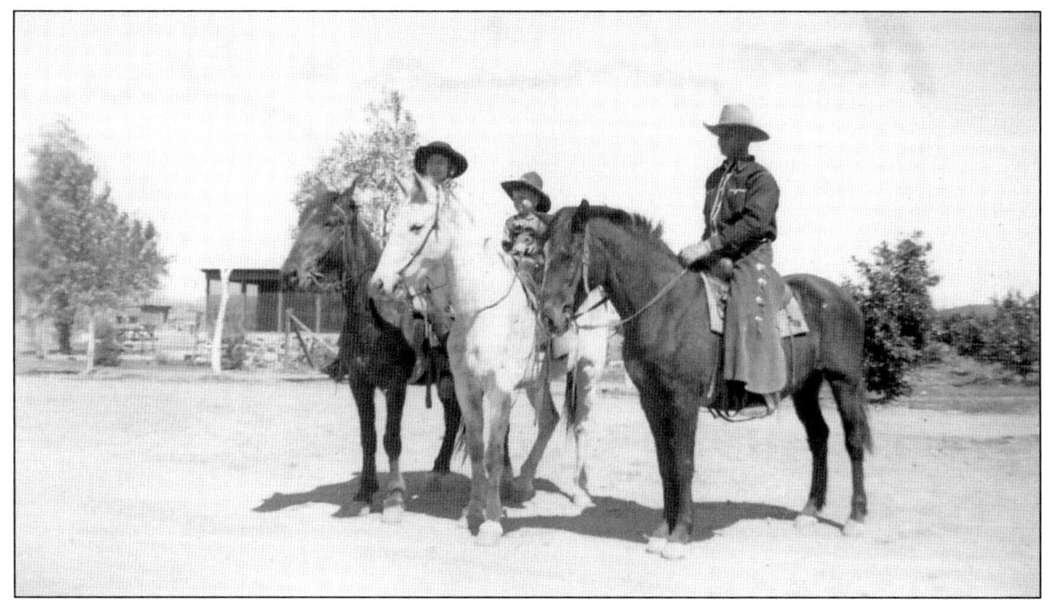

Rose and Jerry Jacka Sr. first put Jerry D. Jacka in the saddle as a newborn. By the time he was four, Jerry was handling his own mount with ease. Note the screened porch on the left side of the Sun-Up Ranch house. Before air-conditioning, Arizonans used the sleeping porch to sleep in during hot weather. (Courtesy of Jerry D. Jacka and Lois Essary Jacka.)

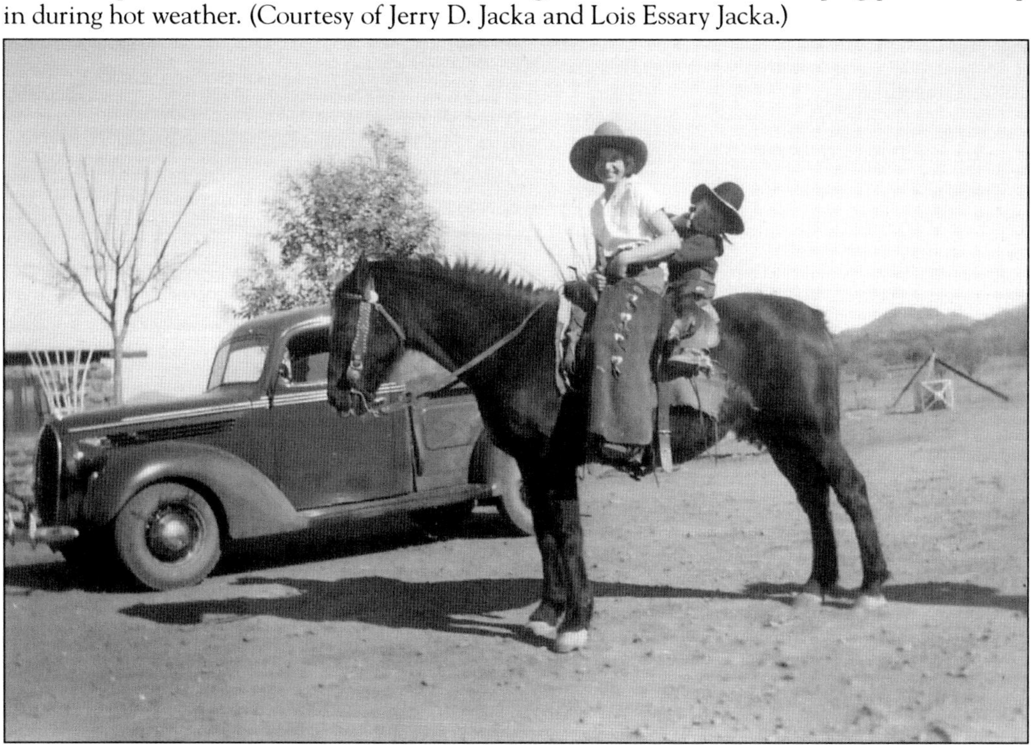

Rose and her son Jerry D. Jacka could trust reliable Nibs to carry them double. Rose's stylish chaps accented with heart-shaped conchos were essential gear for the terrain, protecting the legs from cactus and other potential hazards. Equally important in the hot desert sun was the wide-brimmed western hat. (Courtesy of Jerry D. Jacka and Lois Essary Jacka.)

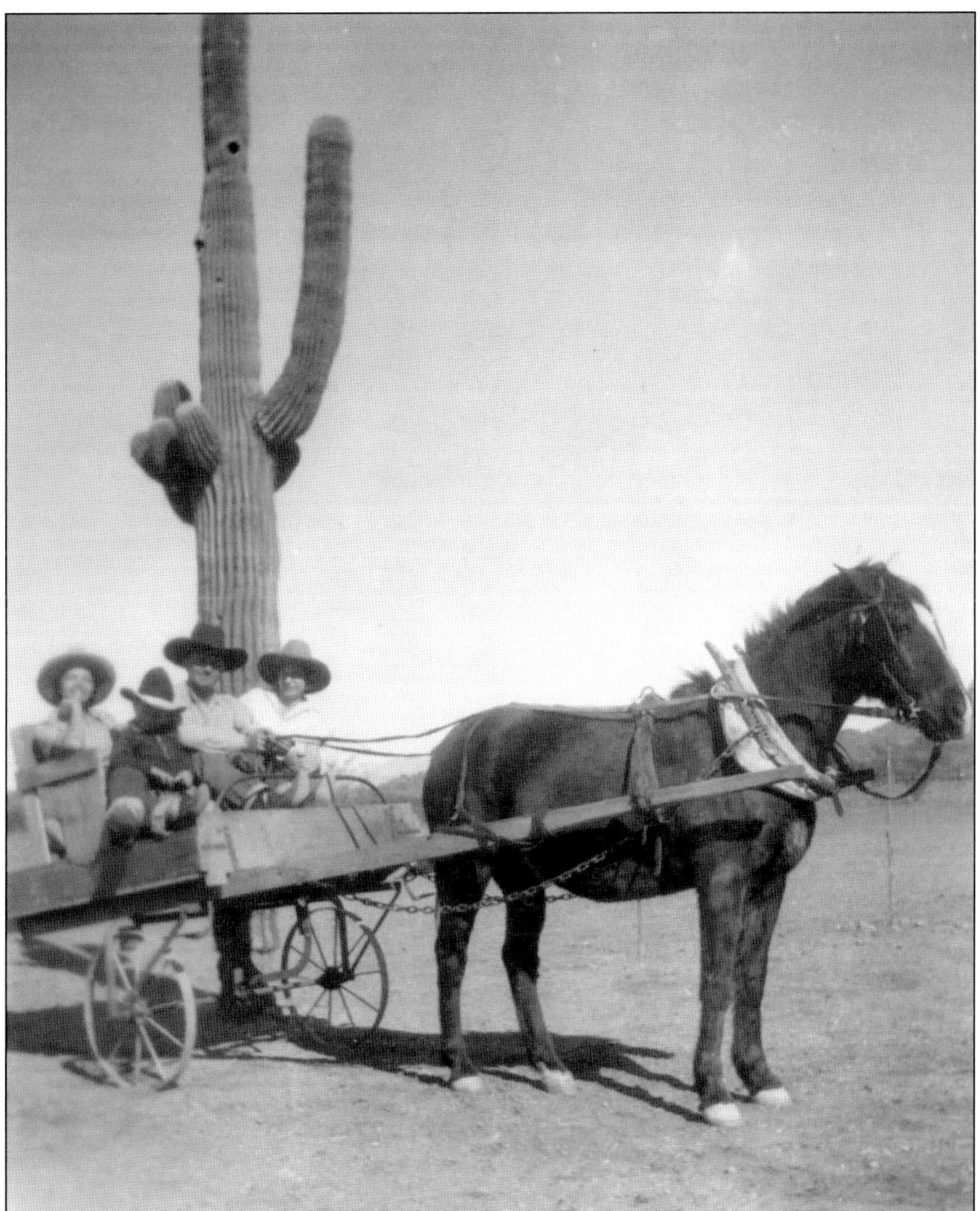

Sunday drives were different in 1930s New River. The Jacka family showed how it was done in a horse-drawn cart. Jerry Jacka Sr.'s cousin Lena Pallas (left) joined the Jackas on this occasion. Lena wholeheartedly loved the ranch and after her death at age 105, her ashes were scattered on the grounds. (Courtesy of Jerry D. Jacka and Lois Essary Jacka.)

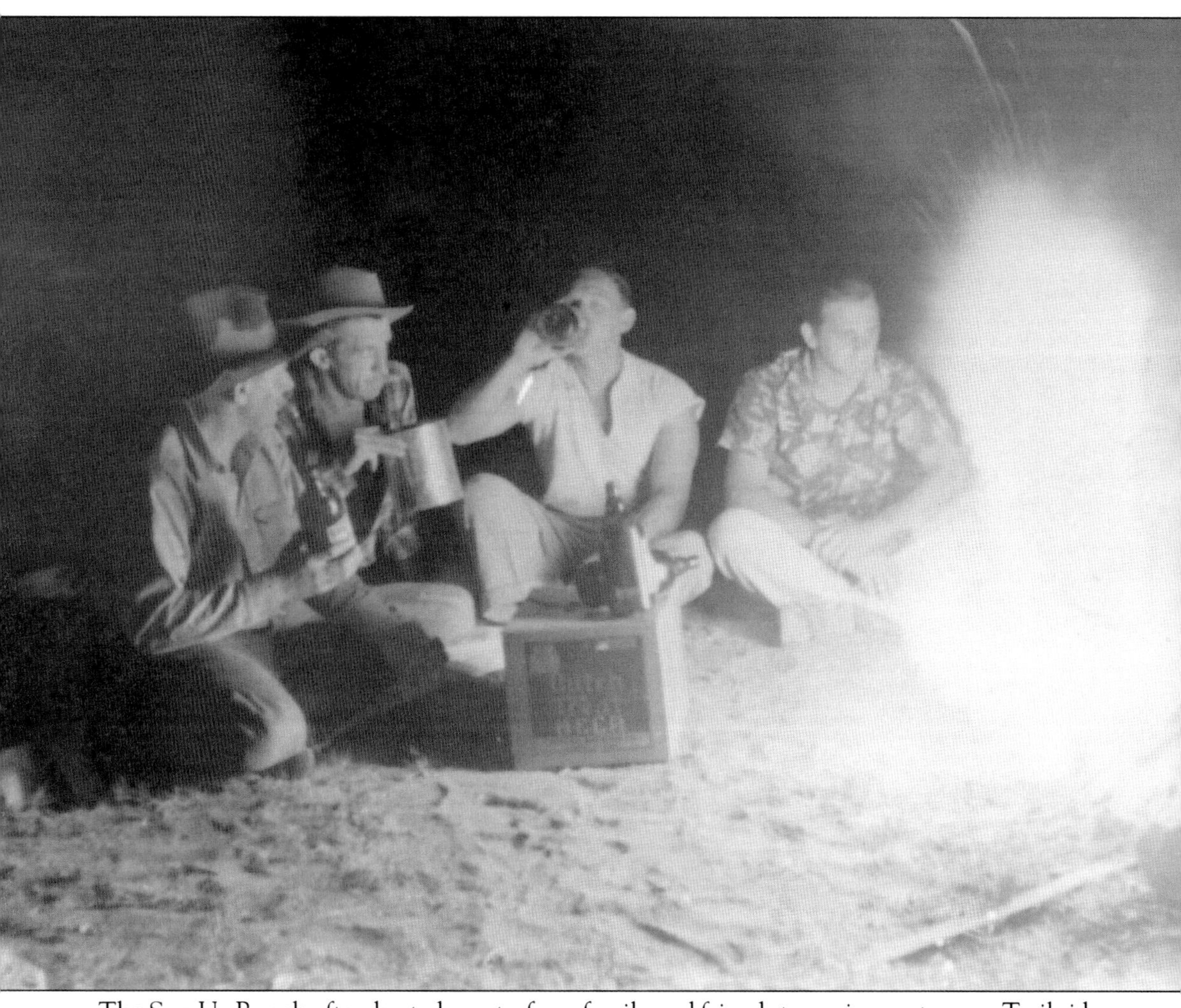

The Sun-Up Ranch often hosted guests, from family and friends to paying customers. Trail rides, campfires, and other gatherings were popular means of entertainment for residents and visitors. Guests here enjoy a campfire at Sun-Up Ranch in the late 1930s. Jerry Jacka Sr. is at far left. (Courtesy of Jerry D. Jacka and Lois Essary Jacka.)

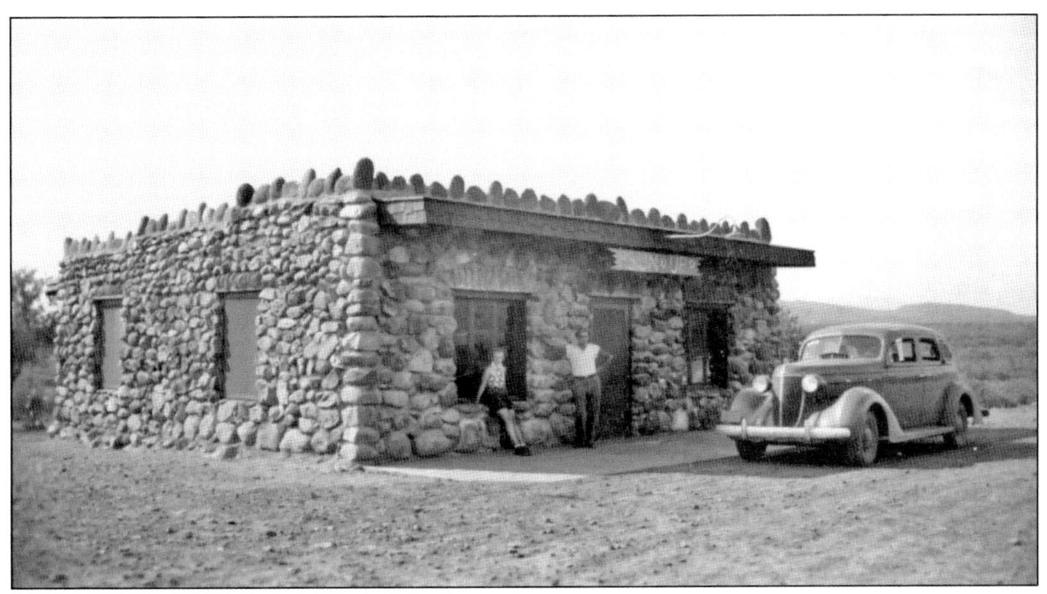

By 1936, the Jackas opened their picturesque Sun-Up Cafe on the east edge of the ranch. Homesteaders forging a living from the desert had to be innovative to survive. The beautiful stone café was one of the Jacka family's successful enterprises and offered travelers along the still-unpaved Black Canyon Highway a place to enjoy a cold soda or an Apache beer brewed by the Arizona Brewing Company in Phoenix. The café served light meals and, as appropriate to a fine Arizona establishment of the time, also sold ammunition. (Both, courtesy of Jerry D. Jacka and Lois Essary Jacka.)

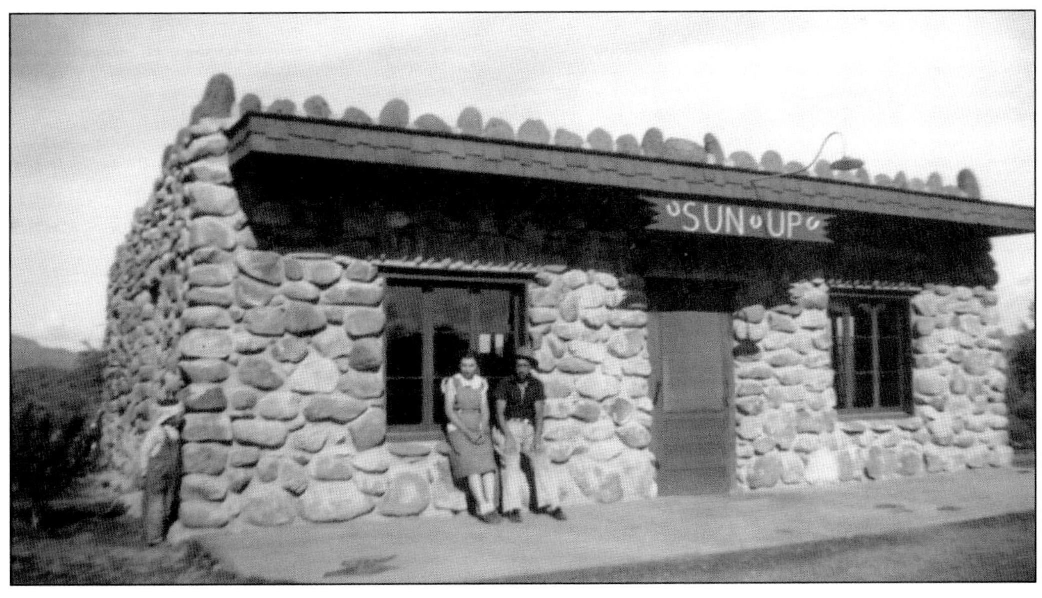

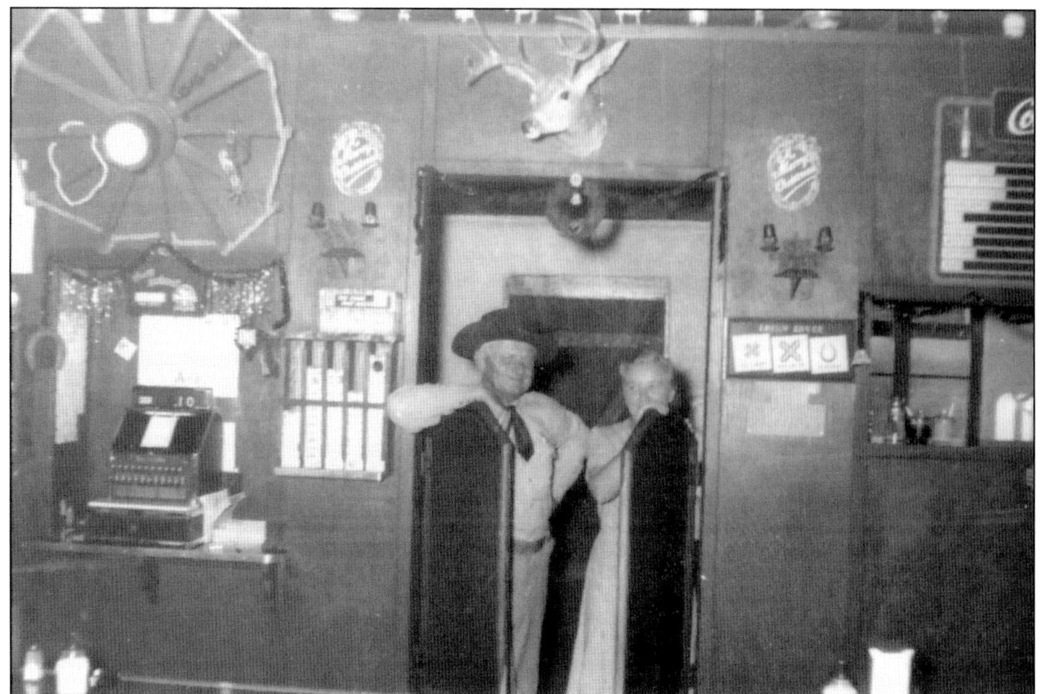

The Sun-Up Cafe, shown above in approximately 1950, initially had neither plumbing nor electricity. The Jackas hauled ice from Phoenix for the icebox and hauled water from the ranch. Closed during the wartime years and later for remodeling, the now plumbed and renovated café reopened in 1953, made accessible by the newly-paved Black Canyon Highway. Sadly, the café, which was hand built of native stone to match the Sun-Up ranch house and cabins, stood in the path of the future Interstate 17 freeway. In 1967, the café was demolished. The same fate befell Elmer King's 69er Cafe, a tavern south of the Sun-Up at what is now the intersection of Interstate 17 and Anthem Way. (Both, courtesy of Jerry D. Jacka and Lois Essary Jacka.)

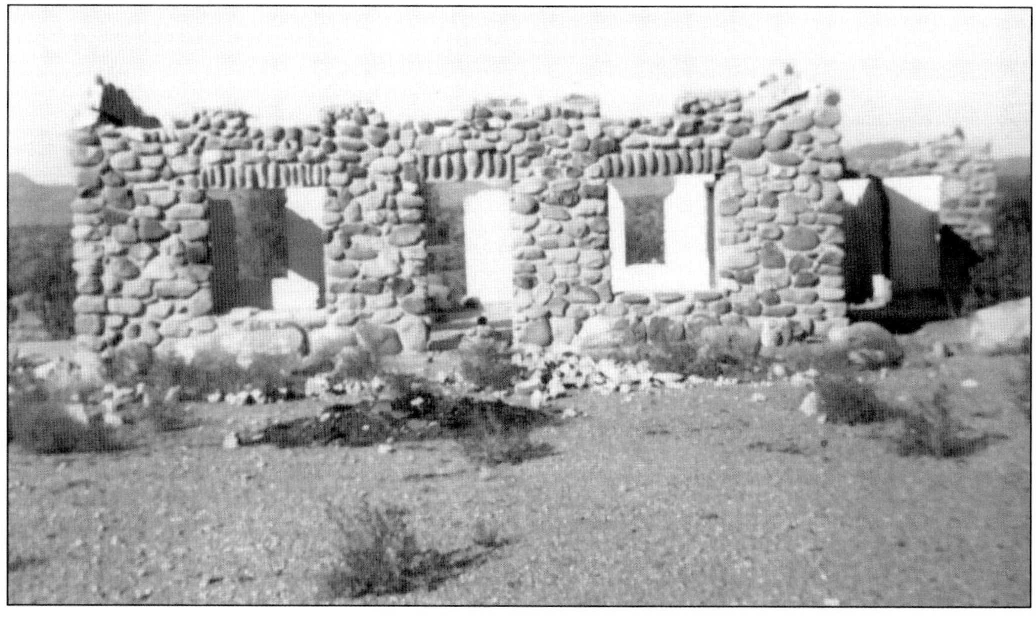

The close-knit New River homesteaders enjoyed dances, parties, and holiday events together. Jerry Jacka Sr. welcomes the new year in the late 1940s in appropriate attire as an Old West gambler at the Sun-Up Ranch New Year's Eve party. (Courtesy of Jerry D. Jacka and Lois Essary Jacka.)

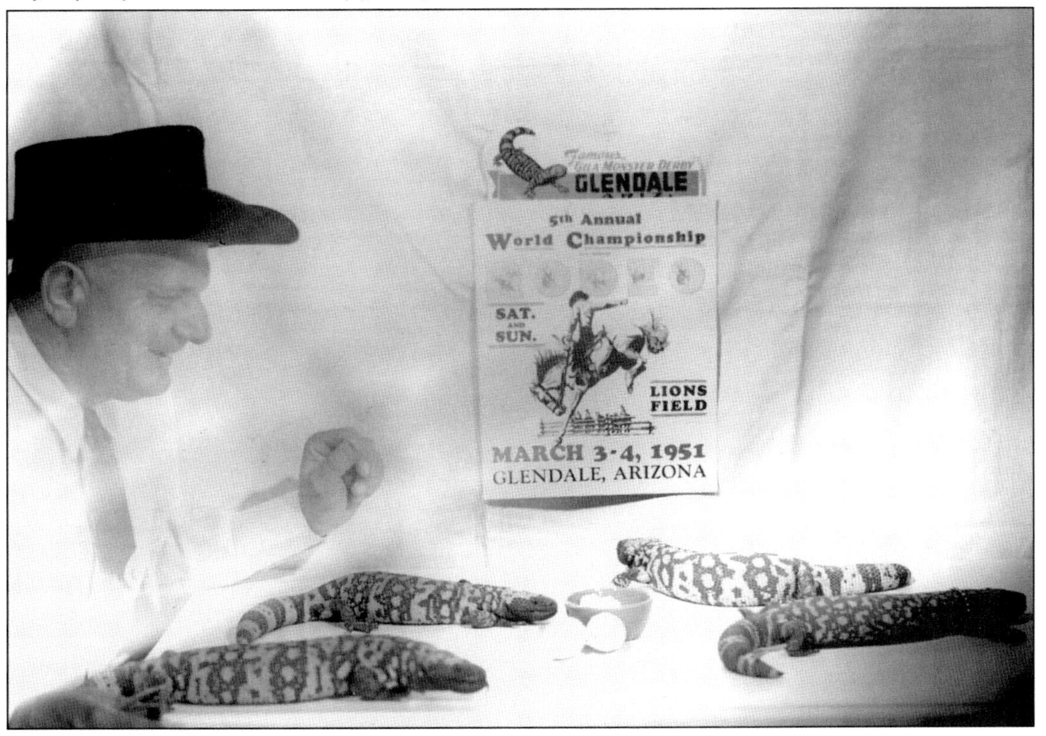

For decades, Jerry Jacka Sr. kept Gila monsters as pets and, from 1949 to 1951, directed the popular (albeit slow-paced) Gila Monster Derby at the Glendale Rodeo. Quite comfortable handling them, Jerry Sr. caught them barehanded despite their dangerous bite. Jerry Sr. was granted a special permit from the state to continue keeping Gila monsters once they received protected status. (Courtesy of Jerry D. Jacka and Lois Essary Jacka.)

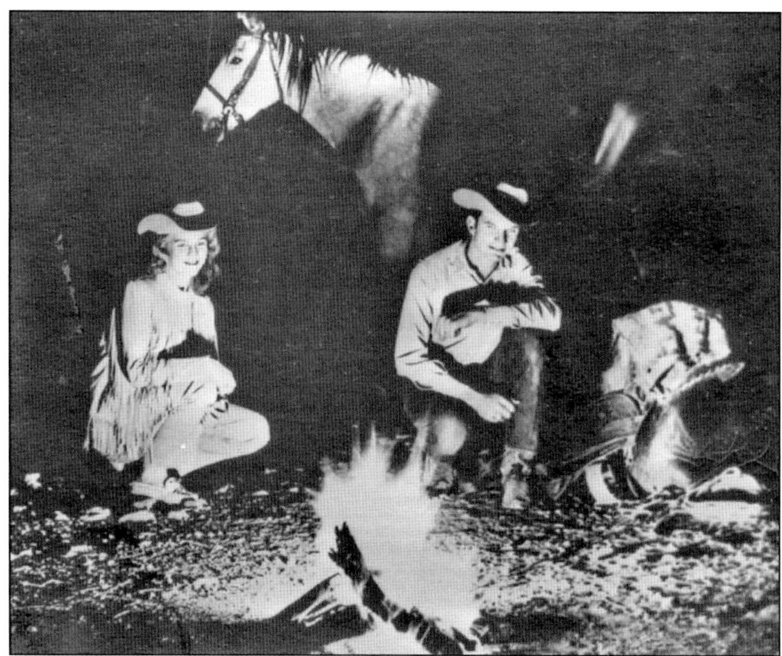

The offspring of homesteaders, Jerry D. Jacka and Lois Essary Jacka attended New River's one-room schoolhouse together as children, later becoming high school sweethearts. Marrying at 18, they lived at Sun-Up Ranch until purchasing the Fred Mayer homestead at the northeast corner of the intersection of today's Anthem Way and Interstate 17. (Courtesy of Jerry D. Jacka and Lois Essary Jacka.)

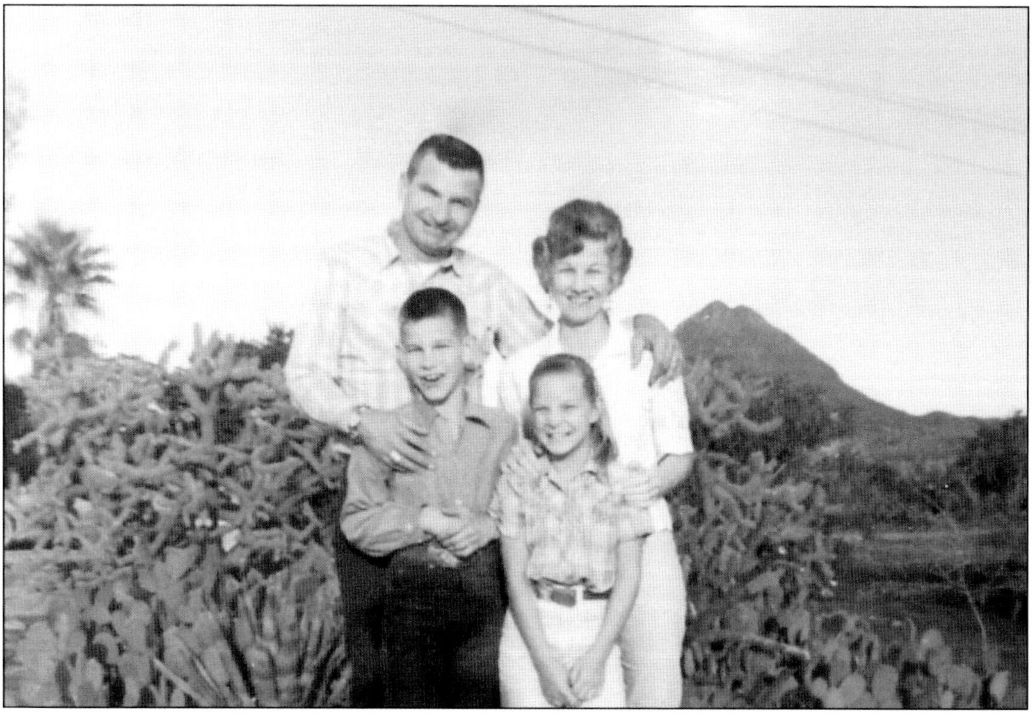

By 1966, Sun-Up Ranch was the lush and fertile place of Rose and Jerry Jacka Sr.'s dreams. Pictured in front of a stand of cholla, prickly pear, and agave are Lois Essary Jacka and Jerry D. Jacka with their children Mike and Cindy. (Courtesy of Jerry D. Jacka and Lois Essary Jacka.

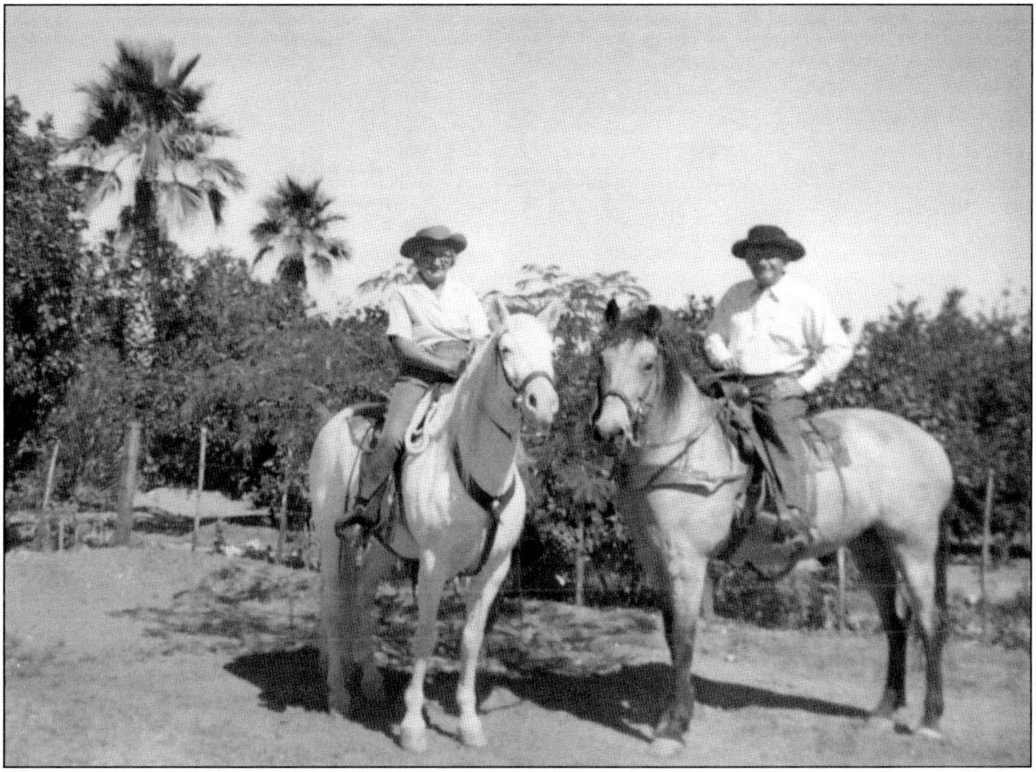

Jerry Jacka Sr. met his future wife, then Rose Josephine Kubes, in his hometown of Chicago after his return from Marine service in World War I. Married in 1927 and in love with the allure of the Southwest, they chose their homestead in Arizona in 1929. Although Jerry had once worked on a cattle ranch in Colorado, Rose was new to horsemanship at the time of their honeymoon, which included many hours on horseback, riding to a remote cabin near Grand Junction. Decades later, the two were still riding together. Shown here in the 1960s, the couple remained in the stone house they built together on the Sun-Up homestead until their deaths. (Above, courtesy of Jerry D. Jacka and Lois Essary Jacka; right, from the book *Sun-Up Ranch: An Arizona Desert Homestead* by Jerry D. Jacka.)

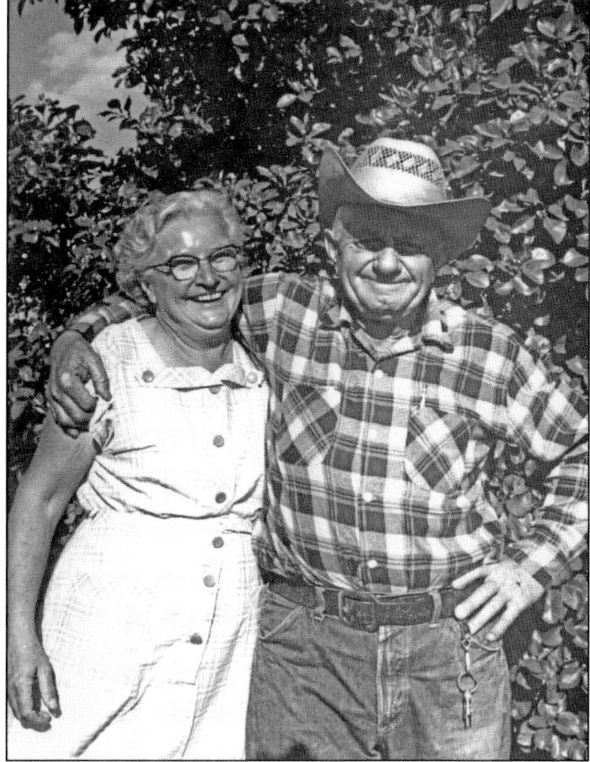

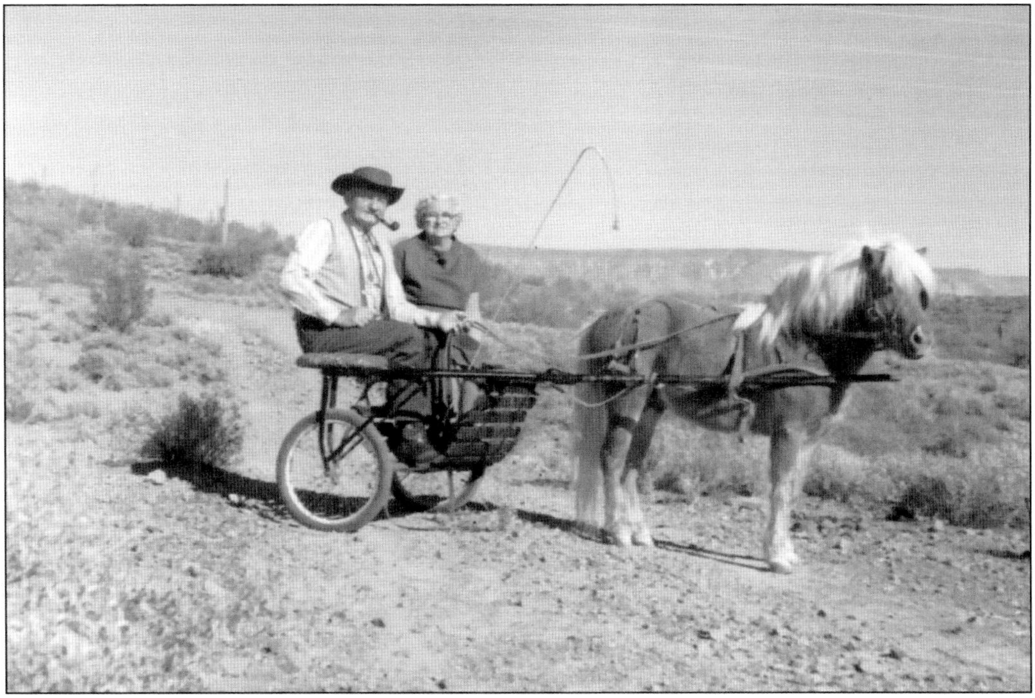

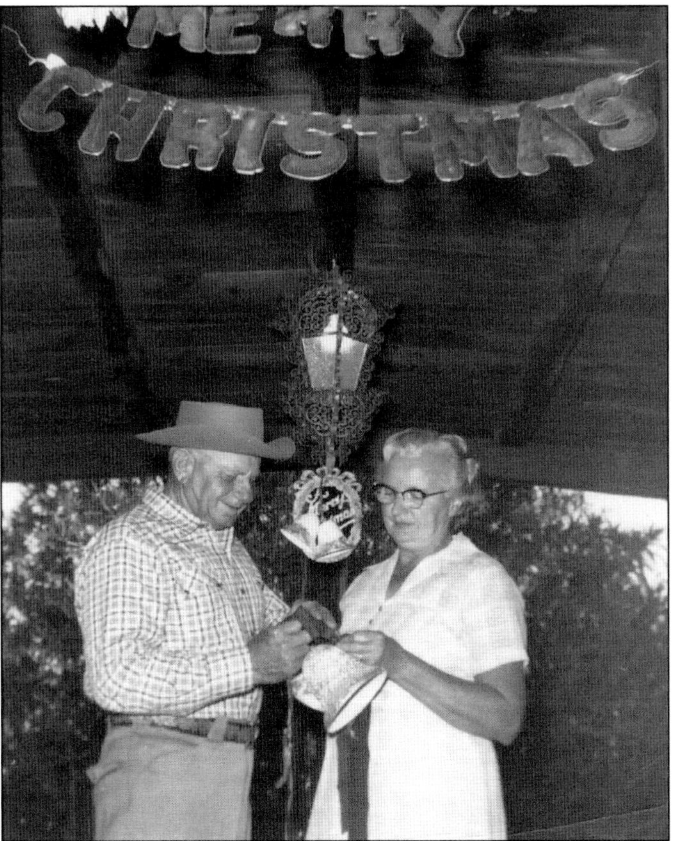

To the very end, Rose and Jerry Jacka Sr. celebrated holidays properly in the homestead tradition. Christmas at Sun-Up Ranch was a special time to share with good company and make memories. Above is a photograph the Jackas included with their Christmas cards one year as they took their pony cart out for a drive snapped in the stunning New River desert they loved. At left, the Jackas decorate for a festive Christmas gathering. New River natives speak fondly of the many good times they had with friends, family, and neighbors. (Above, courtesy of June Evans Bond; left, courtesy of Rene Faires.)

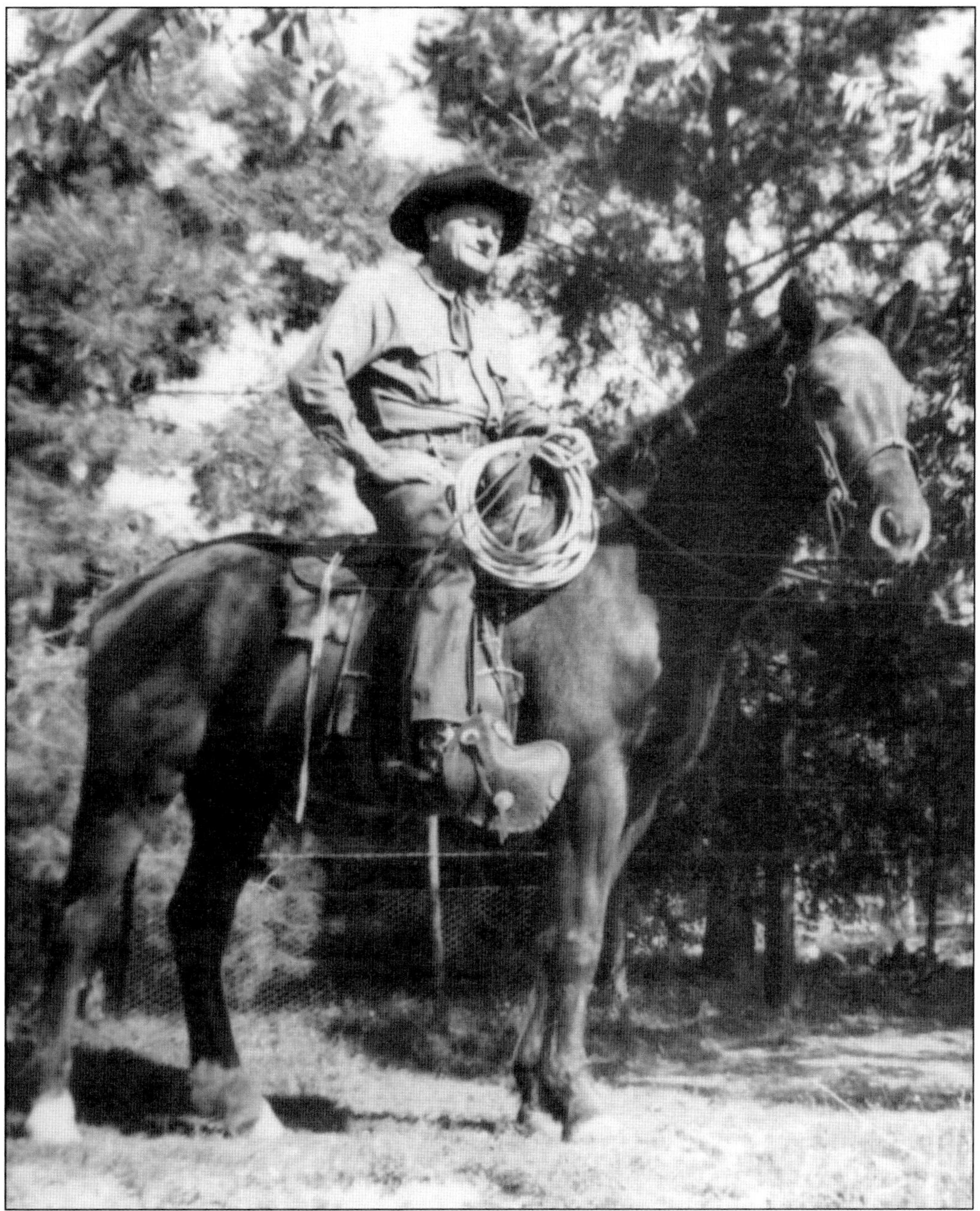

Jerry Jacka Sr. was one of many New River homesteaders who had served in World War I. A Marine during the war, Jerry Sr. was made of the tough, capable stuff that homesteading required and the values needed to help create the community. Fiercely patriotic, during World War II, Jerry worked as a guard at Thunderbird Field, the air base in Glendale, Arizona. (Courtesy of Jerry D. Jacka and Lois Essary Jacka.)

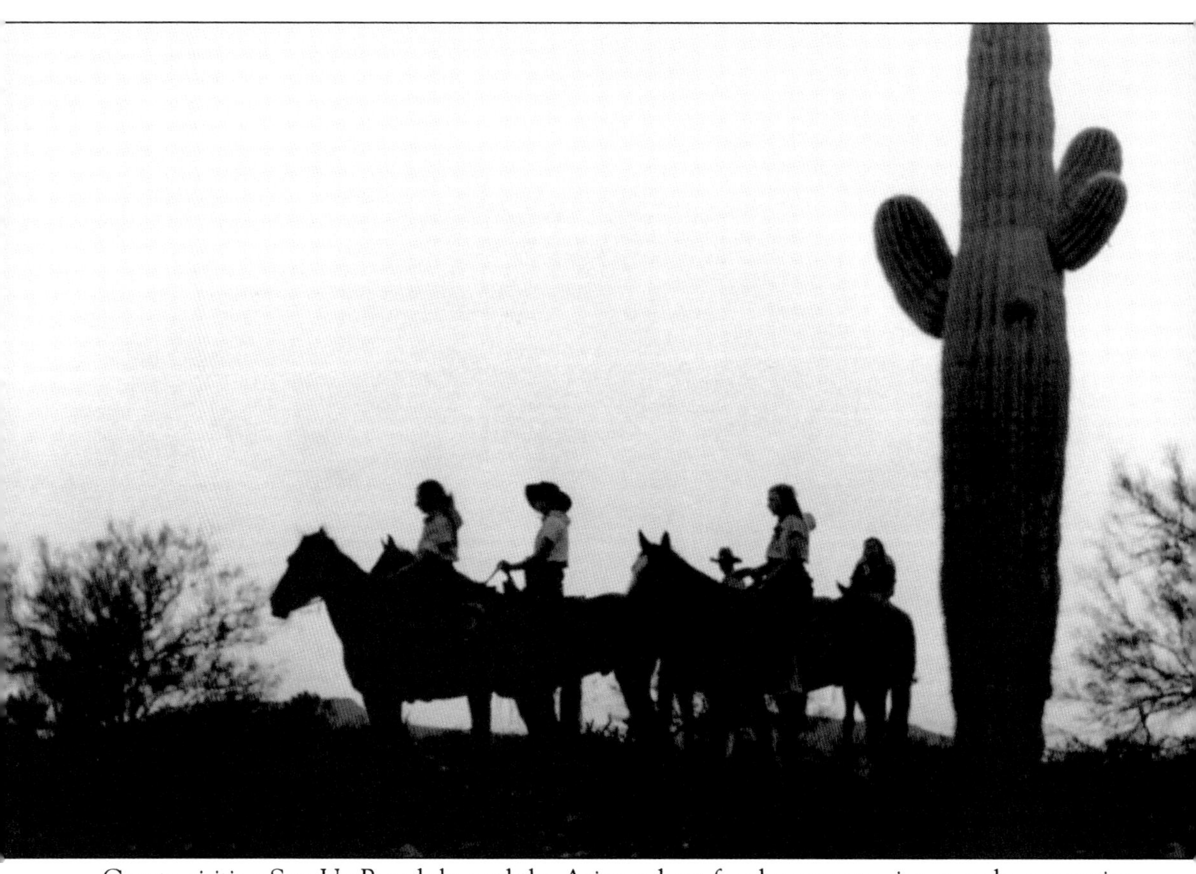

Guests visiting Sun-Up Ranch braved the Arizona heat for the opportunity to make memories like this: a sundown ride in the spectacular desert in the company of like-minded adventurers and stately saguaros. Few sights could beat an Arizona sunset viewed framed between the ears of a horse. (Courtesy of Jerry D. Jacka and Lois Essary Jacka.)

Five

Wrangler's Roost
A Western Guest Ranch

A wooden sign once greeted visitors to Wrangler's Roost dude ranch with the slogan "Out Where the Worst Begins." Although, today, a sign on the gate reads, "Wrangler's Roost Stagecoach Stop, Established 1898," the actual stage line was farther west and had ceased to run long before Chief J. Myers homesteaded the Wrangler's Roost site.

There is a lengthy western tradition of telling tall tales and staging photographs for the amusement and bewilderment of those city folks back east. Cowboys and dude ranch proprietors did—and do—enjoy giving visitors plenty of stories to share on their return back home. Sometimes, those tall tales were told often enough to credulous listeners to become accepted as fact and passed on as history.

Chief J. Myers, Wrangler's Roost's founder, was known for his flamboyant personality and penchant for sharing such tales with the guests. He liked to say he acquired the property—originally a 640-acre homestead—from a jailed bootlegger, receiving the deed in exchange for the bail money. Homestead records, however, indicate Myers paid cash outright for the land, receiving the land patent on February 12, 1937, under the Stock Raising designation. Chief and his companion (known to locals simply as "Mom") began construction on the ranch buildings in the late 1930s, using the native stone abundant on the grounds.

In 1941, Chief sold "the Roost" to Port Halle. There, Port and his wife, Lois, were married. The Halles sold the Roost in 1952, moving into Phoenix so the boys could attend school in town. Television cowboy Lew King, the popular host of the *Lew King's Rangers Show* on KPHO, bought the ranch. Changing hands several times over the years, it has since been subdivided but some of the original stone structures still remain, a glimpse into the rustic allure of the western dude ranches of the past. During its heyday and at the height of public fascination with the Wild West, guests visited the Roost from around the world. From artist Max Meyer to politician Winthrop Rockefeller, they were drawn to the landscape and wildness of New River.

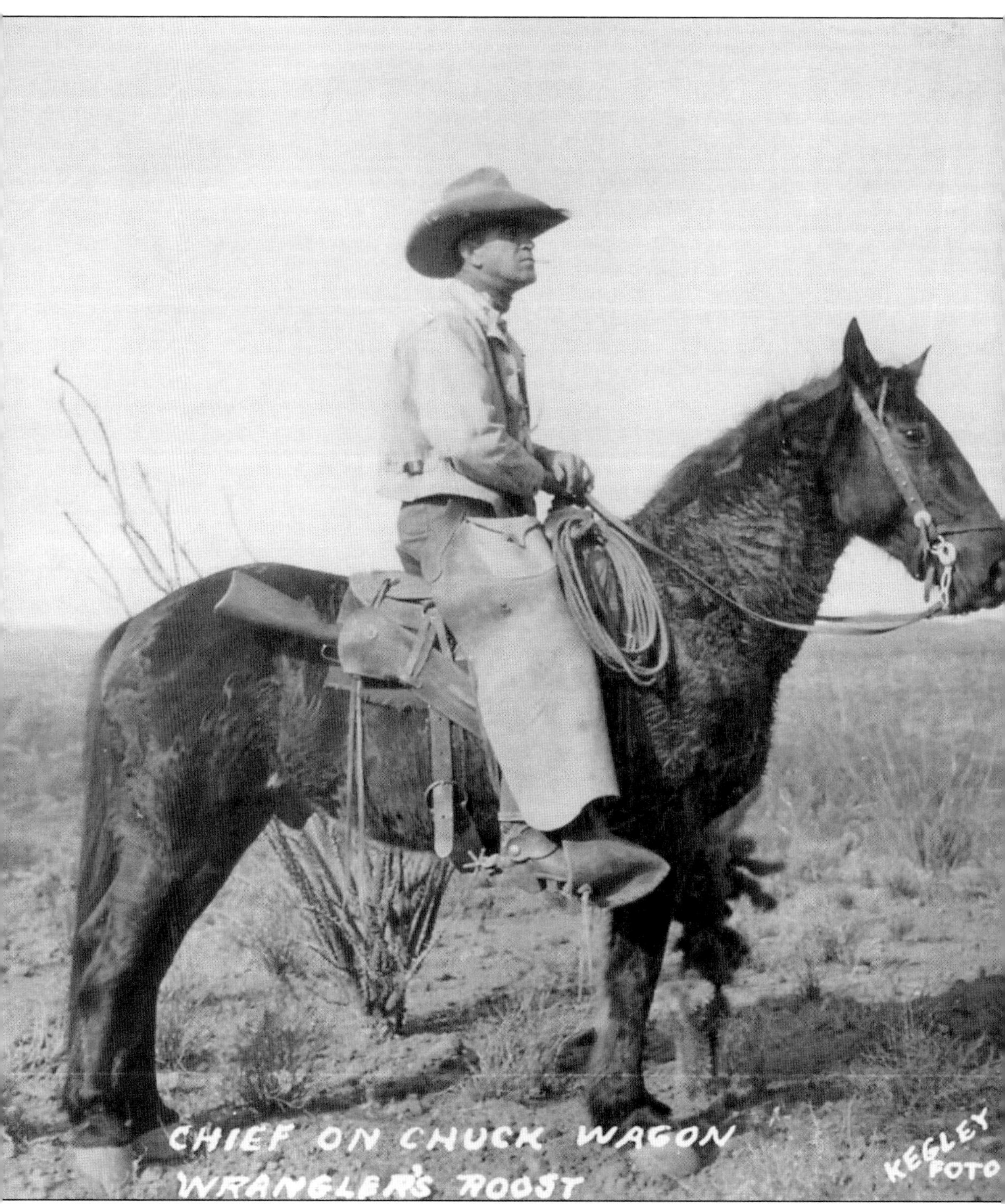

Older natives of New River still remember Chief J. Myers, founder of Wrangler's Roost, invariably describing him as "colorful." Born in Georgia in 1883, Myers died in November 1963. In this photograph from the late 1930s, Myers is on his horse Chuck Wagon. (Courtesy of Jerry D. Jacka and Lois Essary Jacka.)

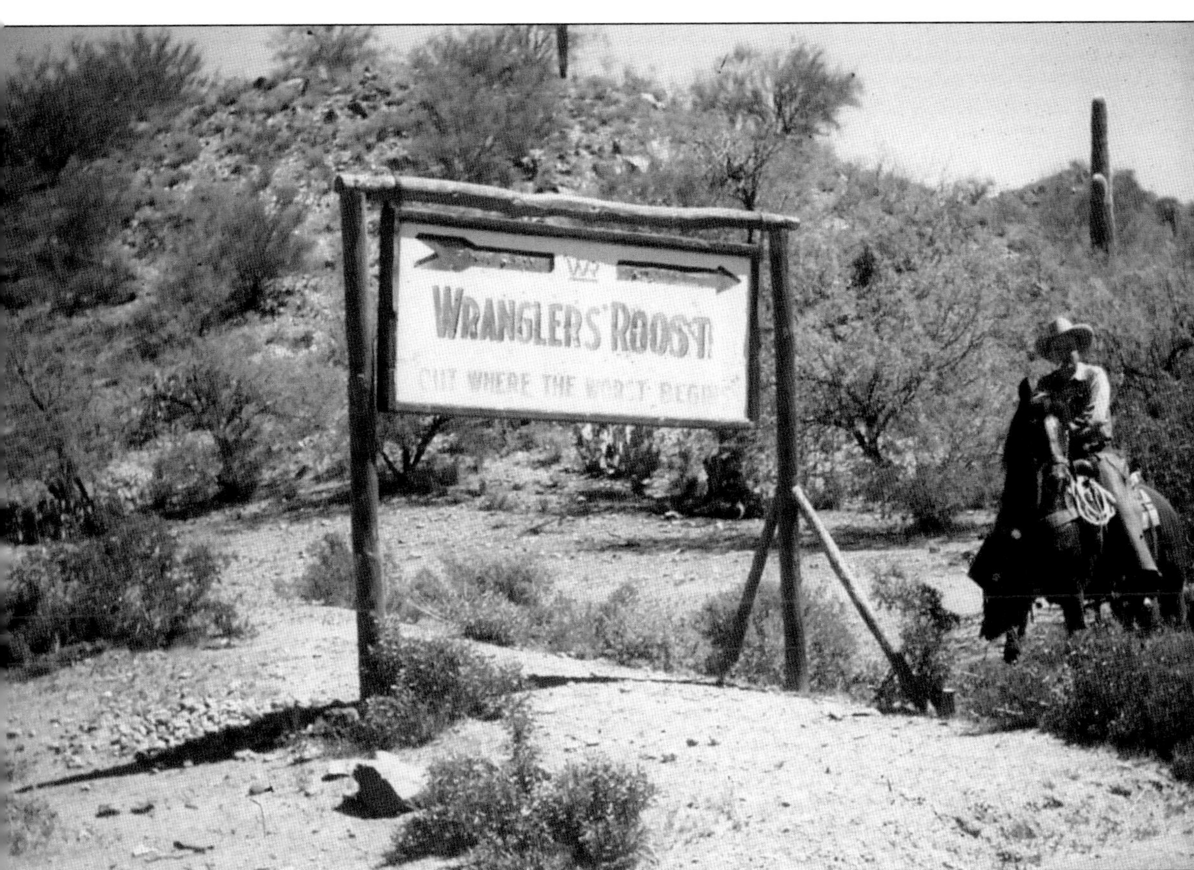

Port Halle sits on horseback near the sign, greeting guests to the ranch. Note the slogan "Out Where the Worst Begins," capitalizing on the tourist perception of the desert as a hostile, daunting land. Later, Wrangler's Roost used the slogan "Out Where the West Begins." (Courtesy of Lance Halle.)

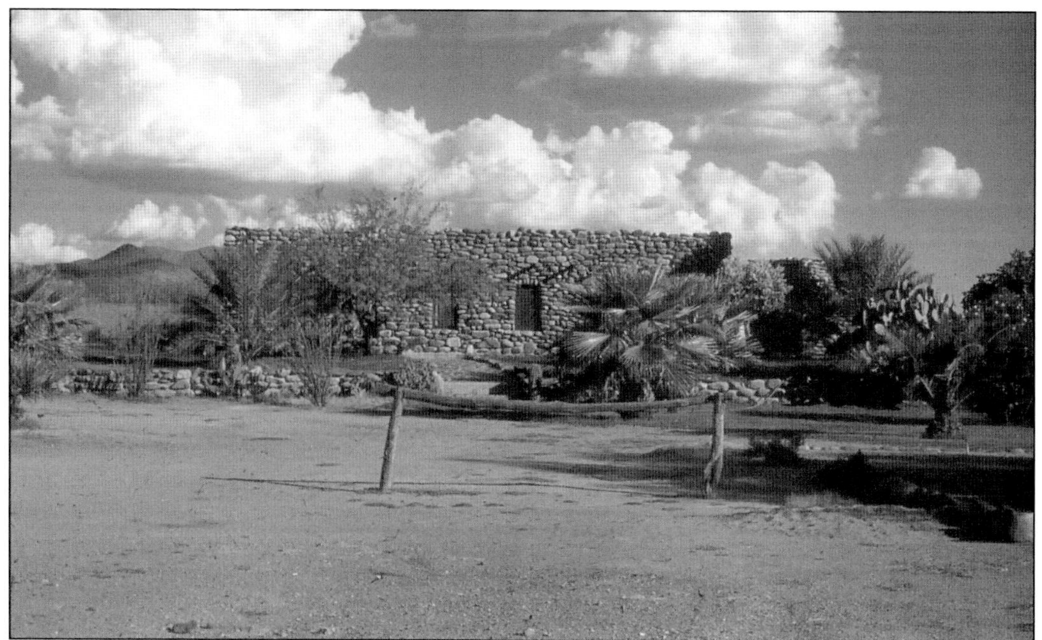

Established in the 1930s by Chief J. Myers, the original bunkhouse at Wrangler's Roost still stands today. The New River area is notoriously rocky; like many early structures, the homestead bunkhouse was built of locally gathered rocks. The palm trees in front, although not native to Arizona, thrive in the arid desert climate. (Photograph by Port Halle, courtesy of Lance Halle.)

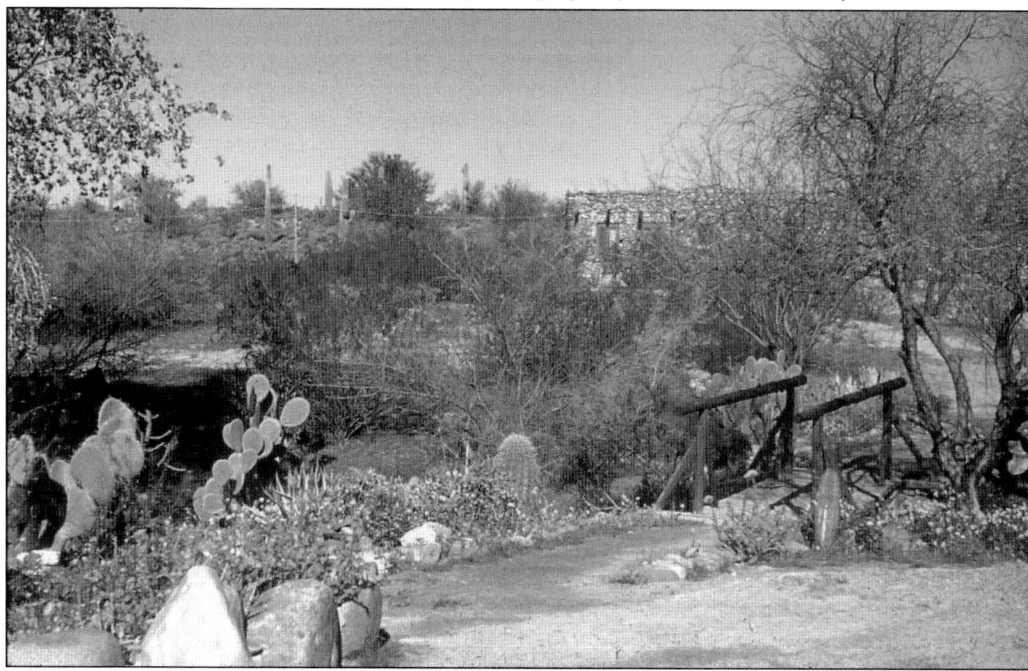

The bunkhouse looked out onto a natural landscape featuring largely native plants. Prickly pear cactus, agave, barrel cactus, creosote bush, and mesquite are among the plants lining the walkway. Arizona's famous cactus, the saguaro, are the tall cacti on the ridge in the background. The saguaro blossom is the official state flower. (Photograph by Port Halle, courtesy of Lance Halle.)

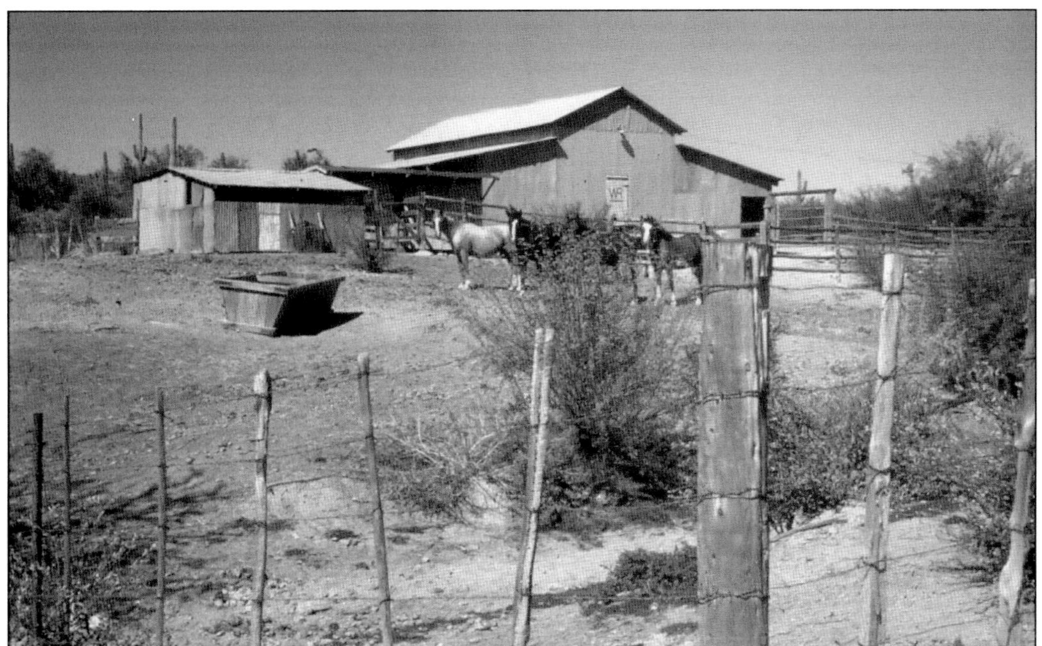

During the heyday of the western dude ranch in the 1940s, guests were drawn by the opportunity to ride horseback through the ruggedly beautiful Arizona desert. Wrangler's Roost boasted a colorful assortment of guest horses and hundreds of miles of trails into the Tonto National Forest to the north. (Photograph by Port Halle, courtesy of Lance Halle.)

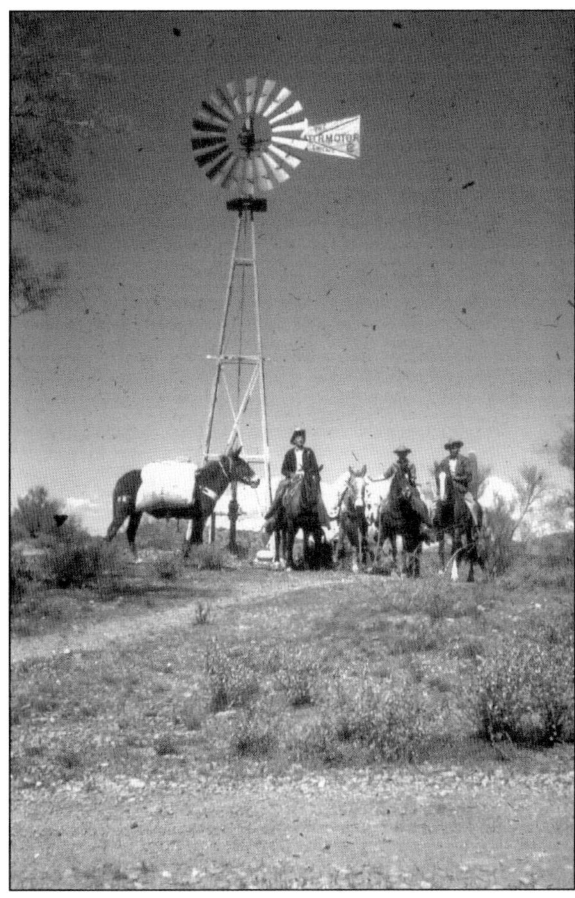

Riders on horseback and their pack animals—a mule and a burro—prepare to head out from the Roost for a pack trip into the desert. The Tonto National Forest, established in 1905 to protect the state's Salt and Verde Watersheds, spans two million acres of undeveloped land accessible for recreational purposes, including hunting and horseback riding. (Photograph by Port Halle, courtesy of Lance Halle.)

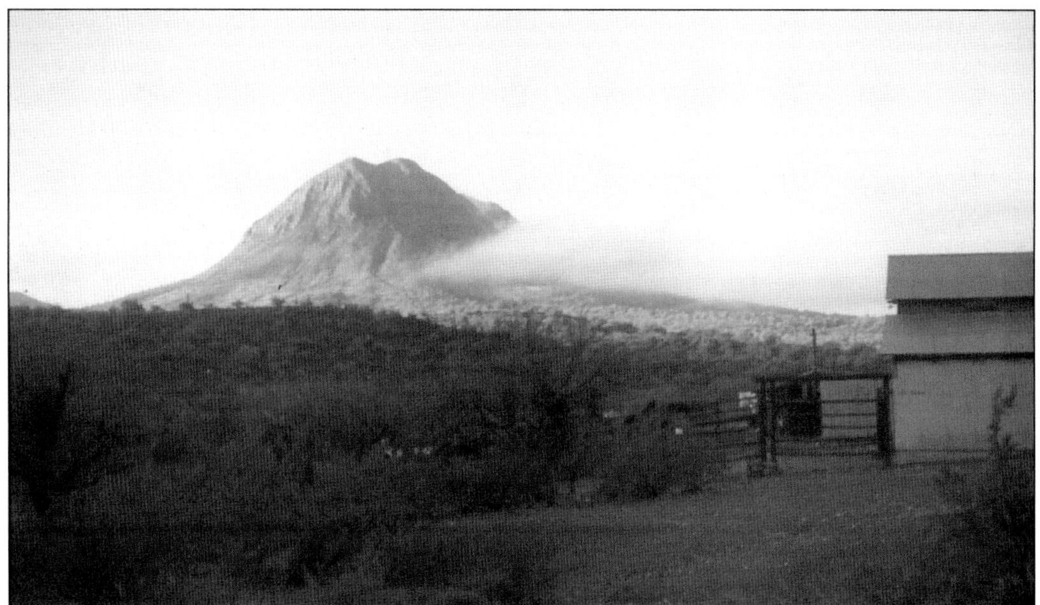

One of New River's most distinctive landmarks, Gavilan Peak dominates the horizon south of Wrangler's Roost. Brush fires and floods are constant hazards to desert dwellers. Here, the smoke from a fire near Gavilan's base drifts to the west beyond Wrangler's Roost barn. From this side, it is easy to see why locals called the peak "Twin Peaks" or "Twin Buttes." (Photograph by Port Halle, courtesy of Lance Halle).

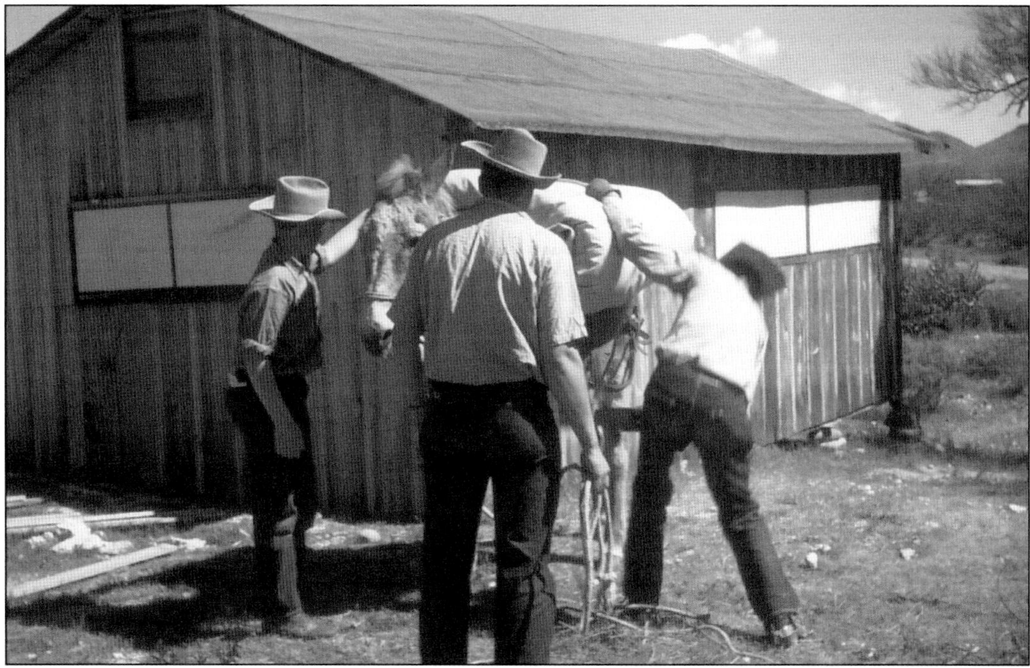

A "wrangler" is the ranch hand responsible for tending and handling livestock, from the horses ridden by the guests to the burros and mules used to pack supplies on long rides. Hardy, sure-footed, and smart, mules and burros required little upkeep compared to the larger, more sensitive horses. (Photograph by Port Halle, courtesy of Lance Halle.)

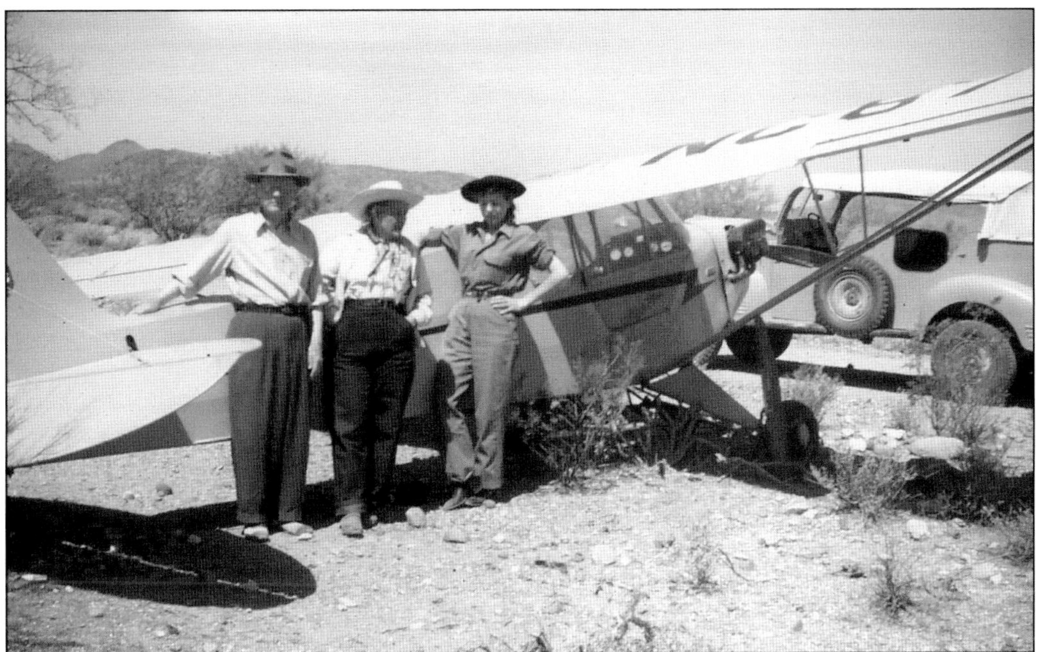
Guests sometimes arrived at Wrangler's Roost via small aircraft, landing at nearby Sharman Landing Strip, a narrow strip bulldozed into the desert. At one end, pilots had to avoid power lines, and at the other, brush. Lance Halle recalls one pilot misjudging weight and departing with one passenger too many. Getting inadequate lift, he narrowly averted tragedy by dipping below the power lines. (Photograph by Port Halle, courtesy of Lance Halle.)

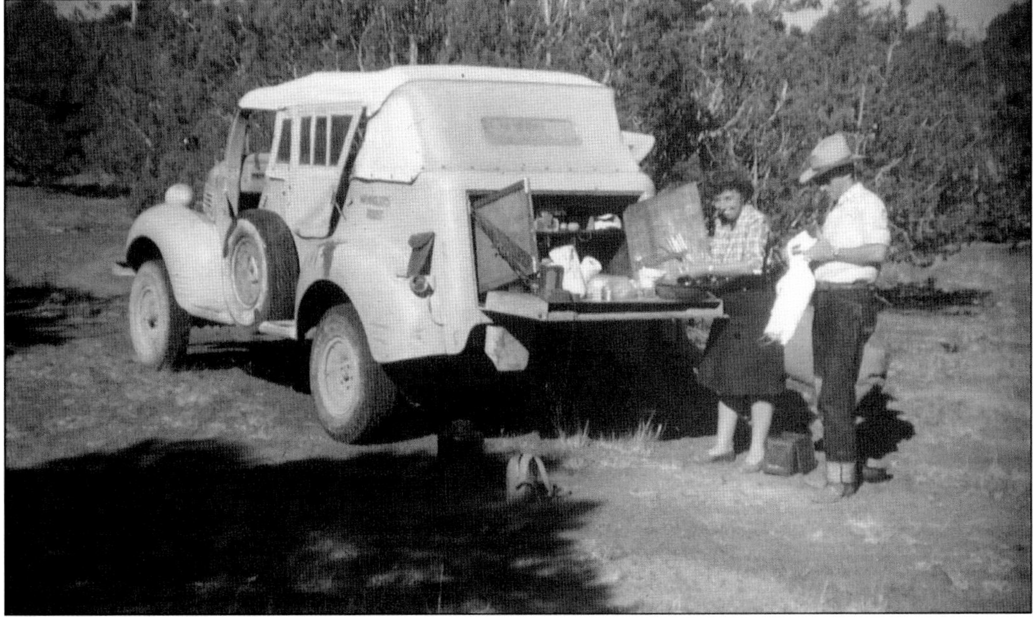
Lois Halle smiles as she sets up the ranch chuckwagon on an expedition into a juniper forest north of Wrangler's Roost. Lance Halle remembers his parents converting former military vehicles into ranch utility vehicles. Durable under desert conditions, they were used for guest transport as well. (Courtesy of Lance Halle.)

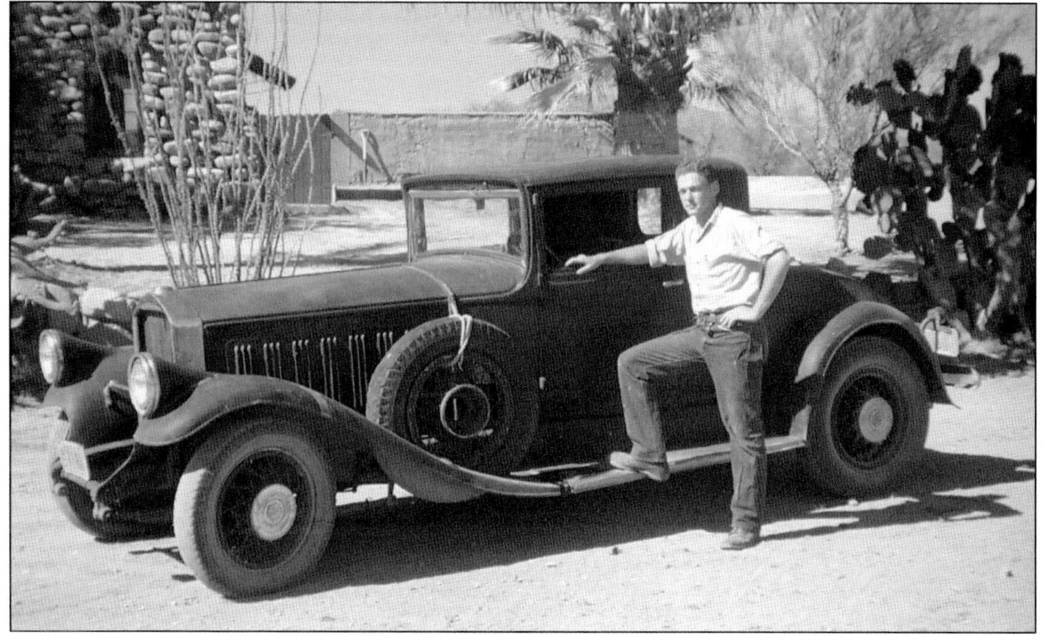

Port Halle's son Pete poses in front of the lodge. Behind his car to the left is an ocotillo, an abundantly growing thorny shrub native to Arizona. To the right is a large prickly pear cactus, popular among native people for its sweet, edible fruit. Tourists often left the state with a jar of prickly pear jelly in their luggage. (Photograph by Port Halle, courtesy of Lance Halle.)

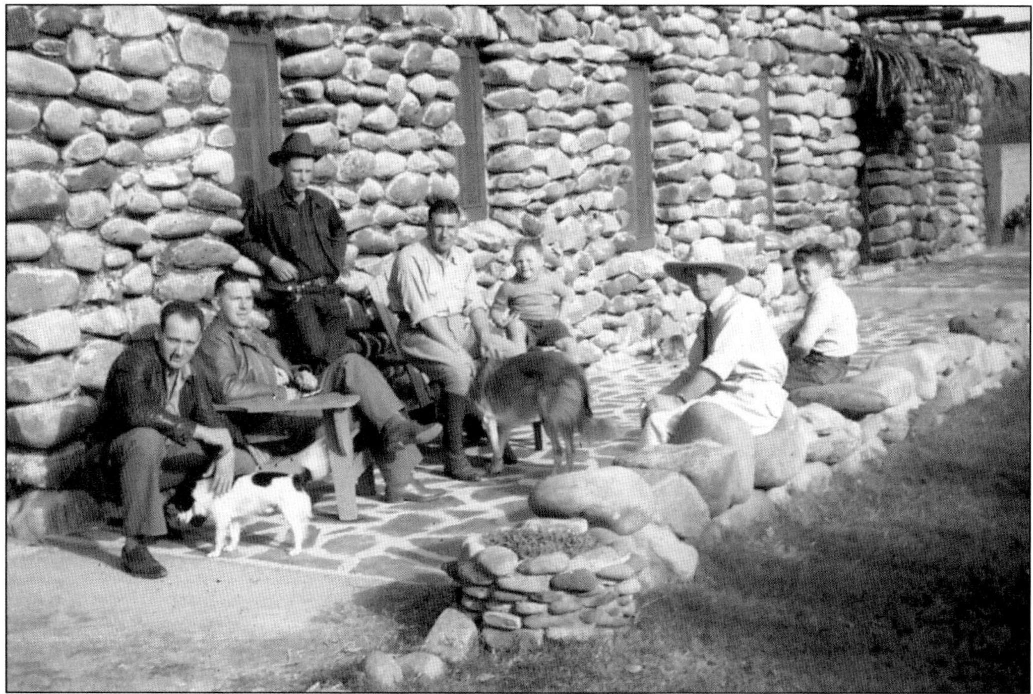

Many dude ranch guests became close friends of the Halle family. Here, visitors assemble for a photograph in front of the bunkhouse. Port Halle sits across from them, second from right. Note the palm fronds incorporated into the building for shade to Port's right. (Courtesy of Lance Halle.)

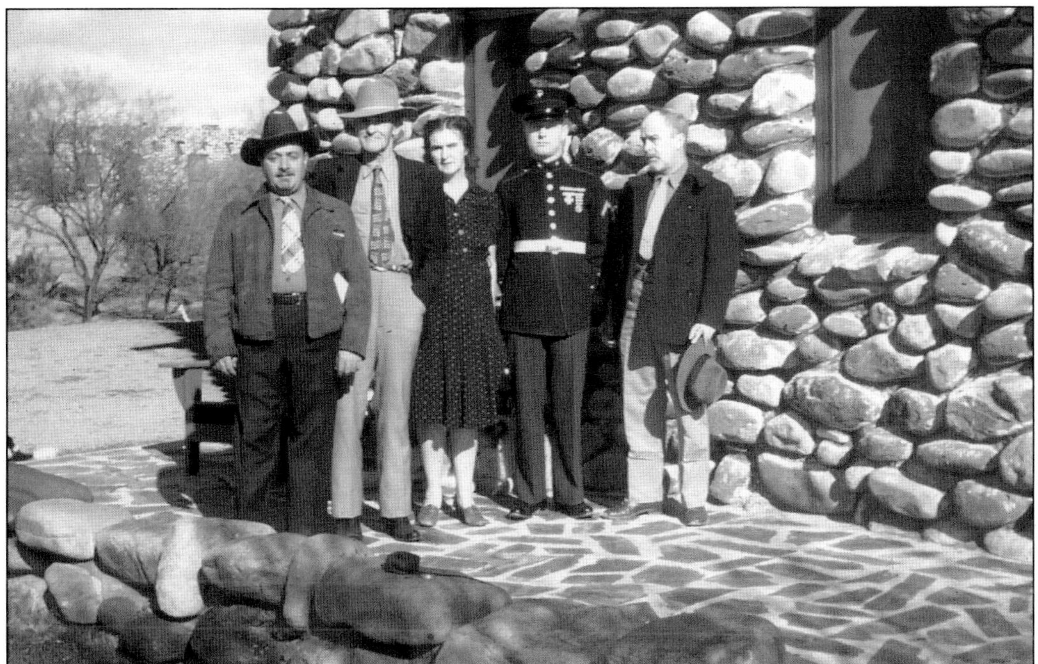

The Roost attracted many international visitors, particularly foreign military officers. It is likely several of the neatly dressed visitors in these two photographs were from overseas. In the image at right, note the English-style boots and rounded-flare breeches worn by the unidentified guest to the left of Lois Halle and the Spanish-style flat-brimmed hat and tunic on the gentleman at right. Lois excelled as the hostess of the Roost and enjoyed getting to know the dudes who visited. Despite the hard work of operating a guest ranch, the rewards were many. (Both, photograph by Port Halle, courtesy of Lance Halle.)

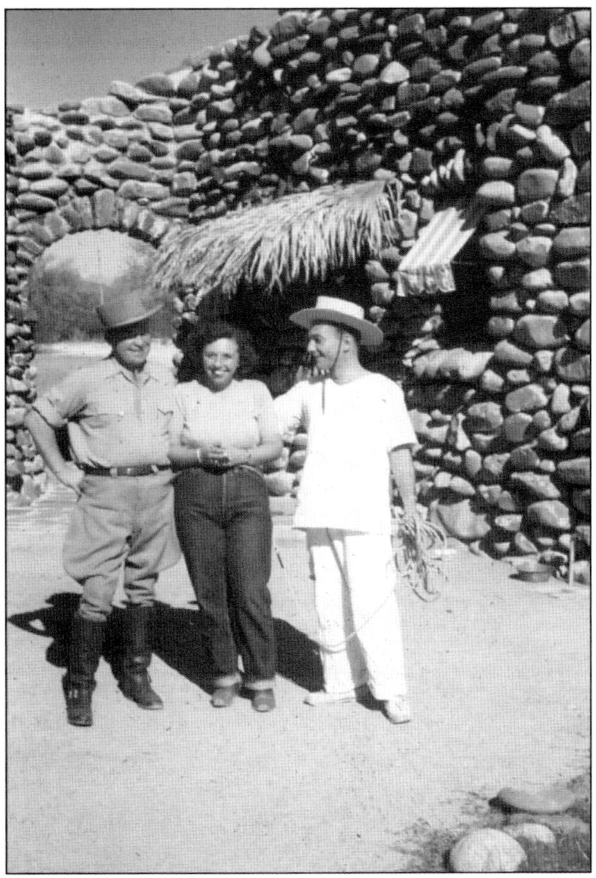

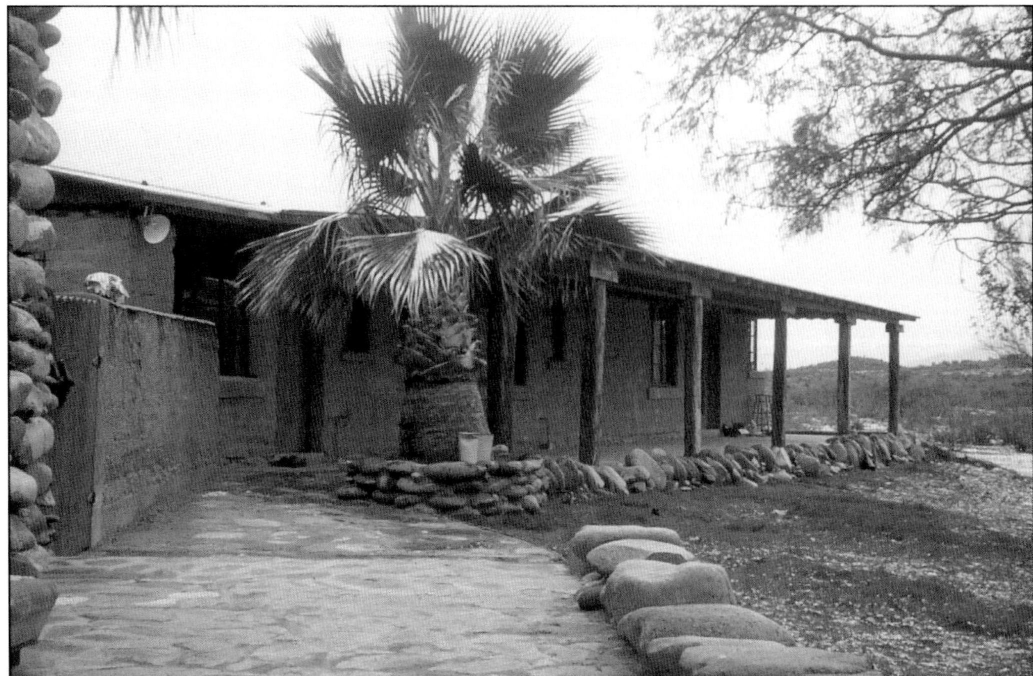

Snow in the desert is a rare delight. Above, melting snow is still visible in patches around the Wrangler's Roost lodge. In the foothills above Phoenix, New River receives more snow than the valley below, but not frequently enough to lose the novelty and joy of seeing it on the desert landscape. The palm trees, with some snow still clinging to the fronds, are not native to Arizona. Note the horse skull ornamenting the wall to the left. In the photograph below, snow graces the old wooden cabin that once stood behind Wrangler's Roost. The bane of desert dwellers and unsuspecting visitors, teddy bear cholla cactus (also known as "jumping cholla") dot the terrain to the right of the cabin. (Both, photograph by Port Halle, courtesy of Lance Halle.)

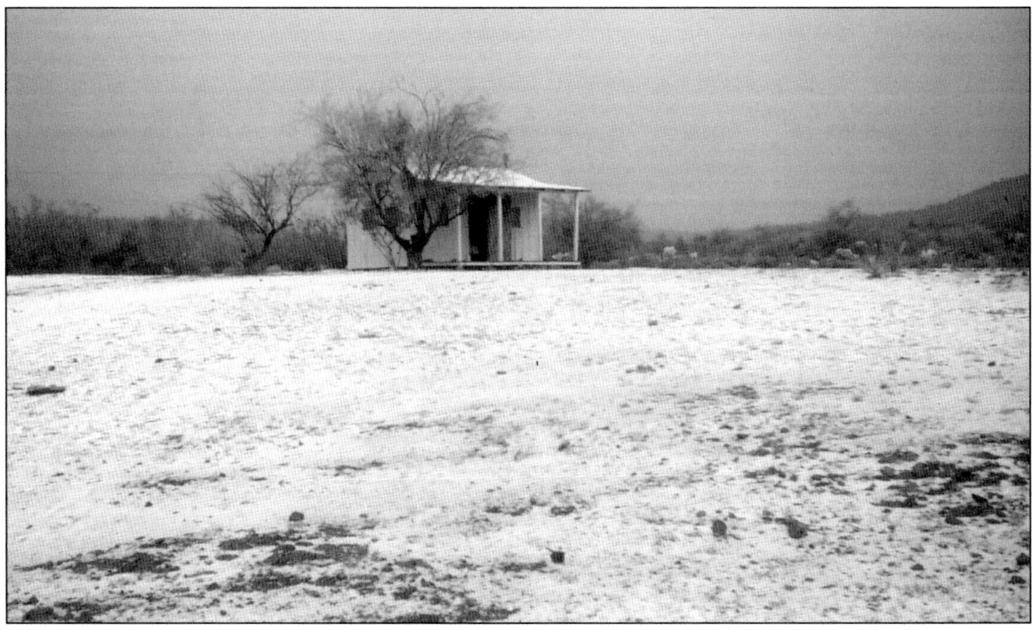

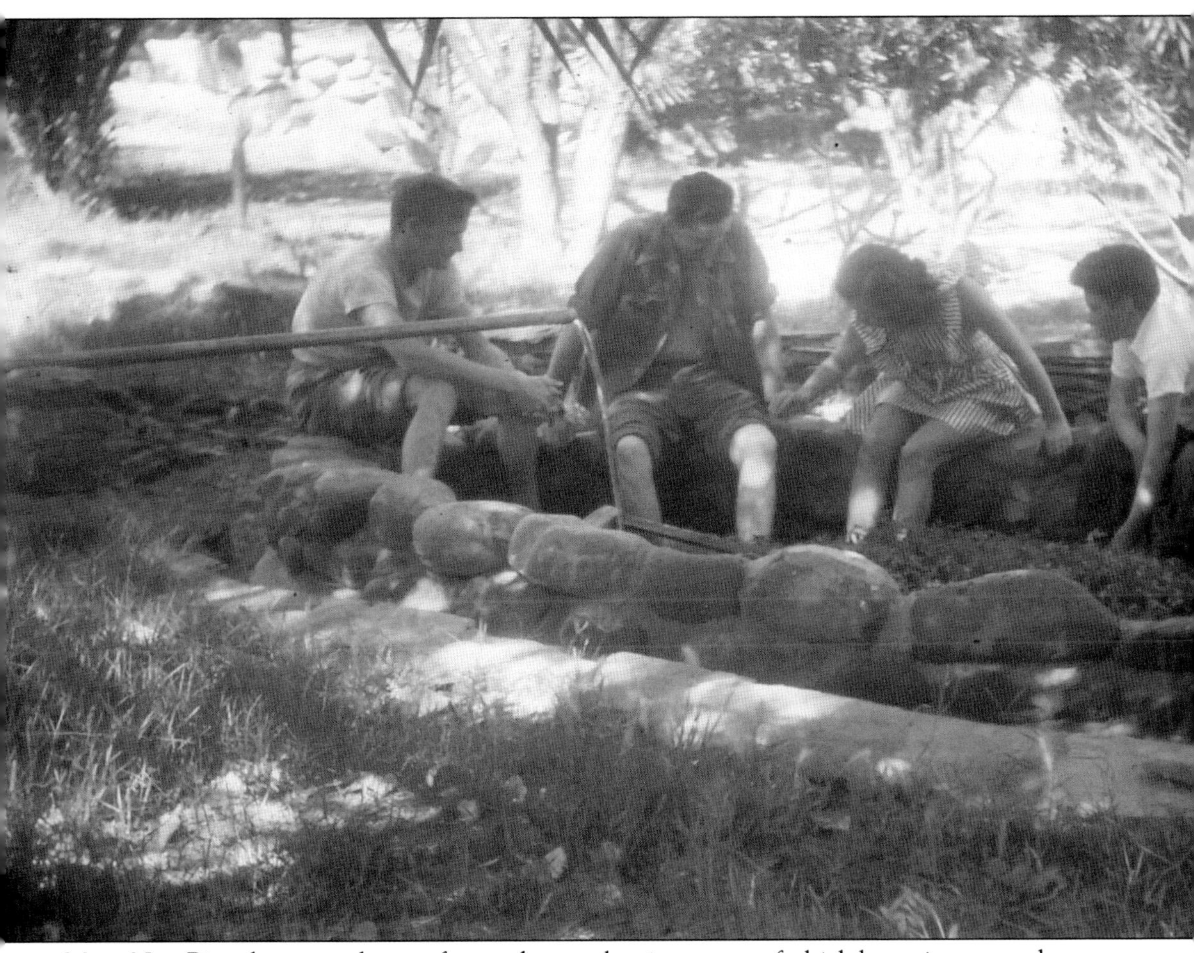

Many New River homesteads once featured natural springs, most of which have since gone dry as the groundwater was depleted. The spring-fed pond at Wrangler's Roost provided an idyllic spot to dip one's feet among the lilies. Springs also attracted rodents, which in turn drew rattlesnakes. (Photograph by Port Halle, courtesy of Lance Halle.)

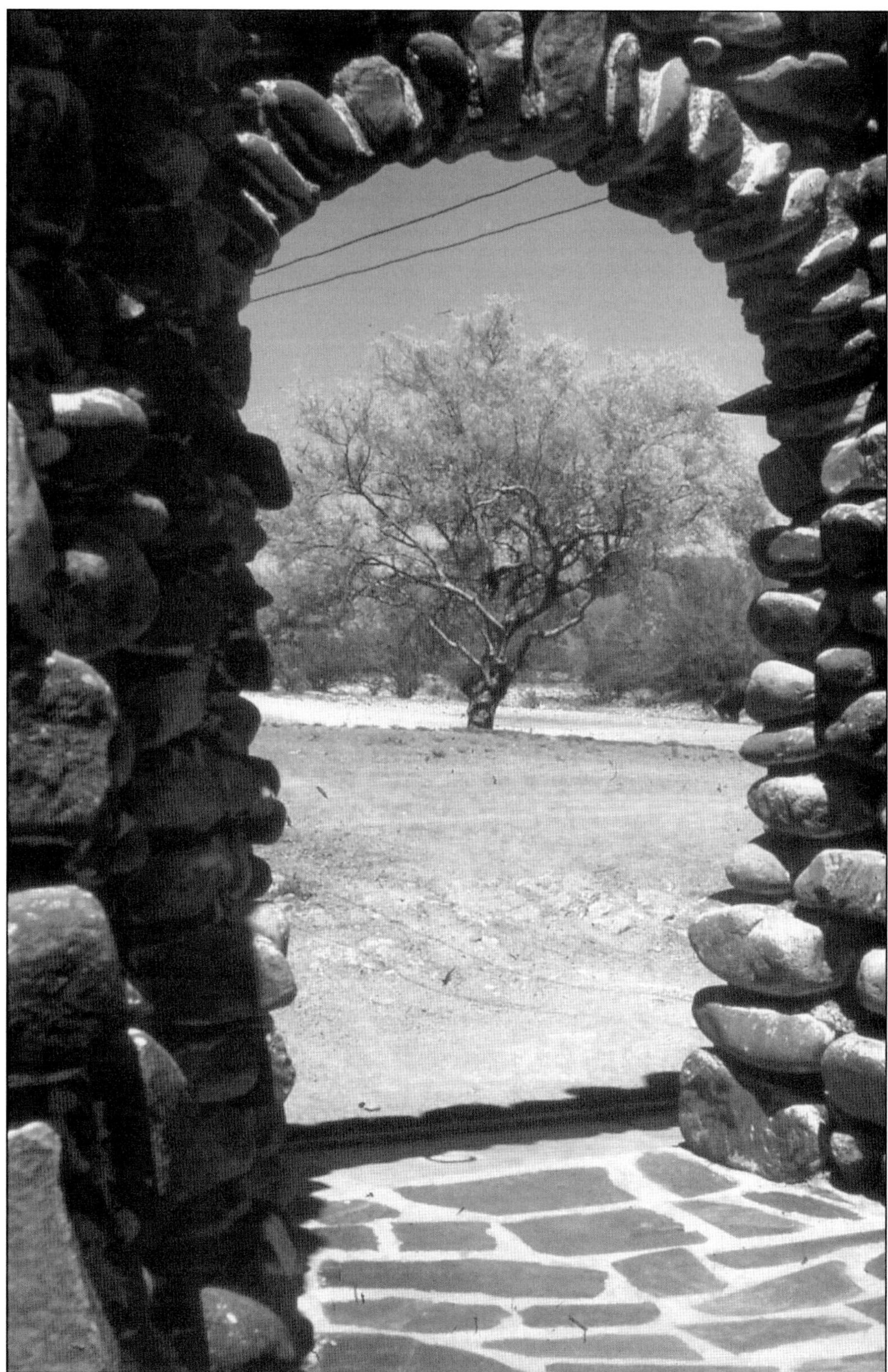

The grounds of Wrangler's Roost were natural and gorgeous rather than posh and artificial. The stone arch and flagstone walkway beautifully frame a view of the native palo verde tree in the background. The thorny palo verde bursts into a profusion of yellow blossoms in the springtime. (Photograph by Port Halle, courtesy of Lance Halle.)

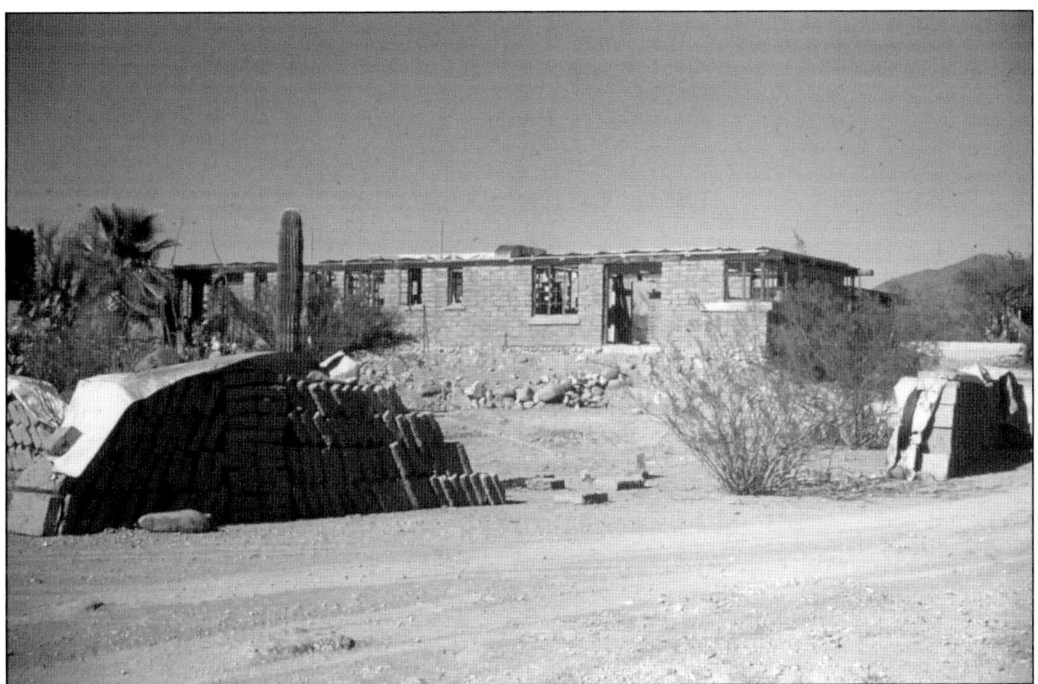

Port Halle began expanding the accommodations at Wrangler's Roost shortly after buying the property. In the foreground of the image above are adobe bricks that were made on-site from native materials. Adobe structures were naturally well insulated against the desert heat and offered quiet, cooler comfort than other materials. Today, although true adobe homes are rare, Arizona architecture still reflects the influence of the once common territorial adobes in the abundance of stucco-finished houses. In the photograph below, note the base of native stone in the lower portions of the walls. (Both, photograph by Port Halle, courtesy of Lance Halle.)

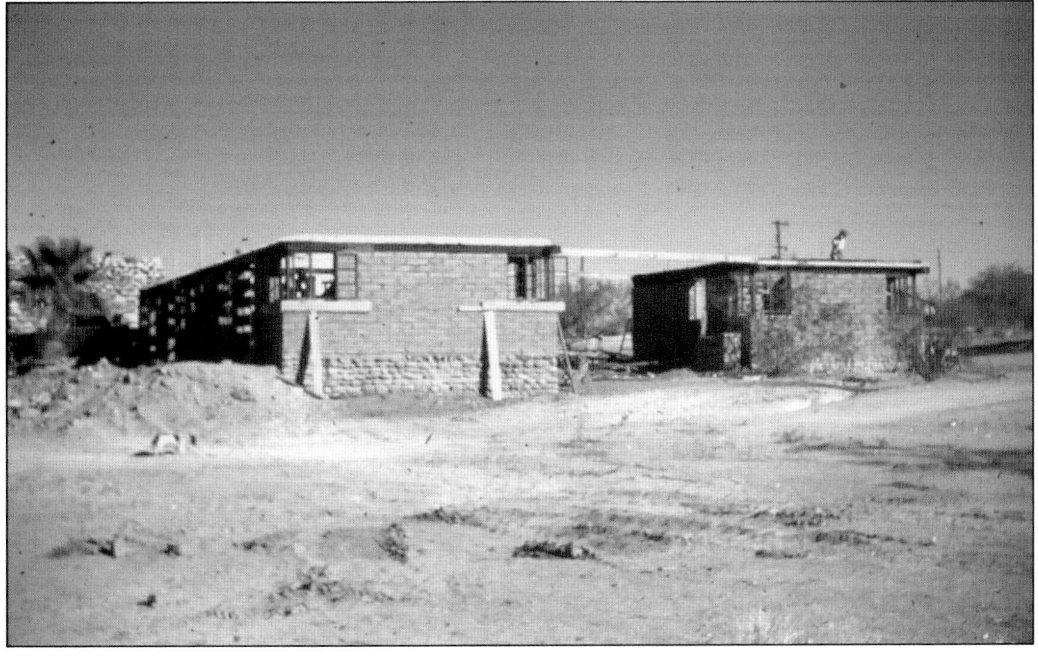

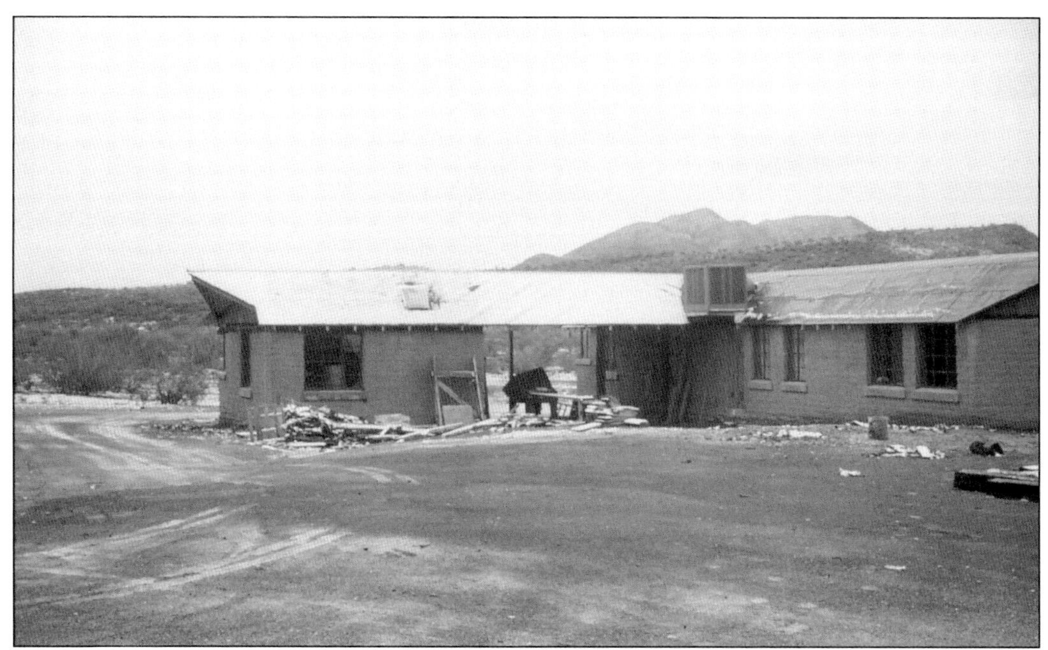

The advent of air-conditioning contributed to Arizona's mid-1900s population boom. Although the early homesteaders toughed out the weather with the help of wet burlap and sleeping porches, guests at Wrangler's Roost had the comfort of controlled climate. Below, the Wrangler's Roost construction crew poses in front of its work truck for this 1940 photograph. The brush in front of the men is the locally abundant native creosote bush, so called for the creosote-like aroma it emits when wet. It is also called greasewood, chaparral, or by its botanical name, *Larrea tridentata*. (Both, photograph by Port Halle, courtesy of Lance Halle.)

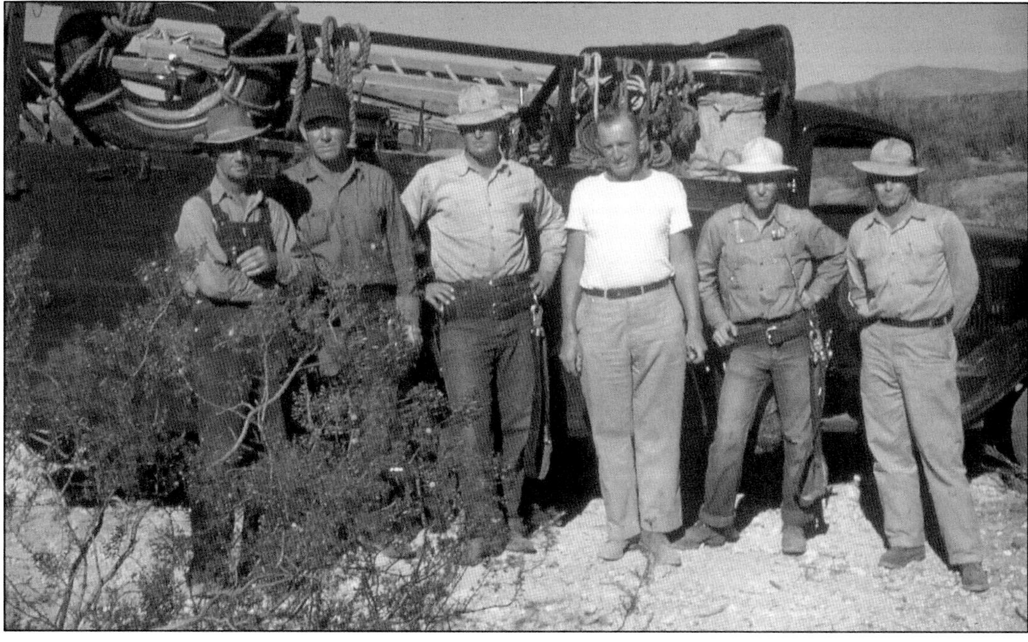

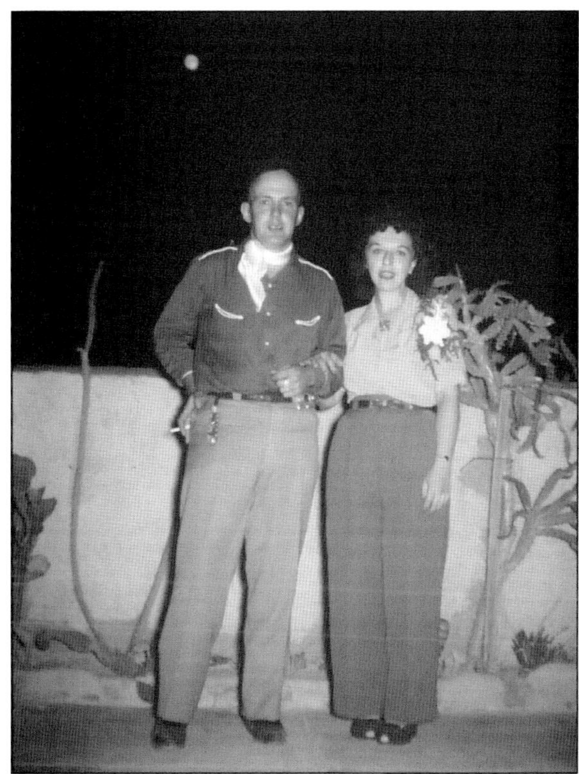

Wrangler's Roost has hosted many weddings throughout its years as a guest ranch, but none as relevant to its own history as that of Port and Lois Halle. In the image at right, Port is dressed appropriately in his boots and slash-pocket western dress shirt with a traditional silk "glad rag" in lieu of a tie. New River native June Evans Bond remembers Port as every bit the westerner. Below, Port's son Pete joins the newly married couple as they cut their wedding cake inside Wrangler's Roost. Soon, Pete's younger brother Lance would be on his way to join the family. (Both, courtesy of Lance Halle.)

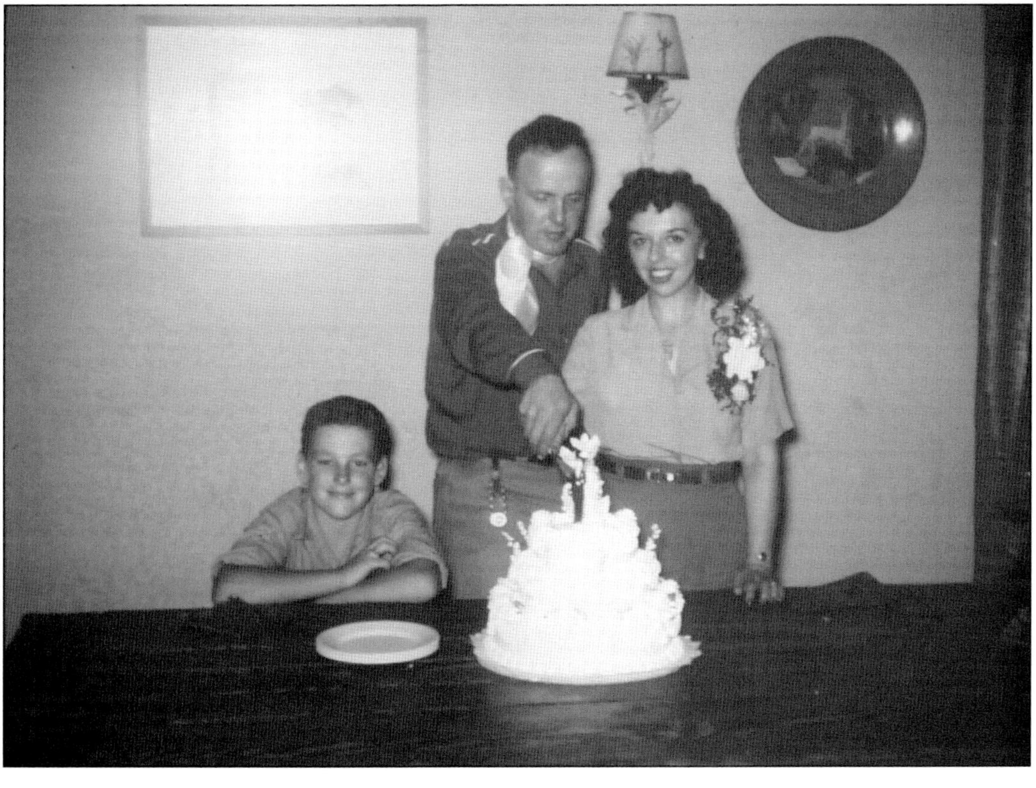

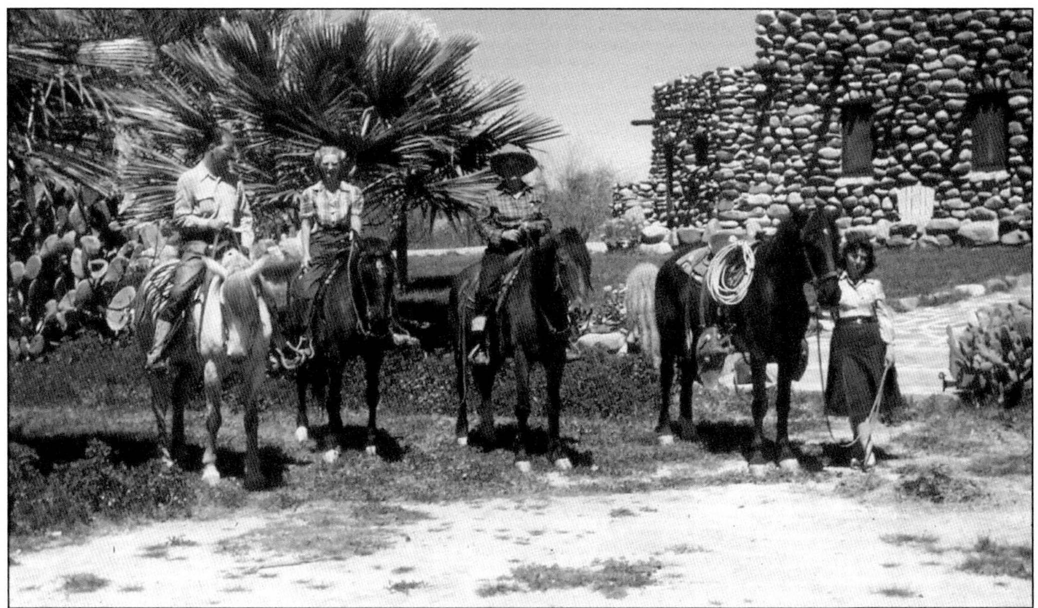

Several years (and owners) after this photograph of Lois Halle (far right) and guests was taken, an interesting character named Richard Ireland owned the Roost. Described by some as a preacher man with a degree in theology, by others as a diviner, Ireland gave psychic performances as he traveled. June Evans Bond recalls instances of Ireland correctly describing to locals things they had done not in his presence. (Courtesy of Lance Halle.)

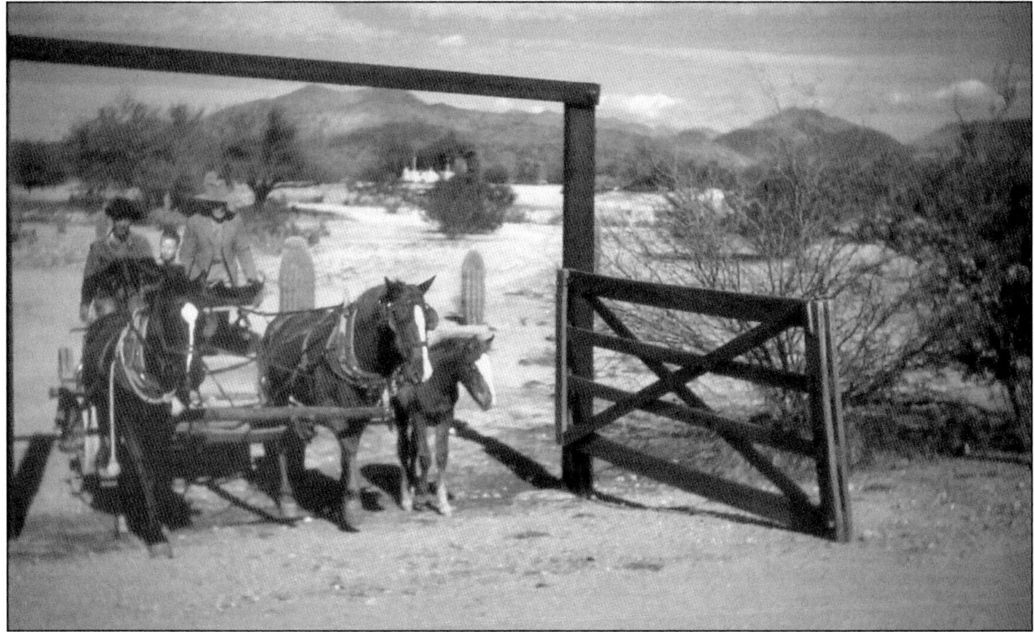

In this 1945 photograph, a sorrel mare with her foal still at side helps draw a wagon on the Wrangler's Roost homestead. Originally, the T-Ranch owned the water rights on the property. Earl Evans, one of the owners of the T-Ranch, allowed Chief J. Myers to homestead on the property if Chief maintained a water trough for the T-Ranch cattle on the north end. (Photograph by Port Halle, courtesy of Lance Halle.)

During the 1940s and 1950s, westerns dominated television and film. Children across America dreamed of living on a ranch, surrounded by cowboys and horses. Lance Halle and his brothers were fortunate to be able to do so. Lance happily recalls his time at Wrangler's Roost. Although the Halle family moved into Phoenix in 1952 so the boys could attend larger schools, they remained in love with the area and returned to New River a few years later. At right, Lance perches on the Roost's corral fence. Below, he smiles in front of the bunkhouse. (Both, photograph by Port Halle, courtesy of Lance Halle.)

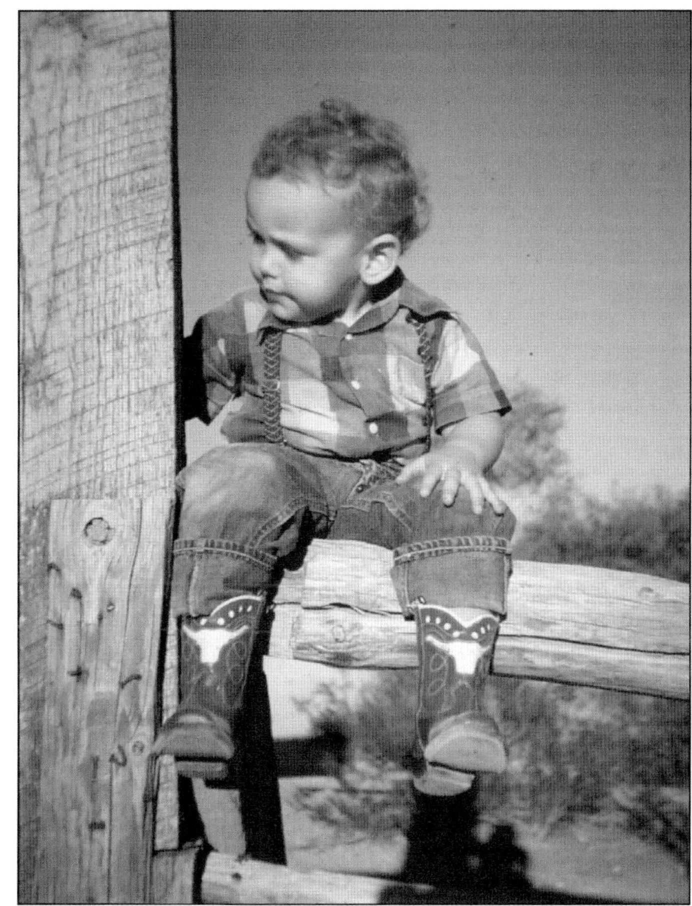

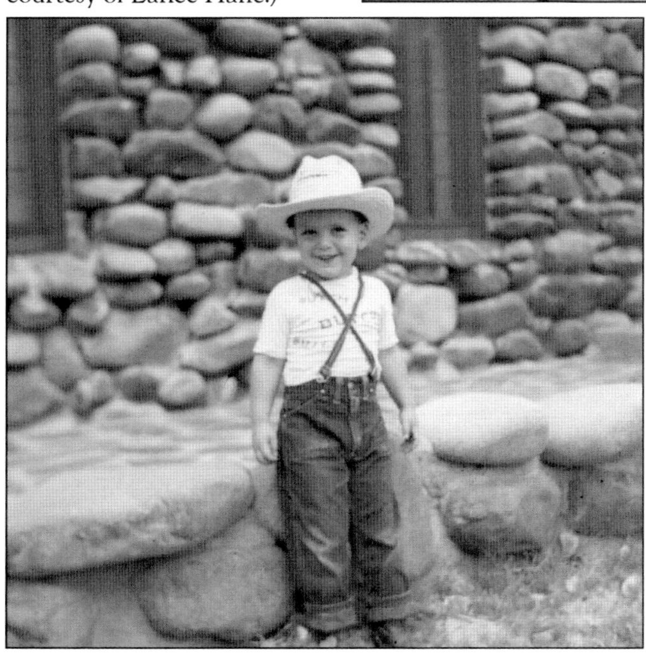

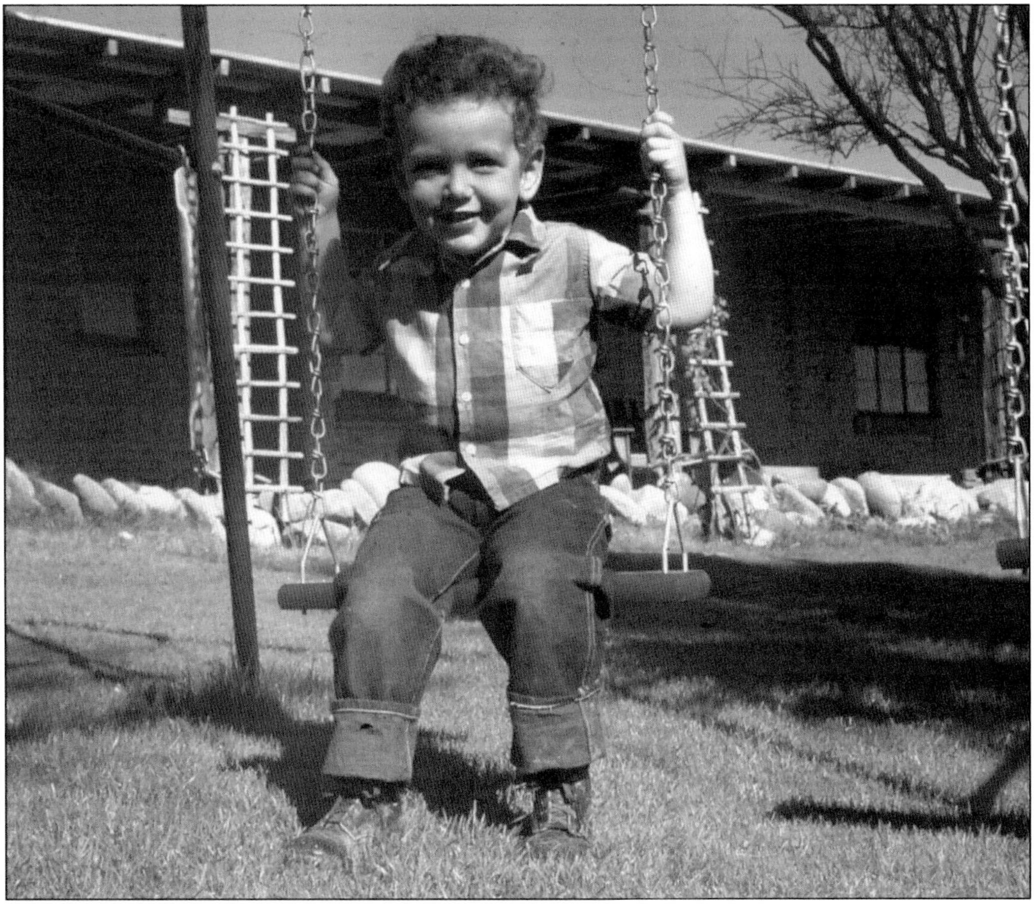

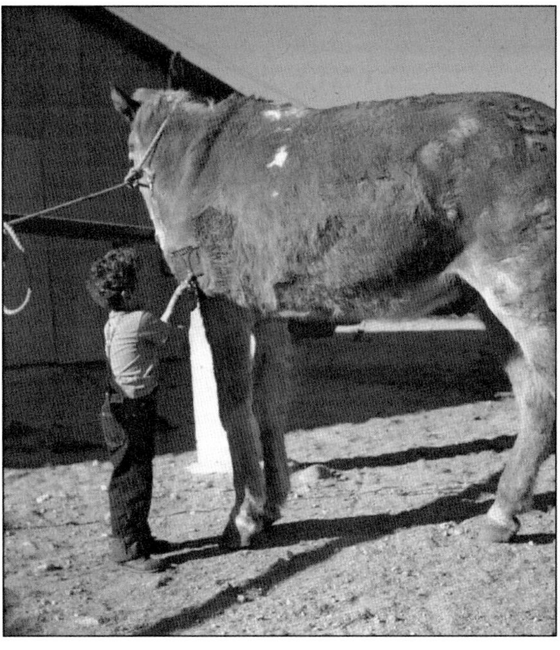

Lance Halle enjoys playing on his swing in front of the adobe lodge of Wrangler's Roost in the 1951 image above. At left, he curries Micho, one of the Roost's burros. Lance's father, Port Halle, was a semiprofessional photographer who worked for some time at a Phoenix camera shop. Port captured everyday life at the Roost on film while Lance's mother, Lois, captured it on canvas with her paintbrushes. Fledgling New River was shaped by the creative hands of its early residents, from the homesteaders who hand built their homes to the artists who chronicled its development. (Both, photograph by Port Halle, courtesy of Lance Halle.)

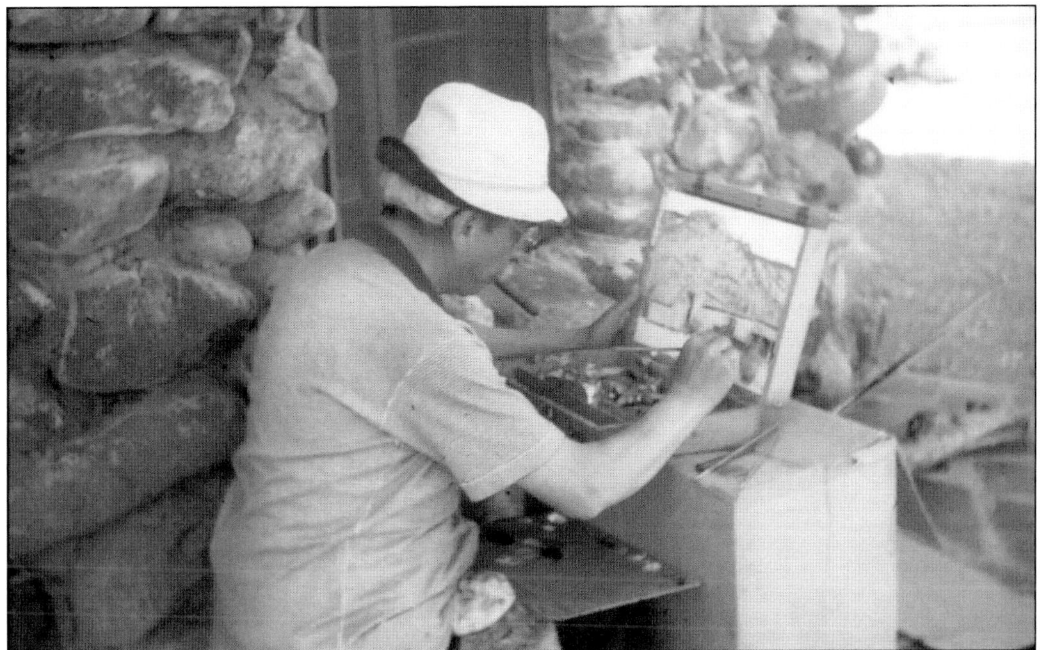

One of several repeat visitors to the Roost was well-known artist Max Meyer. Meyer enjoyed plein air painting in the surrounding desert while visiting. Here, Max paints a view of Indian Mountain, the ruin-topped mesa just east of Wrangler's Roost. (Photograph by Port Halle, courtesy of Lance Halle.)

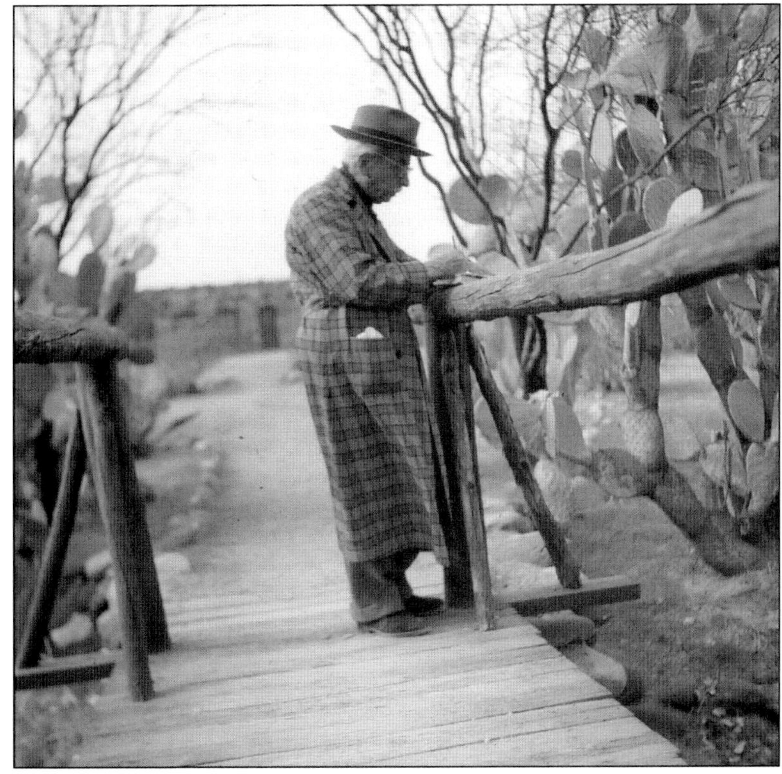

Max Meyer became close to the Halle family and gave Lois Halle art lessons when visiting. A naturally gifted artist, Halle successfully sold many of her original paintings. Here, Max sketches a desert scene from the footbridge in front of the bunkhouse. (Photograph by Port Halle, courtesy of Lance Halle.)

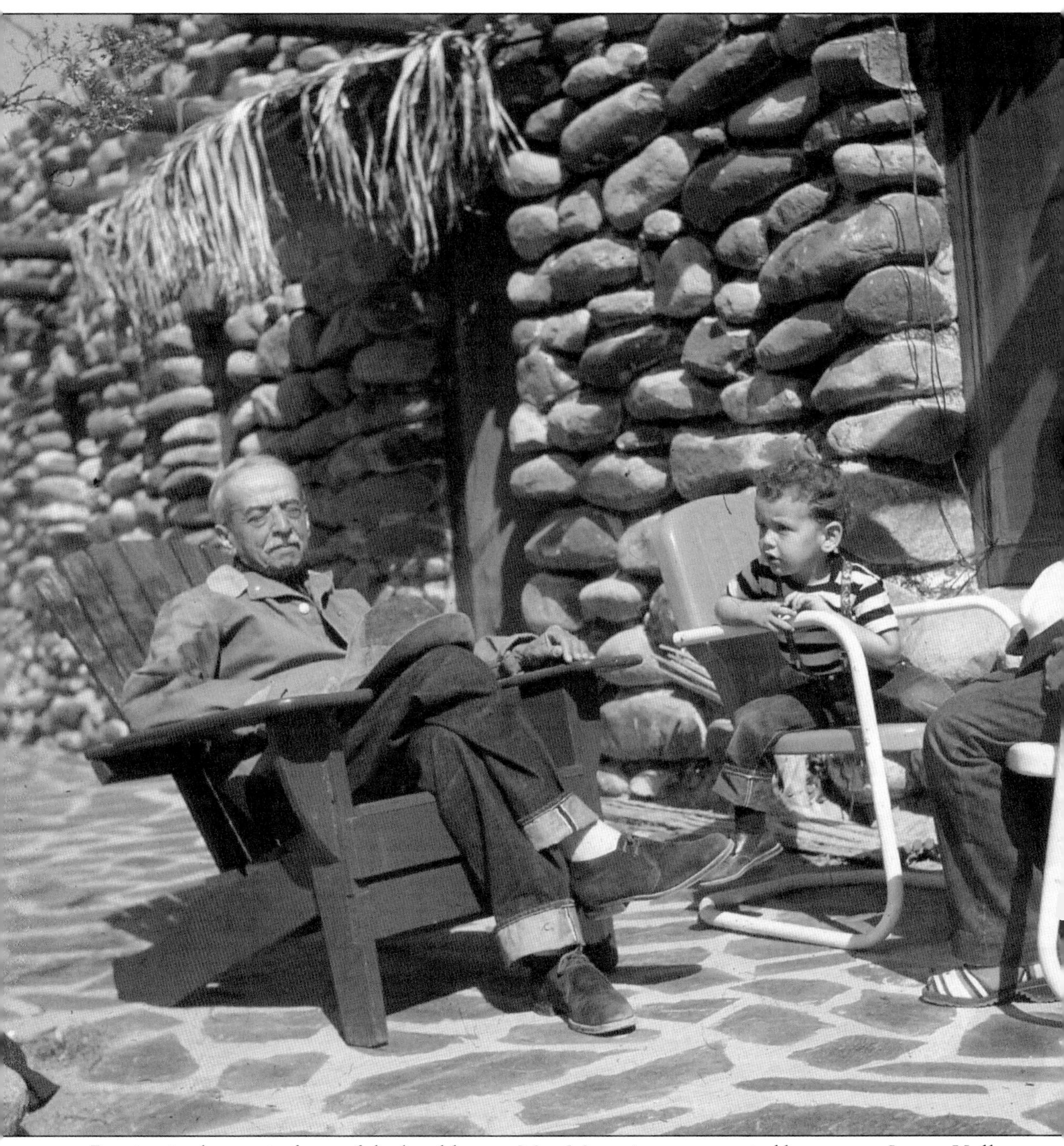

Resting in the sun in front of the bunkhouse, Max Meyer is accompanied by a young Lance Halle in this 1951 photograph. The hospitality industry has long been a key component of Arizona's economy. Wrangler's Roost was one of the few guest ranches in New River. (Photograph by Port Halle, courtesy of Lance Halle.)

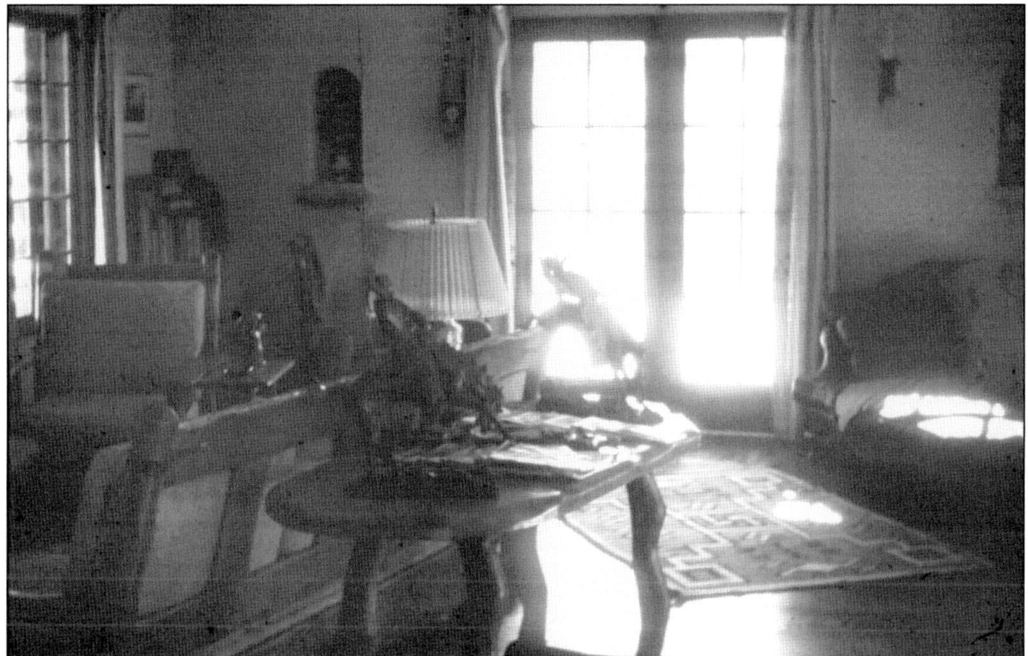

At the height of its popularity as a guest ranch, the lodge was elegantly furnished in an appropriately western motif including an enviable collection of bronze cowboy sculptures. Note the rug in front of the window. Hand-loomed of wool on the reservation by native artisans, authentic Navajo rugs such as this one are valuable collector's items today. (Photograph by Port Halle, courtesy of Lance Halle.)

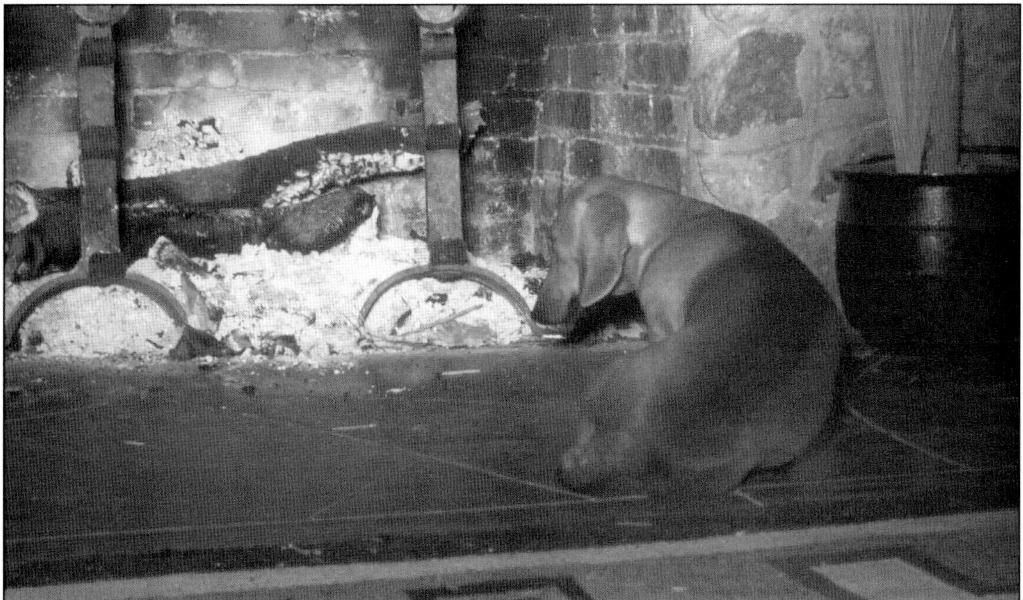

The Halle family's dachshund, Fritzi, curls up in front of the Wrangler's Roost fireplace in this photograph from the 1940s. The cozy lodge was not destined to always be a guest ranch. June Evans Bond remembers a few years after the Halles sold the ranch that it served as lodging for mentally ill patients. (Courtesy of Lance Halle.)

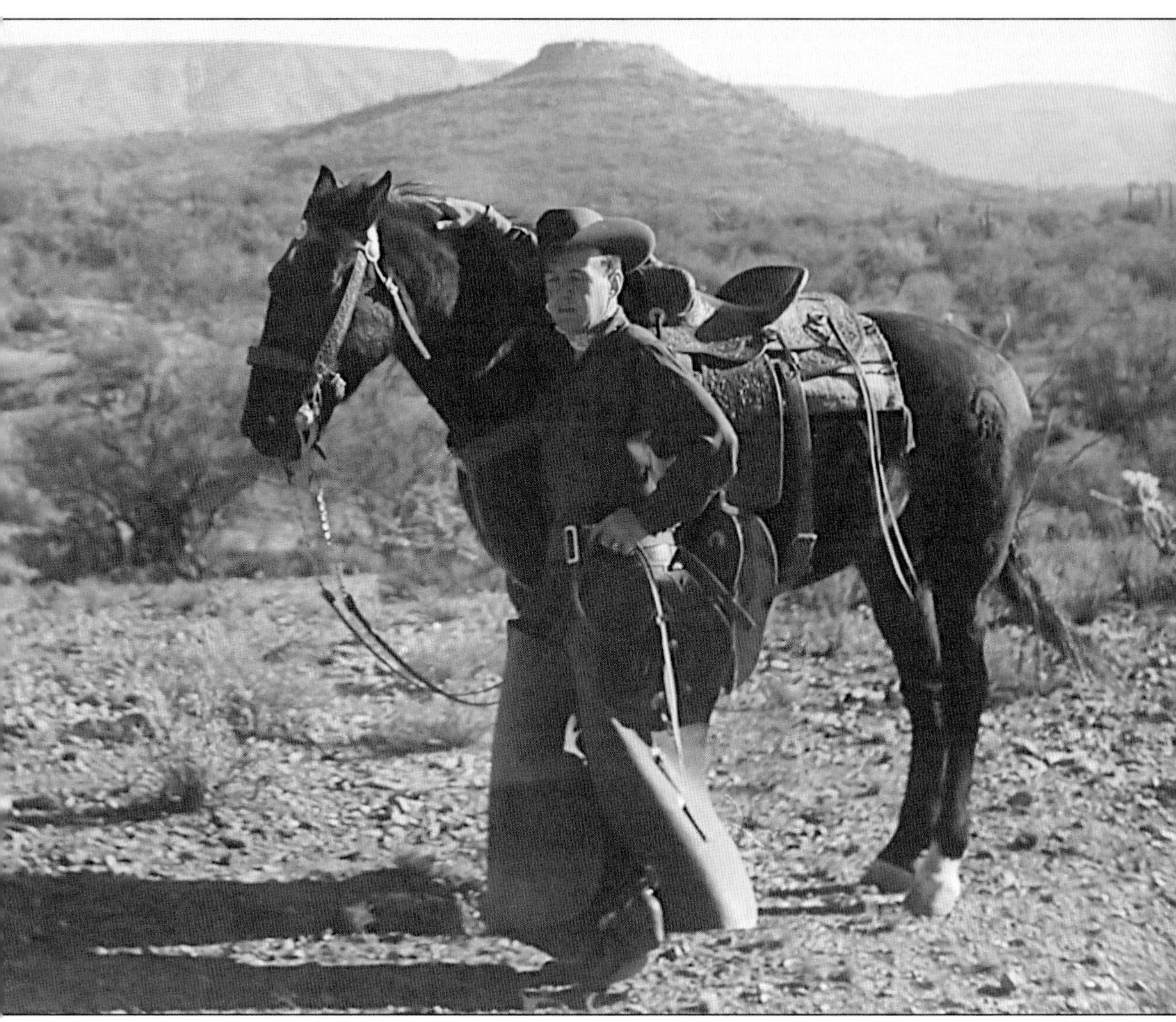

Port Halle, here with his horse Star, could have been mistaken for a movie cowboy. In 1952, Port sold Wrangler's Roost to well-known TV cowboy Lew King. King hosted the popular *Lew King's Rangers Show* on local channel KPHO in the 1940s. It is unlikely King ever lived at the ranch. The small mesa in the background was called Indian Mountain by locals. (Courtesy of Lance Halle.)

Six

A Changing Landscape
New Generations and Newcomers

After the homesteaders established homes, ranches, and families in New River, a limited infrastructure followed. The old Black Canyon stagecoach road not only became fully paved all the way to northern Arizona, but local streets were soon paved as well. The area has quelled incorporation and annexation attempts so far; New River still remains largely a bedroom community, peacefully free of sidewalks and streetlights. For the most part, a person can see the stars at night and hear the ground move beneath his or her feet.

The little one-room school outgrew its original building and location, moving to a new campus on the old Black Canyon stage road north of the old Farrar homestead. Bridges made the river crossings safe, while Daisy Mountain Fire Department now responds to fires and medical emergencies in the area. Of course, the progress accompanied (or, to some extent, made possible) an increasing population and development of the homestead properties and much open land. The old homesteads have been divided and subdivided over again.

By 1975, the general store and Jay Robertson's land office at New River Road and Old Black Canyon Stagecoach Road evolved into the Roadrunner Saloon. New River Station awaits its next incarnation, and although transportation officials have attempted to arrange the straightening of New River Road, residents resisted, and it still snakes its way through the area. Jackass Acres, once a tourist stop, lies vacant near the busy freeway that ran over many of the old haunts. Shangri-La, a nudist ranch, still caters to the clothing-optional residents and travelers, but the livestock ranches have decreased dramatically in number, size and range.

Although of the old homesteads only Sun-Up Ranch is still owned by the original family, many old-timers—some the sons, daughters, or grandchildren of cowboys and ranchers, others from later waves of newcomers—have lived in New River for decades. The area's oldest native, June Evans Bond, has seen 90 years of change in New River. It may have grown up and the lights are on—but it is still home.

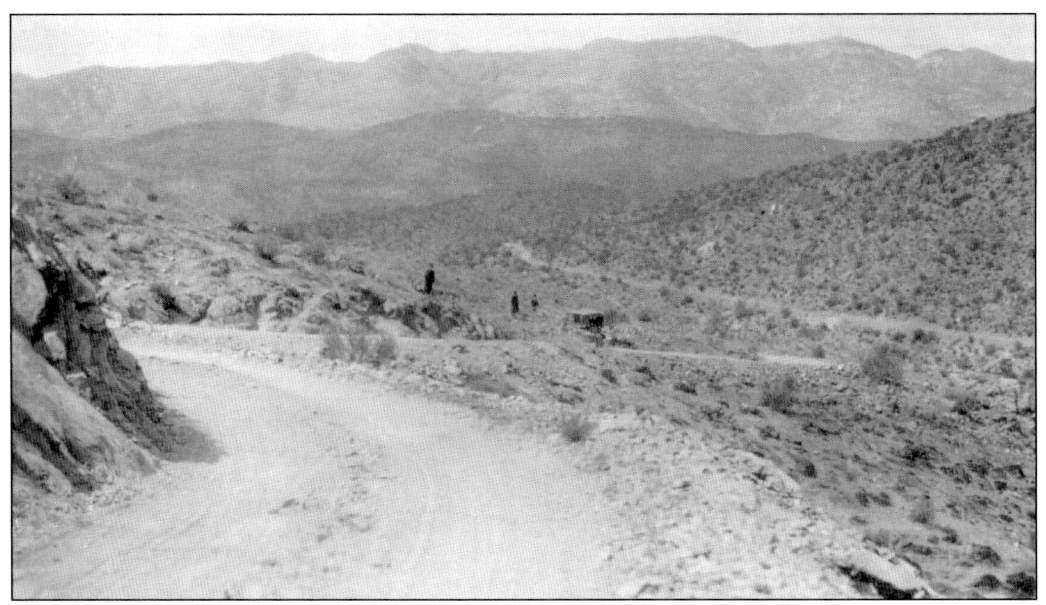

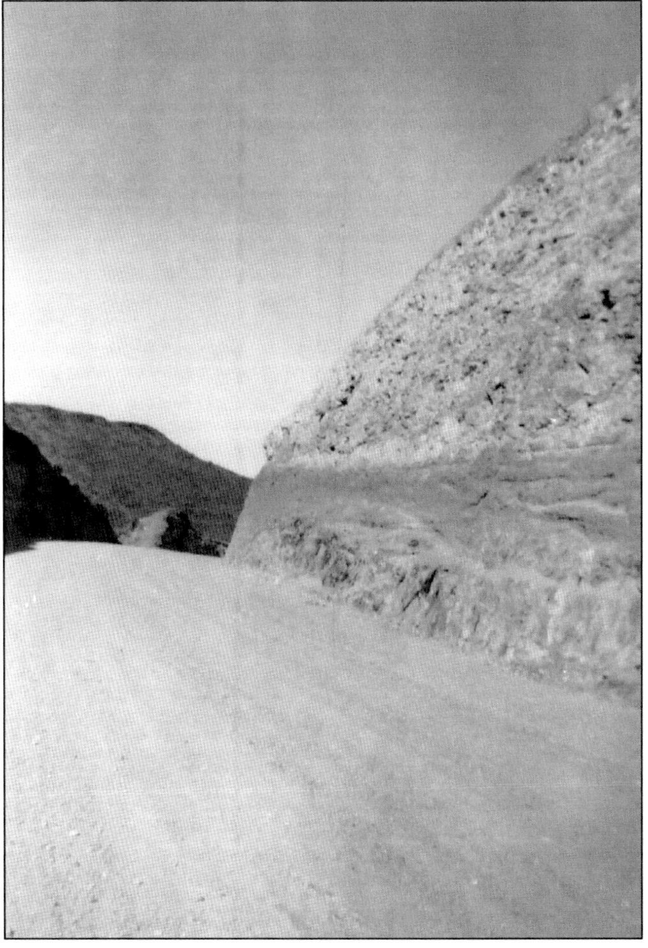

In 1923, the Black Canyon road snaked treacherously through canyons and mountains. The image above shows a family making the slow journey through the Bradshaws on the old road. Originally the "Woolsey Trail" used by pioneer rancher and Indian fighter King Woolsey, and later a stagecoach road, it was described by Frank Alkire as "the toughest freight road in all of central Arizona." As late as 1947, the pavement ended in New River. The 1948 photograph at left shows the cuts made into the mountain to clear the way for paving. (Above, from the book *Sun-Up Ranch: An Arizona Desert Homestead* by Jerry D. Jacka; left, courtesy of June Evans Bond.)

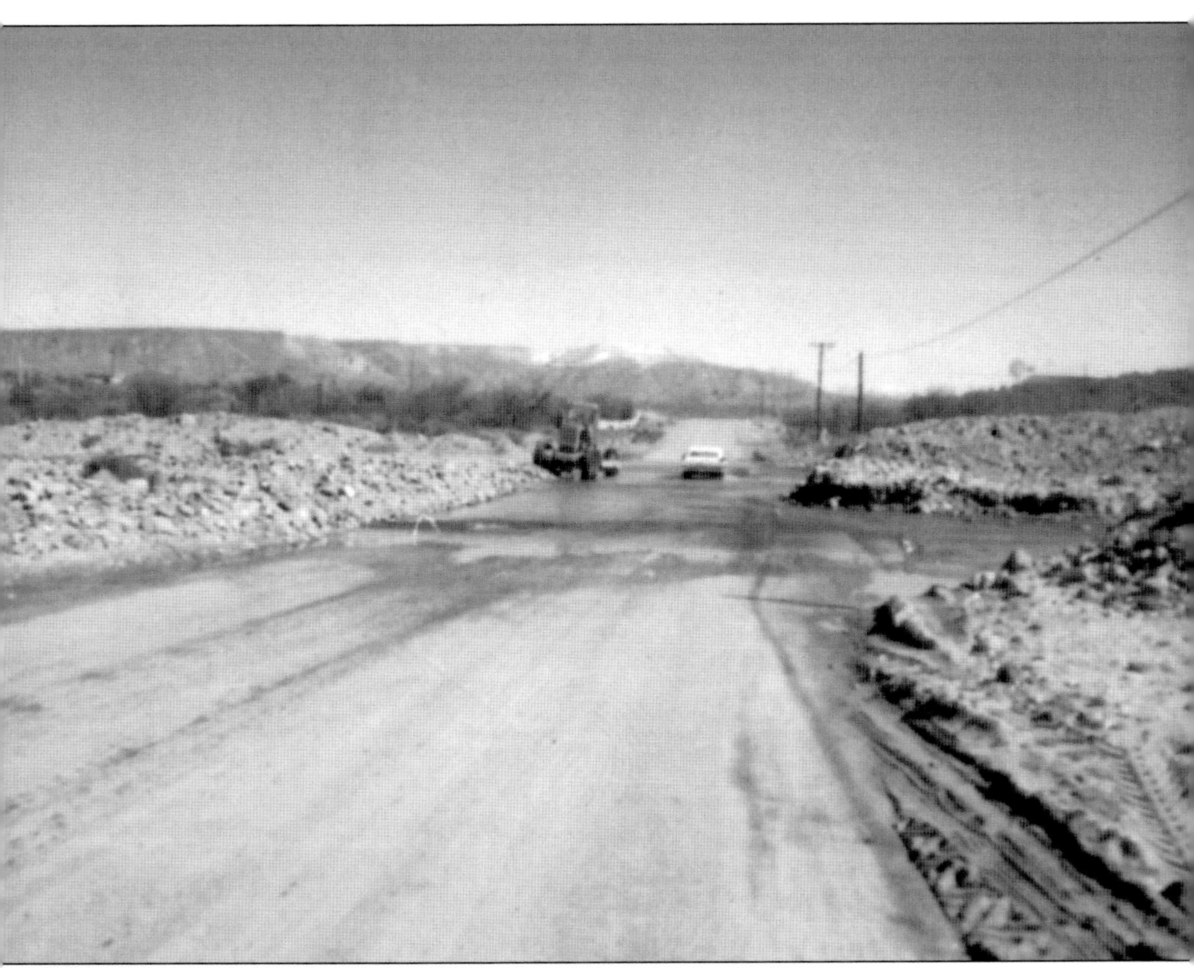

Perhaps even more important than paved roads for those living in New River was the construction of bridges. Old-timers remember the pre-bridge days when a heavy rainfall meant sitting at New River Station with a cup of coffee or taking shelter at a neighbor's house across the river for a night until the flooding subsided. This 1966 photograph shows the water flowing across New River Road. Residents today still grapple with destructive flooding during heavy rainfall. (Courtesy of Leon and Frances Lann Gee.)

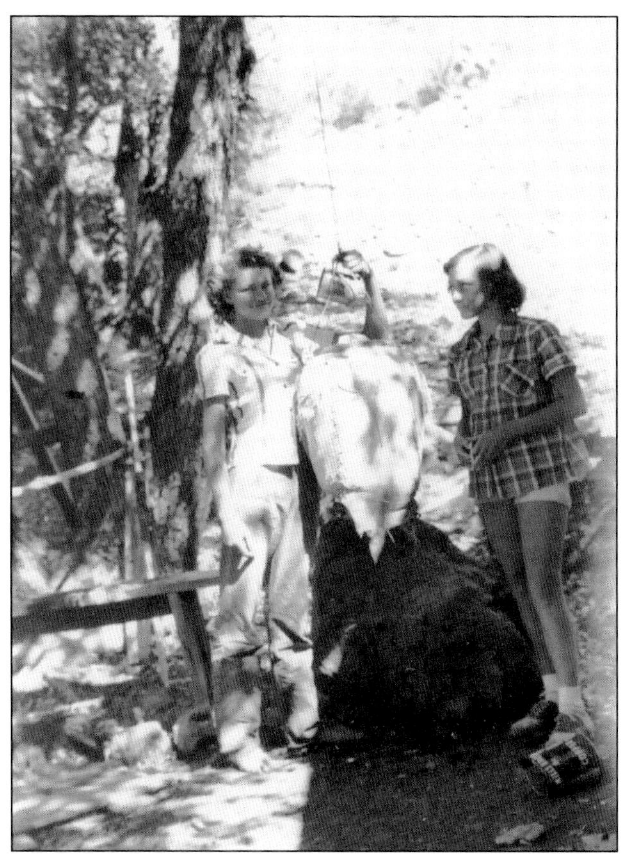

A living bridge to the past, the children and grandchildren of New River's original cowboys, ranchers, and homesteaders grew up with the traditional ways. At left, Frances Lann Gee, daughter of T-Up T-Down cowboy Burrel Lann, is shown on the left in the 1952 photograph with her friend Linda Pigg Neal beside an olla at the head of the river. Ollas are clay water pots often covered with burlap or canvas. Many Southwestern traditions, like the use of the olla, originated with the native peoples. Below, Frances and friends are fishing in upper New River. (Both, courtesy of Leon and Frances Lann Gee.)

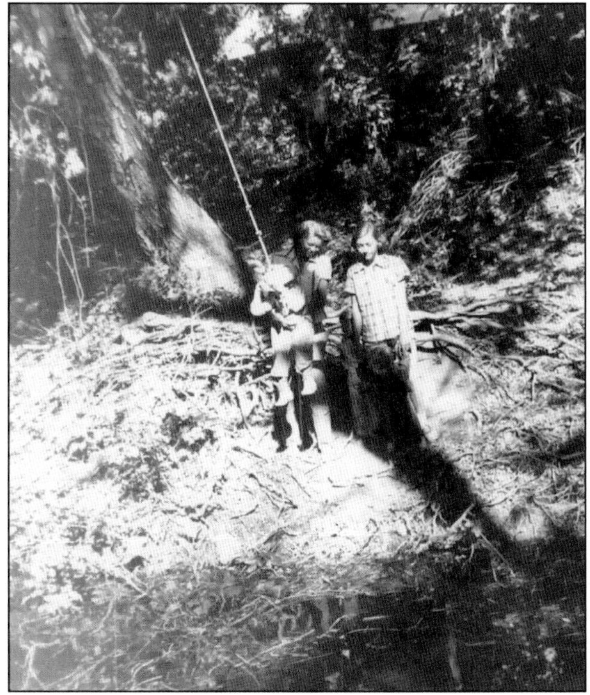

Largely settled by World War I veterans whose own sons were later called to war, New River produced a number of men who served in the military and law enforcement. Natives of area ranches and homesteads, Edward "Woody" Evans (not shown), Frank Bond (left), and Jerry D. Jacka (right) pursued law enforcement careers. In 1957, Bond and Jacka worked as Maricopa County deputies. (Courtesy of Jerry D. Jacka and Lois Essary Jacka.)

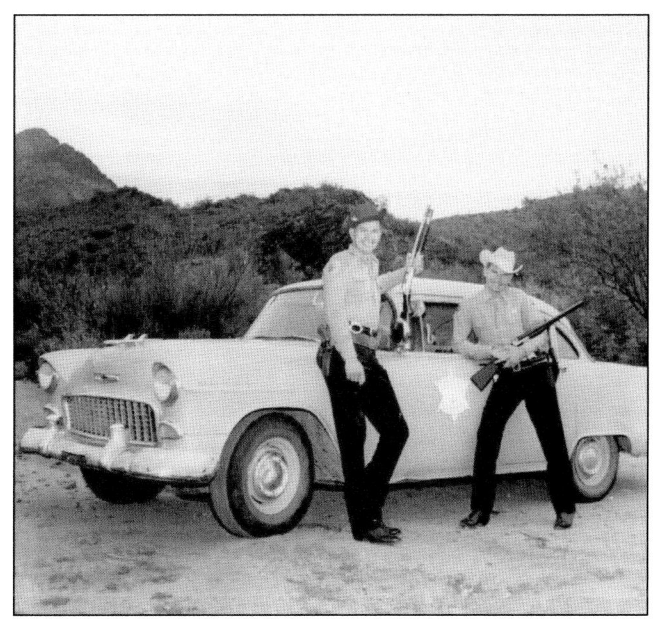

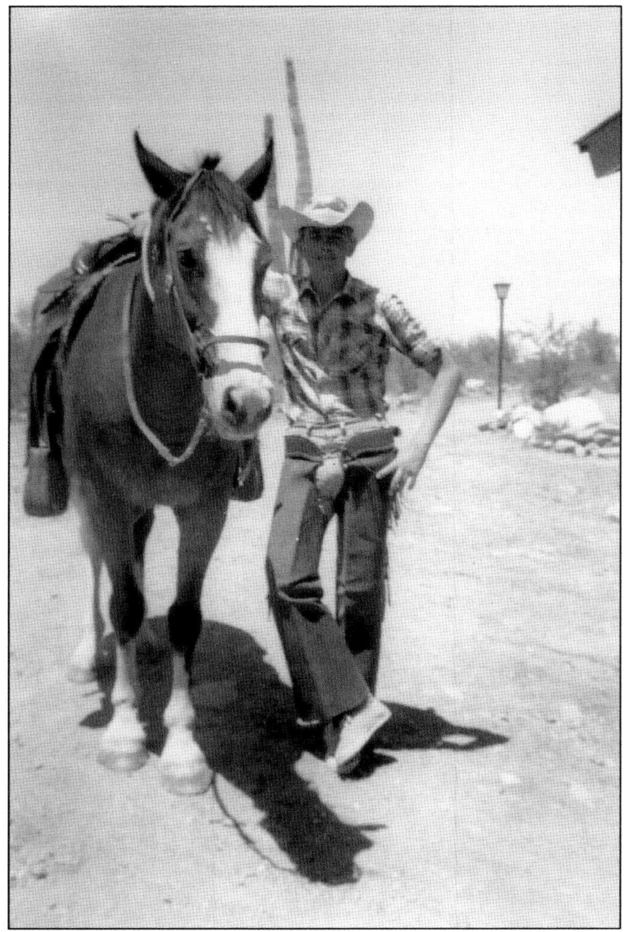

Frank Bond and June Evans Bond, having grown up on New River's ranches, raised their own children with many of the same experiences. Horses, a rural setting, and freedom to roam and explore the desert were some of the benefits of New River childhood. Larry Bond is shown here with Banjo the horse. (Courtesy of June Evans Bond.)

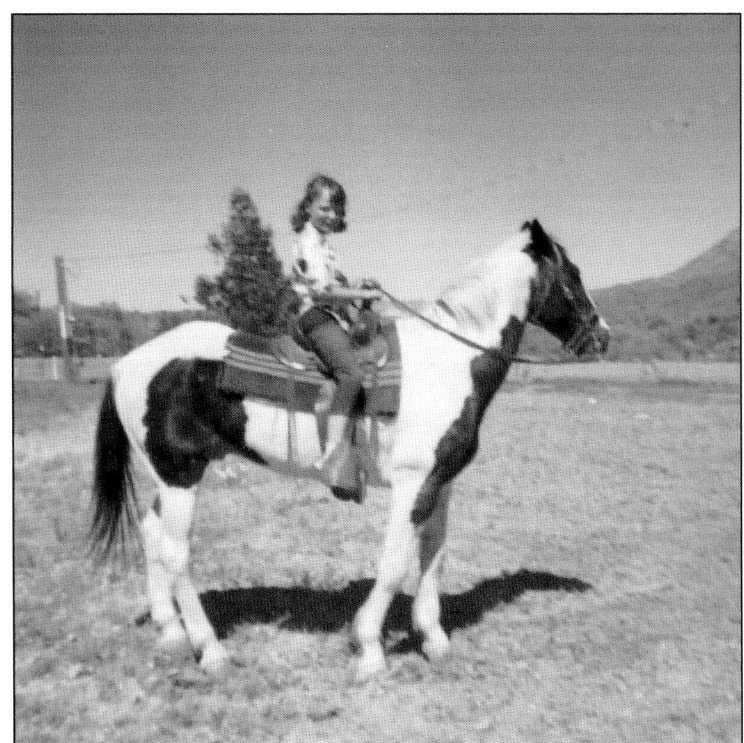

Kristi Bond, the daughter of Frank Bond and June Evans Bond, descended from pioneers. Early members of the Evans family—Kristi's great-great-grandparents—settled in Palo Verde and were the first Anglos interred in the Palo Verde Baptist Church cemetery. The daughter of capable riders, Kristi grew up with horses as well. June Evans Bond recalls one of the mares being bitten by a rattlesnake while pregnant. The foal was born hairless. At left, a teenaged Kristi rides her flashy paint horse. (Courtesy of June Evans Bond.)

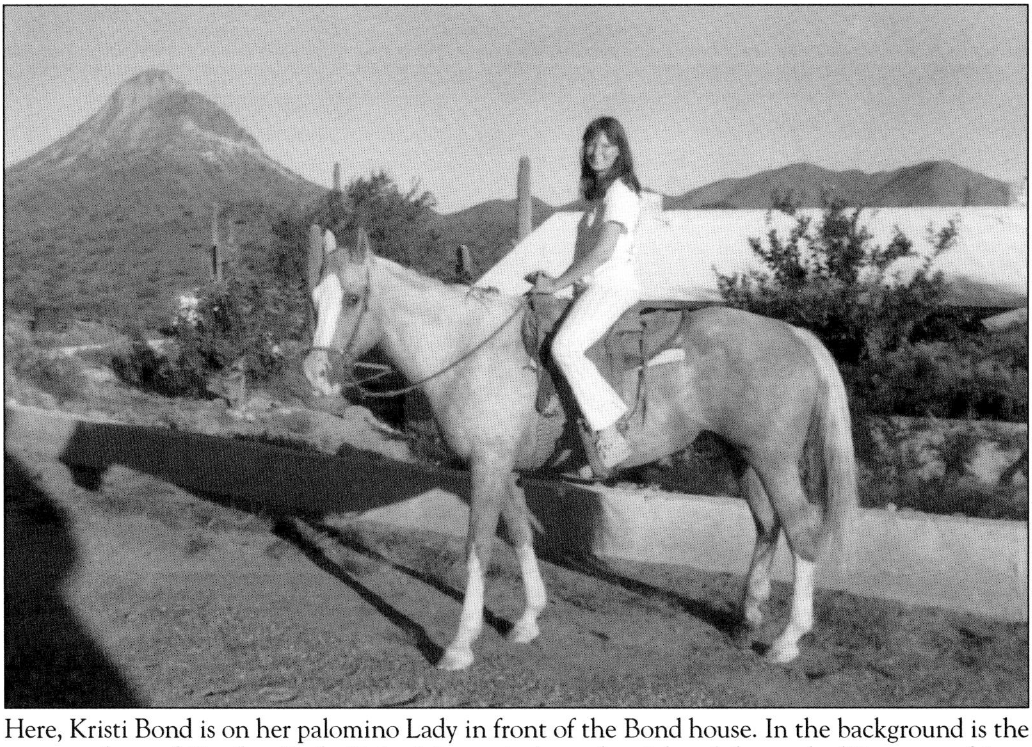

Here, Kristi Bond is on her palomino Lady in front of the Bond house. In the background is the western slope of Gavilan Peak. Daisy Mountain is to the right of the peak. (Courtesy of June Evans Bond.)

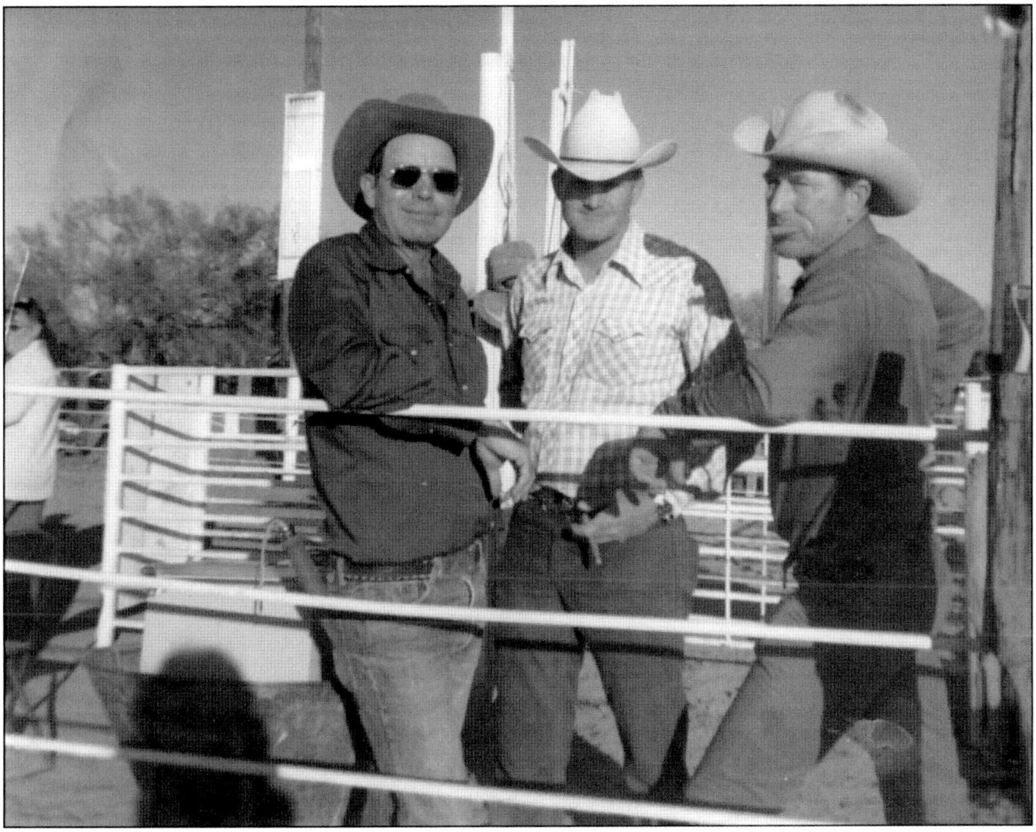

Leon Gee learned to cowboy from Burrel Lann on the T-Ranch and married Burrel's daughter, Frances. Settling at the base of Gavilan Peak in the early 1960s, the Gees built their GK Ranch, raising their own children in the New River ranch tradition. Leon soon learned that a cowboy's salary would not support four kids and turned to other work, but he continued to ride, rope, raise a few cattle, and perform cowboy poetry. Above, from left to right, are Rex Perry, Leon Gee, and Roscoe Franks at GK arena in 1975. At right, Leon and Frances Lann Gee are dressed for winter weather in 1994. (Both, courtesy of Leon Gee and Frances Lann Gee.)

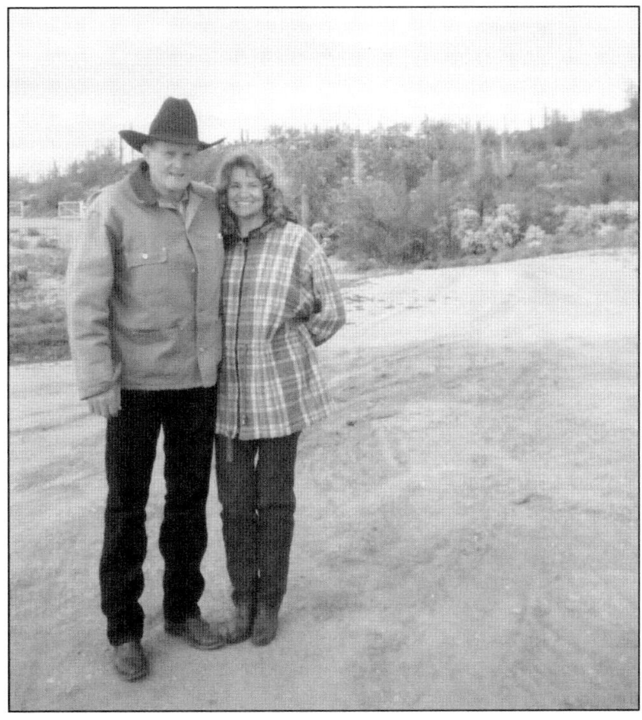

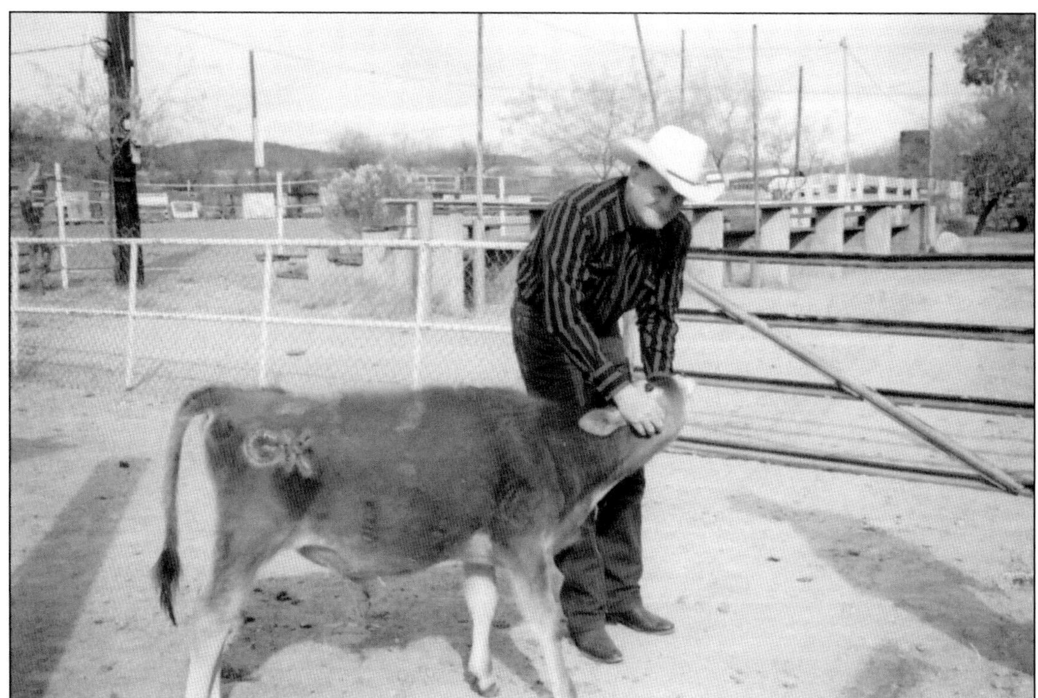

Above, Leon Gee pets a newly branded calf in front of the GK arena. In keeping with the New River tradition, the Gees have been active contributors to the community. For many years, the Gees made their roping arena available to local youth for gymkhanas. Later, the Larkyn Memorial Arena was built at New River's Kiwanis Park to provide a place for equine events. Below, Leon brands one of the Gee calves in the arena with the north face of Gavilan Peak in the background. The GK brand is a registered brand with the state livestock board. (Both, courtesy of Leon and Frances Lann Gee.)

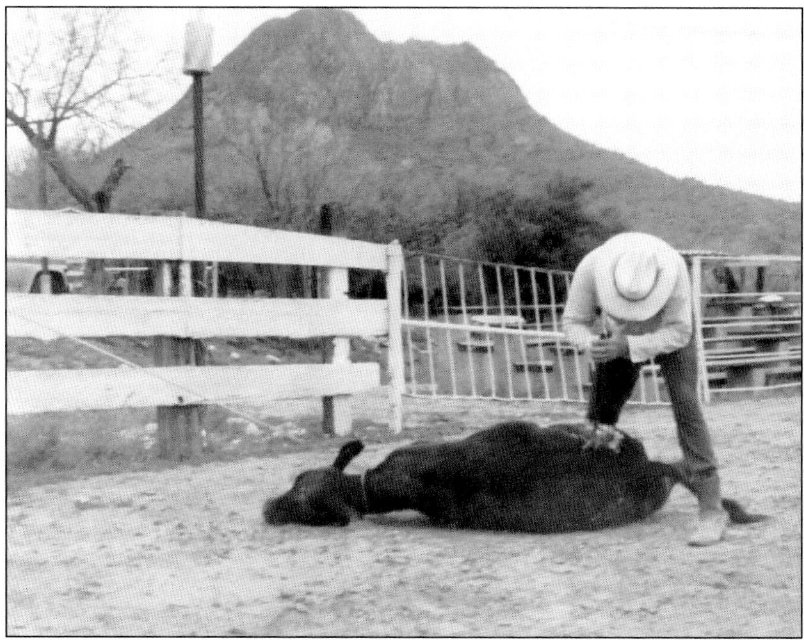

The grandson of a cowboy and ever a cowboy at heart, Leon Gee now performs original cowboy poetry. In these photographs, he is entertaining his audience around a New River bonfire. Bonfires as social settings have long been a part of New River's lifestyle and offer the perfect backdrop for western songs and storytelling. One of Gee's pieces is a tribute to the cowboy skills of his father-in-law, Burrel Lann; others recall Gee's years of working wild cattle on the Bradshaw Strip. A Navy veteran of the Korean War, Gee was later a truck driver and has traveled the old western highways extensively. (Both, courtesy of Leon and Frances Lann Gee.)

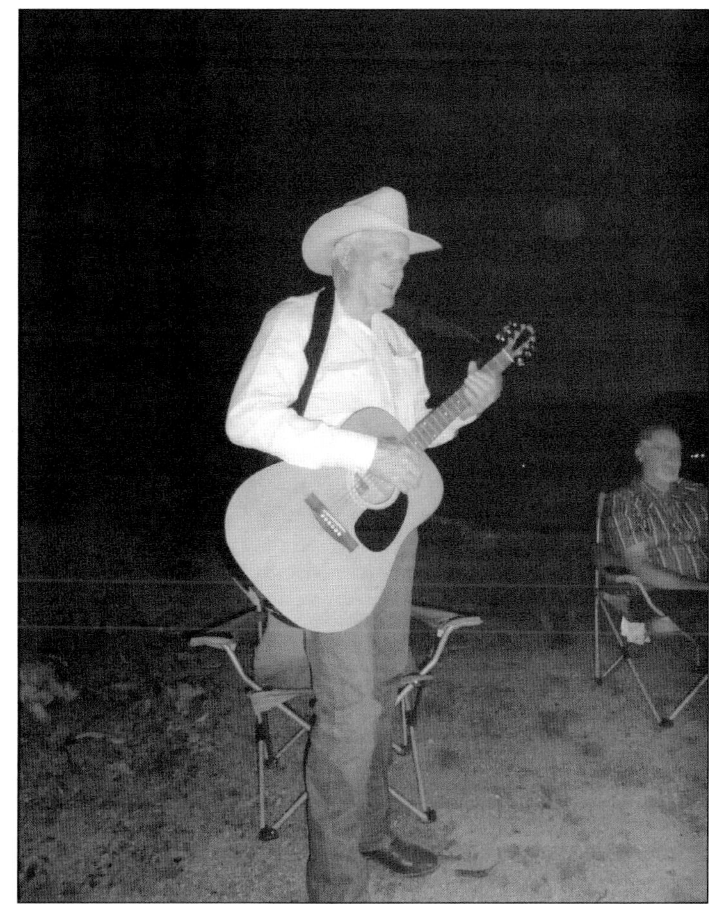

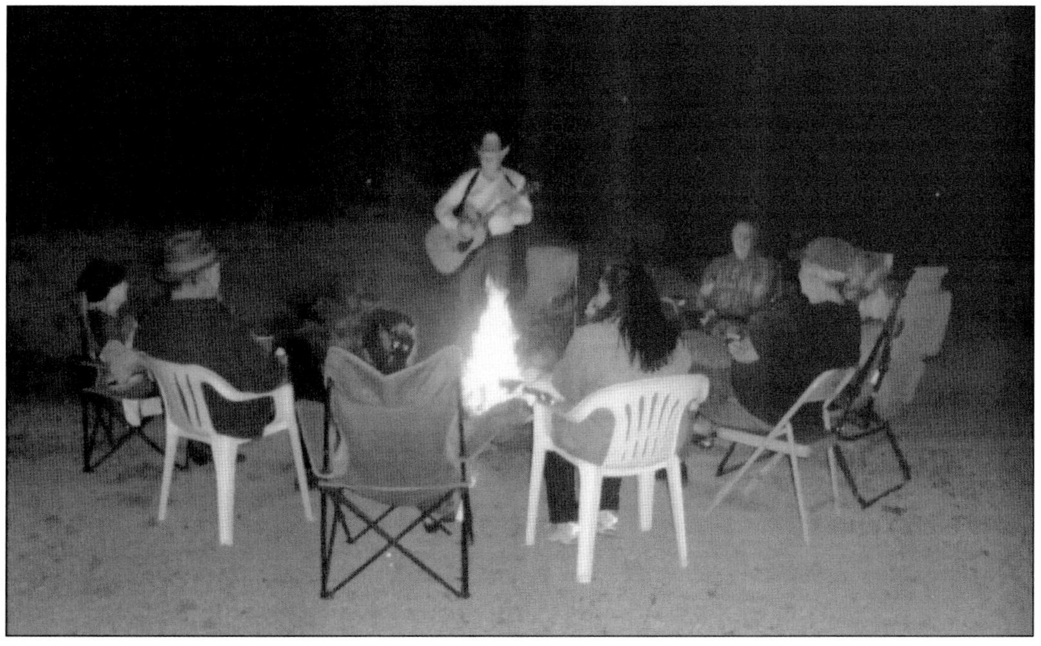

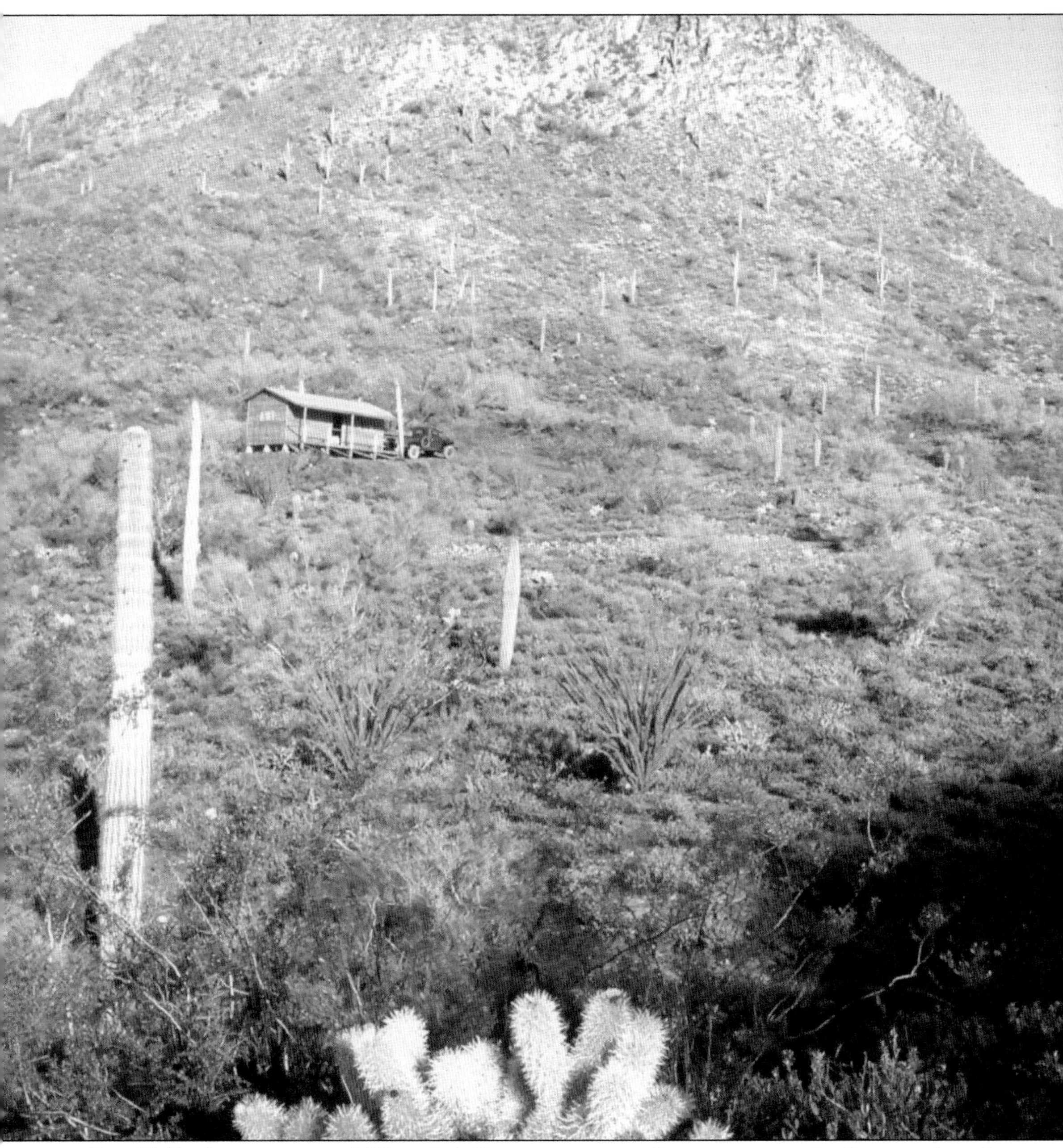

Port Halle, former owner of Wrangler's Roost, once owned some property in Prescott that the government wanted. In exchange, it traded him property on and surrounding Gavilan Peak. The Halle cabin, shown here, was alone on the north slopes of the peak at the time. (Photograph by Port Halle, courtesy of Lance Halle.)

Port and Lois Halle and their family later returned to New River to build their dream home on the side of Gavilan Peak near where the family cabin stood. Halle, an artist, designed the house and incorporated an art studio into the plans. The 1960 photographs on this page show the home while under construction. (Courtesy of Lance Halle.)

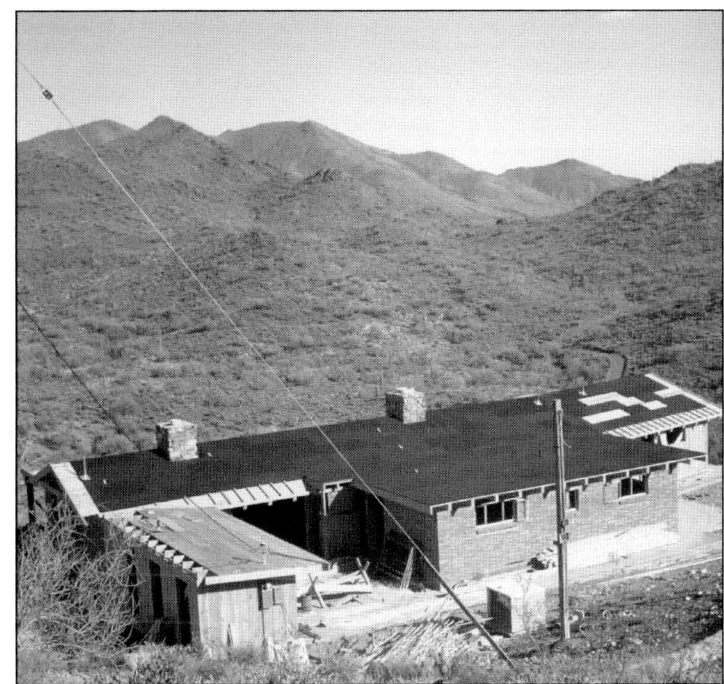

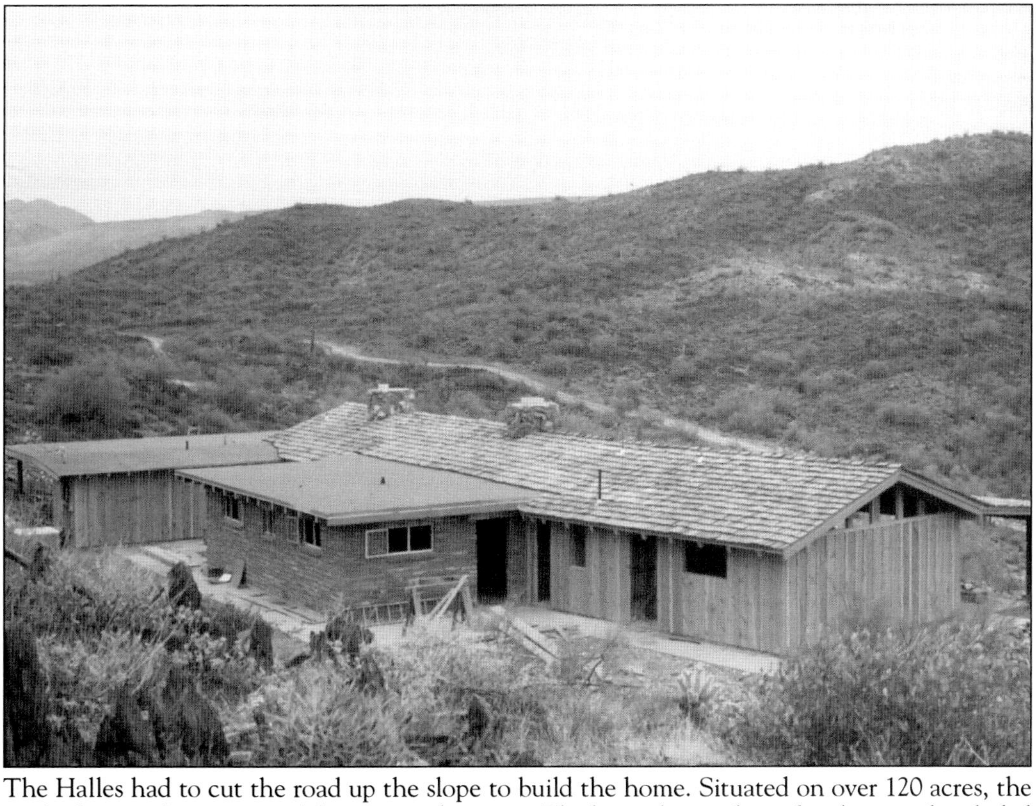

The Halles had to cut the road up the slope to build the home. Situated on over 120 acres, the site had astonishing views of the surrounding area. The house boasted two fireplaces and included specially designed storage for rifles, fishing rods, and tackle. (Courtesy of Lance Halle.)

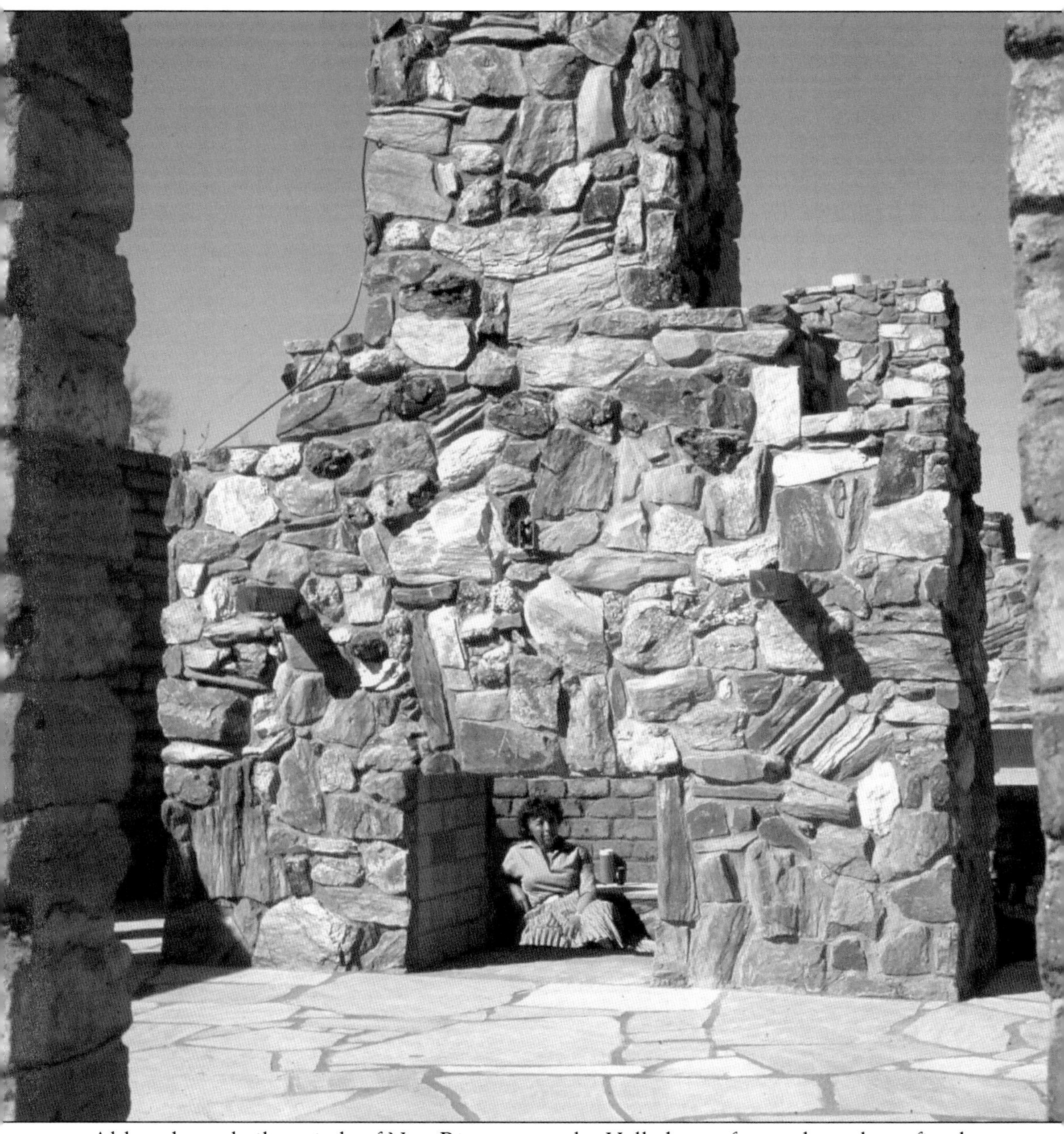

Although not built entirely of New River stone, the Halle house featured two large fireplaces constructed of the abundant local stone. The scale of the fireplaces is dramatically emphasized in this 1960 photograph. Lois Halle sits inside one fireplace of the house she designed. (Photograph by Port Halle, courtesy of Lance Halle.)

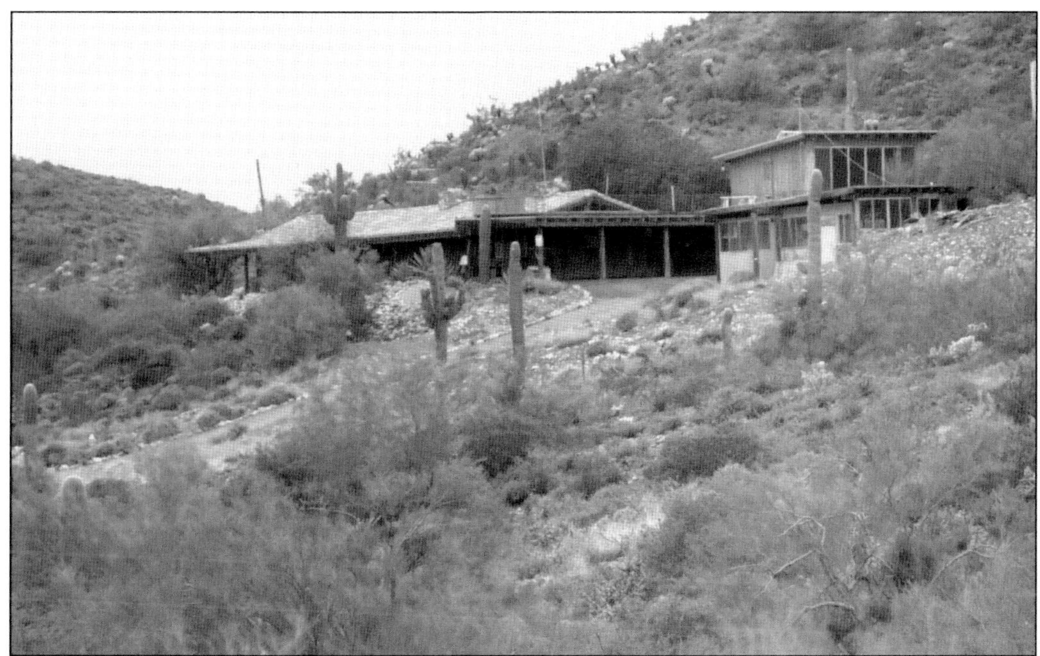

The Halle house, while still standing, has fallen into disrepair and, at onetime, was ground zero for considerable local drama. Controversial munitions manufacturer Charles "Chuck" Byers purchased the property in the 1980s and lived there until 1990, naming it Starflash Ranch. Byers developed explosives on the site. In 1997, federal agents took control of the property and, for several months, made plans to evacuate thousands of neighboring acres and detonate the remaining explosives and outbuildings. Sheriff Joe Arpaio promised to forcibly remove those residents who stated they would not evacuate. During a contentious standoff with New River residents and with the assistance of level-headed state officials, the federal government ultimately backed down. (Both, courtesy of Lance Halle.)

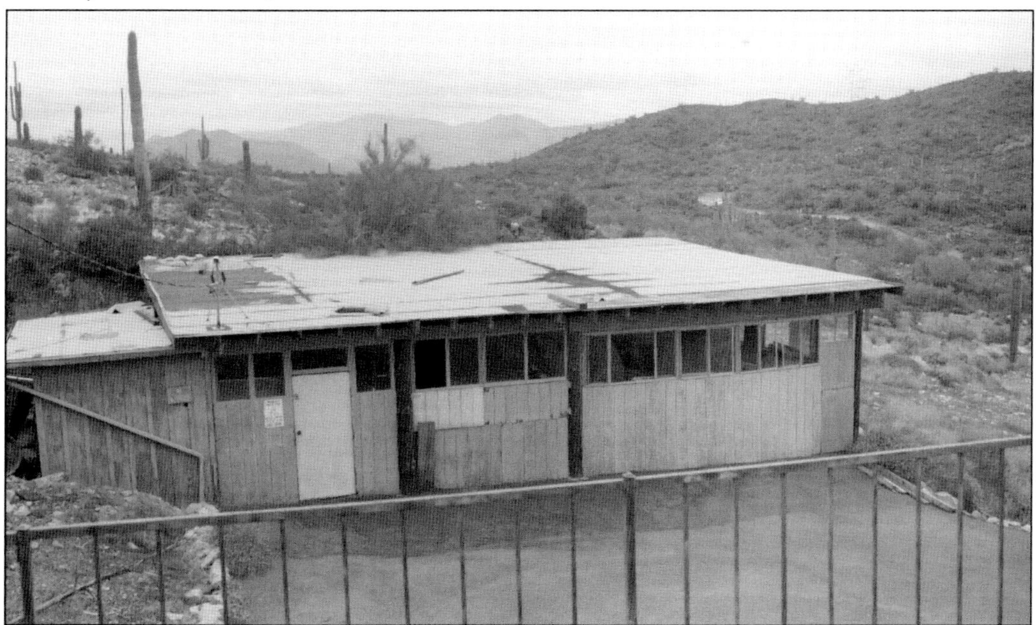

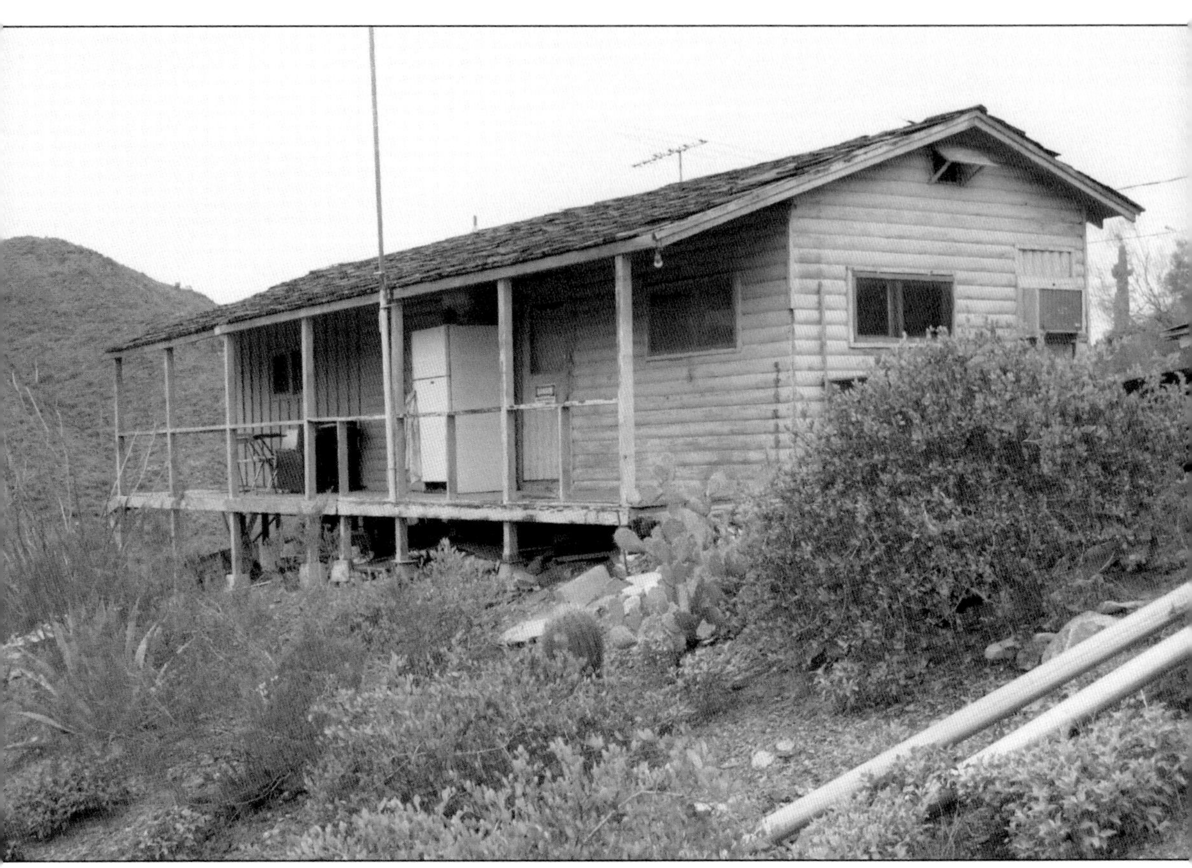

The Halle cabin survived the infamous "siege" on Gavilan Peak. Surrounded by ocotillo, agave, saguaro, barrel cactus, and jojoba bush, the pristine location belies the pattern of turmoil at Starflash Ranch. In 2013, a man helping someone move off the property lost his leg when an explosive detonated underfoot. (Courtesy of Lance Halle.)

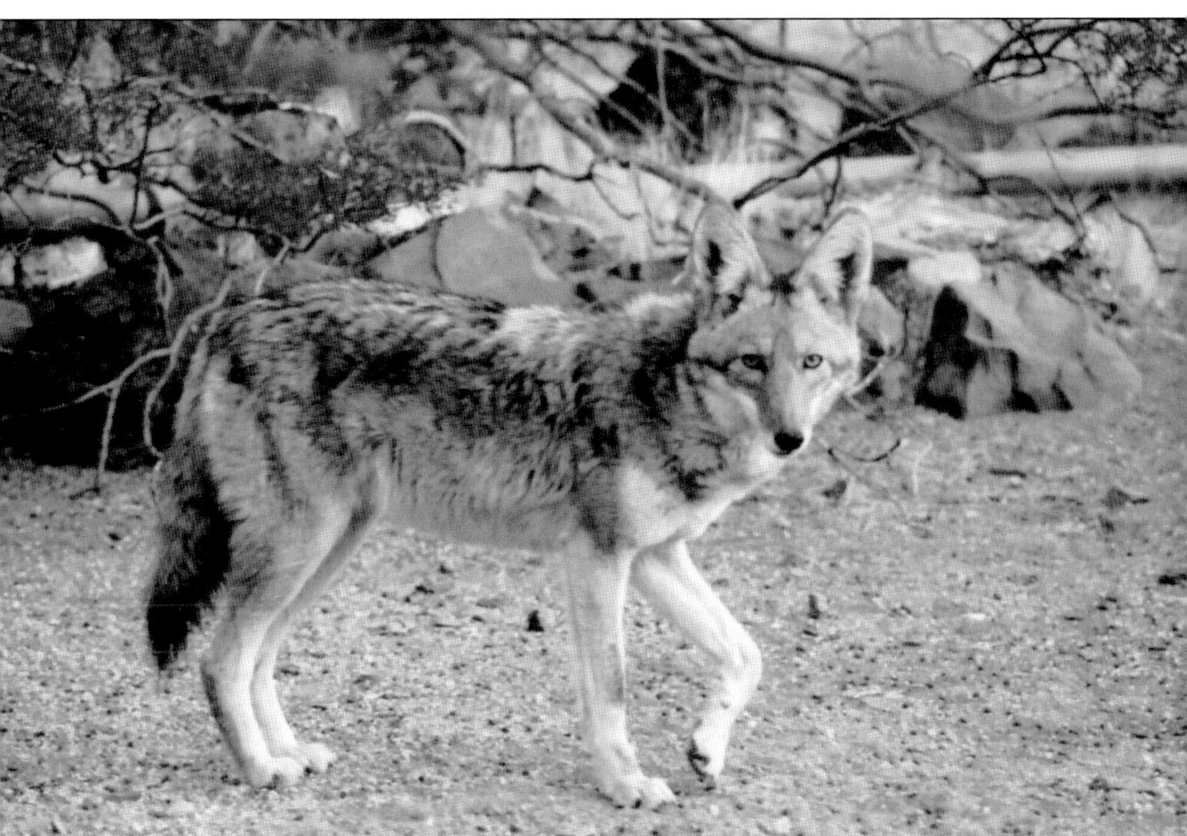

Throughout its history, New River has boasted hardy, capable natives, and perhaps none is as much of a survivor as the coyote. Despite being shot, trapped, and hunted for bounty, the coyote has adapted to meet conditions and has even thrived as development encroached. While the bighorn and the native people have vanished, the coyote remains a daily sight. (Courtesy of June Evans Bond.)

Consistent with our mission to preserve history on a local level, this book was printed in South Carolina on American-made paper and manufactured entirely in the United States. Products carrying the accredited Forest Stewardship Council (FSC) label are printed on 100 percent FSC-certified paper.

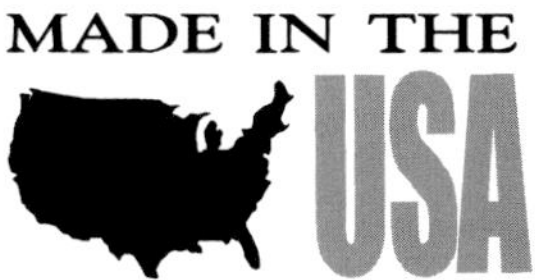